Philosophical Perspectives on Teacher Education

The Journal of Philosophy of Education Book Series

The Journal of Philosophy of Education Book Series publishes titles that represent a wide variety of philosophical traditions. They vary from examination of fundamental philosophical issues in their connection with education, to detailed critical engagement with current educational practice or policy from a philosophical point of view. Books in this series promote rigorous thinking on educational matters and identify and criticise the ideological forces shaping education.

Titles in the series include:

Philosophical Perspectives on Teacher Education
Edited by Ruth Heilbronn and Lorraine Foreman-Peck

Re-Imagining Relationships In Education: Ethics, Politics And Practices
Edited by Morwenna Griffiths, Marit Honerød Hoveid, Sharon Todd and Christine Winter

Education Vygotsky, Philosophy and Education
Jan Derry

Education and the Growth of Knowledge: Perspectives from Social and Virtue Epistemology
Edited by Ben Kotzee

Education Policy: Philosophical Critique
Edited by Richard Smith

Levinas, Subjectivity, Education: Towards an Ethics of Radical Responsibility
Anna Strhan

Philosophy for Children in Transition: Problems and Prospects
Edited by Nancy Vansieleghem and David Kennedy

The Good Life of Teaching: An Ethics of Professional Practice
Chris Higgins

Reading R. S. Peters Today: Analysis, Ethics, and the Aims of Education
Edited by Stefaan E. Cuypers and Christopher Martin

The Formation of Reason
David Bakhurst

What do Philosophers of Education do? (And how do they do it?)
Edited by Claudia Ruitenberg

Evidence-Based Education Policy: What Evidence? What Basis? Whose Policy?
Edited by David Bridges, Paul Smeyers and Richard Smith

New Philosophies of Learning
Edited by Ruth Cigman and Andrew Davis

The Common School and the Comprehensive Ideal: A Defence by Richard Pring with Complementary Essays
Edited by Mark Halstead and Graham Haydon

Philosophy, Methodology and Educational Research
Edited by David Bridges and Richard D Smith

Philosophy of the Teacher
By Nigel Tubbs

Conformism and Critique in Liberal Society
Edited by Frieda Heyting and Christopher Winch

Retrieving Nature: Education for a Post-Humanist Age
By Michael Bonnett

Education and Practice: Upholding the Integrity of Teaching and Learning
Edited by Joseph Dunne and Pádraig Hogan

Educating Humanity: Bildung in Postmodernity
Edited by Lars Lovlie, Klaus Peter Mortensen and Sven Erik Nordenbo

The Ethics of Educational Research
Edited by Michael Mcnamee andDavid Bridges

In Defence of High Culture
Edited by John Gingell and Ed Brandon

Enquiries at the Interface: Philosophical Problems of On-Line Education
Edited by Paul Standish and Nigel Blake

The Limits of Educational Assessment
Edited by Andrew Davis

Illusory Freedoms: Liberalism, Education and the Market
Edited by Ruth Jonathan

Quality and Education
Edited by Christopher Winch

Philosophical Perspectives on Teacher Education

Edited by

Ruth Heilbronn and Lorraine Foreman-Peck

WILEY Blackwell

This edition first published 2015
© 2015 Ruth Heilbronn and Lorraine Foreman-Peck
Editorial organisation © Philosophy of Education Society of Great Britain

Registered Office
John Wiley & Sons, Ltd, The Atrium, Southern Gate, Chichester, West Sussex, PO19 8SQ, UK

Editorial Offices
350 Main Street, Malden, MA 02148-5020, USA˙
9600 Garsington Road, Oxford, OX4 2DQ, UK
The Atrium, Southern Gate, Chichester, West Sussex, PO19 8SQ, UK

For details of our global editorial offices, for customer services, and for information about how to apply for permission to reuse the copyright material in this book please see our website at www.wiley.com/wiley-blackwell.

Library of Congress Cataloging-in-Publication Data applied for

978-1-1189-7766-8 (paper)

A catalogue record for this book is available from the British Library.

Cover image: Front cover image © Ellie Foreman-Peck

Set in 11.25/13.5pt Times by SPi Publisher Services, Pondicherry, India

Printed in Singapore by C.O.S. Printers Pte Ltd

1   2015

Contents

Preface

Teacher education is in a state of flux across the globe. While in some countries public investment in research-informed teacher education continues, in others it is being downsized and the balance between different spaces for teacher education tipped in favour of new types of employment-based learning, following the pattern of 'Teach for America'. In England specifically, the White Paper for Education (DfE, 2010), heralding the most radical reforms in the sector for several decades, has reopened fundamental questions about the future role of the university in teacher education.

The empirical, conceptual and normative grounds for reforming teacher education remain, however, subject to debate (BERA/RSA, 2014). For example, while there may be broad consensus that school-based learning is necessary to the preparation of new and beginning classroom teachers, there is no agreement as to whether this is sufficient. What do the different spaces for teacher education contribute to becoming and continuing to be a good teacher? Does higher education learning, engagement with research, and theoretical understanding matter to teachers' professional development? If they do, why? What knowledge, values, dispositions and skills do teachers need to educate others well and how might they best develop them (Orchard and Foreman-Peck, 2011)?

Looking back over the history of state-funded teacher education in England since the forerunner to the English Department of Education was set up in 1839, to oversee the public funding of education, there have been recurrent themes in public debates around teachers' roles, knowledge and qualities, and about their relationship with different models of teacher education and with education research. In the current context of heated discussion around the nature of teaching and of teachers' professional knowledge, and, by extension, about the appropriate sites for teacher education, pausing to reflect on meanings and their framing, prior to moving into action (see MacIntyre, 1984), may be a particularly important exercise in 'mak[ing] fragile the seeming causality of the present' (Popkewitz, 2013, p. 2), and this is the purpose of this book.

In fact, narratives of state-funded teacher education have several long-standing tensions at their core, two of which are particularly significant to themes in this volume. First, a *philosophical tension* between ethics and knowledge in the construction of teaching practice, and second, a *political tension* between the role of the state, of universities, of the church, and of schools and colleges in shaping and controlling teacher education and the supply of teachers.

This volume contains a range of philosophical perspectives and characteristic preoccupations that may be brought to bear on these particular concerns. At the same time, it recognises that, while questions such as those sketched above may be viewed as characteristically philosophical, they cannot be isolated from the policy context or from practice in teacher education. With this in view, the Philosophy of Education Society of Great Britain (PESGB) sponsored a series of 48-hour research symposia on the theme 'Philosophical Perspectives on the Future of Teacher Education' (PPfTE), over an 18-month period between May 2011 and November 2012, with participants from teacher educators and philosophers of education (Oancea and Orchard, 2012). Further sponsorship from four Higher Education Institutes enabled these to take place at the Department of Education, University of Oxford; Moray House, University of Edinburgh; the Centre for Philosophy in Education, Institute of Education, University of London; and the Graduate School of Education, University of Bristol. A core group of approximately 20 attended each symposium, which allowed discussion in depth among all participants.

There was little sense of complacency about the future or nostalgia about the past of teacher education in any of the symposia. Rather, discussions were characterised by proposals for change based on principled arguments about what it takes to become a good teacher. This presented participants with a relatively blank canvas, and gave philosophers and teacher educators a shared space in which to frame and articulate the core problems discussed. The symposia experience was a source of mutual learning and has led to publications to disseminate discussions – notably, some that were overtly philosophical, (e.g. Winch, 2012), others self-defined as 'educational' (e.g. Ellis, 2012).[1]

Philosophers contributing to the PPfTE represented in this book not only highlighted logical contradictions in current policies and practices, but also provided well-argued a priori accounts of what ought to be found in any suitable alternative. Colin Wringe (Chapter 2 in this volume) was one of many contributors who used philosophical argument to question the representation of teaching as a craft in current policy discourse. Chris Higgins (Chapter 4), for example, appealed to very different traditions in philosophical thought to evaluate the notion of the 'good teacher'.

As Viv Ellis (2012) argued at the first PPfTE symposium, the practice of education does not fall within the boundaries of neat and discrete disciplinary packages; critical and systematic reflection on education stems from many traditions, voices and modes of enquiry. Teacher education is no exception. However, an important place for characteristically philosophical reflection on all aspects of educational practice remains. The papers in the present volume offer a collection of sustained philosophical responses to crucial questions for the future of teacher education raised though the PPfTE series. The editors have focused on the explicitly philosophical contributions to the PPfTE symposia and have brought together a diverse selection of powerfully argued papers pursuing moral, ontological and epistemological questions in relation to the future of teacher education.

Philosophical reflection on the future of teacher education continues, for example in an initiative to support ethical deliberation with beginning teachers (working with the Higher Education Academy) and the contribution to a prominent enquiry into research in teacher education (BERA/RSA, 2014). Most importantly, philosophers and teacher educators are engaging in conversation in their everyday professional lives, as evidenced by their participation in the PPfTE symposia and in sessions at professional conferences, and by the generous response of the institutions and individuals who were invited to engage with the initiative. For many of them, teacher education and its future is not simply something to think and write about, not simply the object of critique, but a space for 'ontologically transformative' and 'constructive' educational practice in its own right (Aldridge and also Hogan, in this volume). These discussions continue to enrich our understanding of how teachers learn to teach and to be teachers, and this book seeks to share that understanding in ways that we hope will prove enlightening to other teachers, teacher educators, researchers and policy makers.

Janet Orchard and Alis Oancea

NOTE

1 A second strand of publication has developed from an adapted and extended version of the PPfTE research symposium format, this time teacher education-led and driven by concern for a particular issue, 'What and how do teachers learn from experience?' This event, supported by the Society for Educational Studies and the Oxford Centre for Sociocultural and Activity Theory Research in Oxford, included contributions from philosophers and led to the publication of an edited book (Ellis and Orchard, 2014).

Acknowledgements

We would like to thank the publishers of the following for permission to reproduce these articles in this volume:

Heilbronn, R. (2013) Wigs, Disguises and Child's Play: Solidarity in Teacher Education. *Ethics and Education*, 8:1, 31–41. Published by Taylor & Francis, www.tandfonline.com.

Higgins, C. (2010) The Good Life of Teaching: An Ethics of Professional Practice. *Journal of Philosophy of Education*, 44:2–3, 189–208. Wiley-Blackwell.

Hogan, P. (2013) Cultivating Human Capabilities in Venturesome Learning Environments. *Educational Theory*, 63:3, 237–252. University of Illinois, Wiley-Blackwell. This chapter first appeared as a paper which was part of a contribution to a symposium on love and pedagogy.

Notes on Contributors

David Aldridge After teaching and leading in religious education and philosophy departments in secondary schools for ten years, David Aldridge moved to Oxford Brookes University, where he is now Principal Lecturer in Philosophy of Education and Programme Lead for Secondary Initial Teacher Education, MA Programmes in Education, and the Educational Doctorate (EdD). His main research interests are phenomenology and philosophical hermeneutics, and he has published in *Journal of Philosophy of Education*, *Educational Philosophy and Theory* and *Journal of Beliefs and Values*.

Gert Biesta is currently Professor of Educational Theory and Policy and Head of the Institute of Education and Society, University of Luxembourg. He has published widely on the theory and philosophy of education and the theory and philosophy of educational and social research. Recent work focuses particularly on teaching and teacher education and on the roles of theory and theorising in educational research. He is editor-in-chief of the journal *Studies in Philosophy of Education*, and co-edits two book series on the theory and philosophy of education with Routledge. Recent books include *Good Education in an Age of Measurement* (2010) and *The Beautiful Risk of Education* (2014), both with Paradigm Publishers USA. He is also co-author of a chapter on the philosophy of teaching in the forthcoming edition of the AERA *Handbook of Research on Teaching*.

Lorraine Foreman-Peck is an Honorary Research Fellow at Oxford University's Department for Educational Studies. She has taught in inner-city secondary schools in London and Newcastle upon Tyne and at the Universities of Newcastle, Northumbria, Oxford Brookes and Northampton, where she was Reader in Education. She has been a Visiting Professor at Northumbria University. Her recent research has included empirical and philosophical investigations into museum pedagogy, responsive evaluation methodology, and teacher well-being. In 2010 she co-authored *Using Educational Research to Inform Practice: A Practical Guide to Practitioner Research in Universities and Colleges* (Routledge) with C. Winch.

Fiona Hallett is a Reader in Education at Edge Hill University (UK) and Joint Editor of the *British Journal of Special Education.* She is interested in inclusive educational practices and has researched the lived experiences of children in mainstream and special schools and students in higher education. She is also interested in the ways in which research methodologies position the researcher and the researched and is currently using visual methodologies for an international project on inclusion.

Ruth Heilbronn researches and lectures at the UCL Institute of Education, where she has led various teams engaged in teacher education, having previously taught in inner London secondary schools and worked as an LEA adviser. Her publications include research on the induction of newly qualified teachers, for the Department for Education, and *Teacher Education and the Development of Practical Judgement* (Continuum, 2008). In 2010 she co-edited *Critical Practice in Teacher Education* with John Yandell (IoE Press) and has recently published on ethical teacher education. She is an executive member of the Philosophy of Education Society of Great Britain.

Chris Higgins is Associate Professor and Program Coordinator of Philosophy of Education in the Department of Education Policy, Organization and Leadership at the University of Illinois at Urbana-Champaign, where he serves as Editor of *Educational Theory* and holds affiliate appointments in the Unit for Criticism and Interpretive Theory and the Center for Translation Studies. He was Co-Director of an NEH Summer Institute for College Teachers entitled 'The Centrality

of Translation to the Humanities: New Interdisciplinary Scholarship'
(2013) and Director of the Illinois New Teacher Collaborative
(2011–2012). He has served as Program Chair of the Philosophy of
Education Society and now serves as General Editor of the Society's
Yearbook, *Philosophy of Education*. His scholarly work concerns the
ethical and existential dimensions of the practice of teaching. His
book, *The Good Life of Teaching: An Ethics of Professional Practice*
(Wiley-Blackwell, 2011), draws on virtue ethics and neo-praxis philosophy (e.g. Hannah Arendt, John Dewey, Hans-Georg Gadamer,
Alasdair MacIntyre, and Michael Oakeshott) to examine the nature of
meaningful work and the place of self-cultivation in teaching. His
work also explores the dynamics of the teacher–student relationship
(freedom and authority, dialogue and recognition, transformative education); teacher education (the role of the arts and the humanities, the
cultivation of reflection and professional judgement); aesthetic education (the arts and the educated imagination; creativity and social
change); the nature of schooling (progressive and radical theories;
what makes a public school public); and higher education (liberal and
vocational aims; hermeneutics and translation; humanism and the
humanities; political economy of the university).

Pádraig Hogan is a senior lecturer at the National University of
Ireland Maynooth, where he leads the Research and Development
programme 'Teaching and Learning for the 21st Century' (TL21). His
research interests are mainly concerned with issues of quality in
educational experience and with the enhancement of educational
policy and practice. He has published widely and his most recent
book is *The New Significance of Learning: Imagination's Heartwork*
(Routledge, 2010).

James McAllister is director of first year education studies in the
School of Education, University of Stirling and is a qualified primary
school teacher. His doctoral study at the University of Edinburgh
entailed an analysis of philosophical and policy literature related to
school discipline, pupil behaviour and teacher authority. His publications have involved philosophical exploration of epistemology and
education; how school discipline might be more educational; emotion

education; physical education; the curriculum for excellence in Scotland; the ethics underpinning educational research; and the role and importance of the body in education. He has two articles forthcoming that explore the thought of the Scottish philosopher John MacMurray on school discipline and emotion education and on the importance of learning through bodily senses and with love.

Mary McAteer has worked for over 30 years as a teacher, local authority consultant and educator, in a range of senior pastoral and curriculum roles. Since moving into higher education in 1999 she has held a range of posts including Senior Lecturer and Principal Lecturer, and programme lead for Master's-level Professional Development Programmes in two different universities. Her current post is Director of the Specialist Primary Mathematics Programmes in Edge Hill University, where she supports a range of Master's-level practitioner research projects, and also supervises doctoral studies. She has a particular interest in the notion of ethical deliberation and the changing nature of ethical issues facing the practitioner researcher during the life of a project.

Alis Oancea is Associate Professor in the Philosophy of Education and Deputy Director for Research at the Department of Education, University of Oxford. She writes on philosophy of research, research ethics, knowledge dynamics, policy and governance, higher education, contemporary challenges for philosophy of education, and science and technology studies. She is currently leading an AHRC study on the cultural value of arts and humanities research, and co-editing the *Review of Education* (Wiley). Publications include *Quality in Applied and Practice-Based Research* (Routledge, 2007), *Education for All* (Routledge, 2009) and *Research Methods in Education* (Sage, 2014). She is secretary to the Oxford branch of the Philosophy of Education Society of Great Britain and was part of the executive group of the Society's Philosophical Perspectives on Teacher Education initiative.

Janet Orchard is Co-Director of the PGCE Programme at the Graduate School of Education, University of Bristol, having previously taught in secondary schools for over 14 years. Her publications focus on professional education, specifically the contribution of philosophy to teacher education. She co-authored 'The Contribution of Educational Research to Teachers' Professional Learning – Philosophical Understandings' with Christopher Winch and Alis Oancea for the BERA/RSA Teacher Education Inquiry, and in 2014 she co-edited *Learning Teaching from Experience: Multiple Perspectives, International Contexts* (Bloomsbury) with Viv Ellis. She has been a co-opted member of the Executive of the Philosophy of Education Society of Great Britain since 2008, with specific responsibility for engagement with teacher education, the capacity in which she convened the Philosophical Perspectives for Teacher Education initiative.

Paul Reynolds is Reader in Sociology and Social Philosophy at Edge Hill University. His research interests are in radical theory, ethics and critique, and, germane to his contribution here, radical pedagogy and the possibility of moral agency in professional practice. Amongst his research involvements is co-directorship of the International Network for Cultural Difference and Social Solidarity; and Co-Convenor of the International Network for Sexual Ethics and Politics and co-editor in chief of its journal with Barbara Budrich Publishers. He is also a member of the editorial board of *Historical Materialism: Research in Critical Marxist Theory* and has held and holds other examinerships and advisory board memberships.

Damien Shortt teaches English literature on Edge Hill University's Secondary Undergraduate teacher-training programme. His research interests lie in a broad number of areas including the ethics of teaching, teachers' standards and codes of conduct, the management of behaviour in schools, and the place of English in the National Curriculum. His current research into behaviour management aims at exploring the philosophical foundations of individual schools' behaviour management policies, in order to map the synergies and tensions between their stated means and ends. Recent publications include articles in the *European Journal of Teacher Education* and the *Journal of Teaching and Teacher Education*, and a chapter entitled 'Who Put the Ball in the English Net? Postnationalism in Dermot Bolger's In High

Germany', in Carmen Zamorano Llena (ed.), *Redefinitions of Irish Identity in the Twenty-First Century: A Postnationalist Approach* (Peter Lang, 2010).

Colin Wringe is an Honorary Fellow of Keele University where he was previously a Reader in Education. His publications in Philosophy of Education include *Children's Rights: a Philosophical Study* (Routledge, 1981), *Democracy, Schooling and Political Education* (Unwin, 1984), *Understanding Educational Aims* (Unwin, 1988), *Moral Education: Beyond the Teaching of Right and Wrong* (Springer, 2006) and numerous articles, mostly published in the *Journal of Philosophy of Education*. He gained his first degree at St Edmund Hall, Oxford and his PhD at the London Institute of Education, and has been a member of the Philosophy of Education Society of Great Britain since its foundation in 1963, having served two substantial terms as the Society's Treasurer. He taught in schools for a number of years before moving to higher education and retains a close interest in the practice of classroom teaching, particularly in his original curriculum subject (Modern Foreign Languages) regarding which he has written two books and edited the subject's main professional journal. The focus of his current research remains the point, purpose and nature of the educational enterprise and their implications for the initial education and continuing professional development of teachers.

Editors' Introduction

Education 'policy borrowing', as indicated by Carrie Winstanley (2012), is taking place on a global scale. Antoni Verger, Hülya Altinyelken and Mireille de Koning (2013) report on the situation in Indonesia, Jamaica, Namibia, Uganda, Peru, India and Turkey, countries all experiencing similar changes. Further examples are found in the US Race to the Top initiative, and the implementation of national professional standards for teachers in Australia and New Zealand. These education policies share basic features and assumptions. They are based on standards or competencies for teachers and test and examination results for students, so that teachers' identity and work is now situated in what Stephen Ball (2001) has characterised as a culture of performativity.

Present policy on teacher education raises specifically philosophical questions that we seek to address in this book, focusing on four key questions: Is the account of teacher training and education in current policy statements adequate to the practical and ethical demands they will face? If the account is lacking, in what respects is it deficient? Are current arrangements for teacher education and training adequate to meet possible deficiencies in the official account? Is there a better way of thinking about preparation for teaching? In addressing these issues our contributors employ a variety of approaches to the philosophy of education. Some authors employ a broadly analytical approach to concepts and arguments. Others start with key writers or philosophical texts to illuminate a practical concern in the education of teachers.

The book is organised around three central philosophical concerns, which address the questions above in different ways. The first is the knowledge required by teachers; the second is about teachers as ethical agents; and the third is ontological, that is – what is it to *be* a teacher? These concerns necessarily overlap and are inextricably related in several of the chapters.

All three contributors to the first section of the book ask questions about the nature of practitioner knowledge and what preparation for teaching might be. How practitioner knowledge is conceived has a bearing on the kind of teacher education that is promoted and enshrined in policy. If teaching is predominantly conceived as a science, for which empirical evidence of effectiveness can be amassed – as, for example, promulgated by David Reynolds (1991) – it follows that teachers can be 'trained' to believe in and rely on the efficacy of methods based on the findings of empirical research which makes claims about 'what works'. The argument against what is seen as an effectiveness mantra has been much rehearsed, but still has considerable purchase in today's educational climate despite vigorous challenges to the school effectiveness and school improvement movement (see, for example, Slee, Weiner and Tomlinson, 1998). Gert Biesta addresses the question of teacher knowledge in Chapter 1 on 'competence, evidence and wisdom' by considering the proposition that teaching should be conceived as an evidence-based practice and also that standards and competences are appropriate mechanisms for training teachers and judging their performance and quality. The chapter argues that both ideas fail to capture the reality of teaching and are therefore insufficient and potentially problematic as reference points for teacher education. Based on the assumption that teaching is a multidimensional teleological practice, that is, a practice constituted by aims, it argues that central to good teaching is the ability to make situated judgements about what is educationally desirable. This is not a matter of the application of evidence, nor should it be understood as a competence. Instead Biesta sees this as something that requires the exercise of 'practical educational wisdom', which he develops in relation to Aristotle's account of *techne, poesis* and *praxis*. Teacher education, Biesta claims, should focus on the cultivation of 'practical educational wisdom' and the wider 'virtuosity' of teaching.

Colin Wringe contrasts two aspects of preparation for teaching, namely the knowledge, techniques and skills necessary for teaching the content of a particular subject effectively, and the more transformative knowledge and understanding needed to enable teachers to achieve a sophisticated and open-minded conception of what education is supposedly about, beyond the mere transmission of curricular content and skills. In particular, the chapter argues that given the diversity of legitimate educational aspirations and the unpredictability of human responses, good teaching cannot simply be a matter of applying tried and tested techniques and procedures but requires wise and conscientious judgements in what are essentially individual situations. The chapter further argues that in the discussion and practice of teacher education it is all too common for those with particular perspectives on this task to emphasise one of these two aspects to the neglect of the other. Both merit equal attention.

In the last chapter in this section James McAllister discusses the idea of a university and school partnership, arguing that in the current context in England and Scotland, where school-based training is possible without any higher education component, the role of the university has become *too* grounded in educational practice, to the exclusion of educational theory. With reference to J. H. Newman, the chapter argues that staff in education faculties in universities have an important role to play in helping educators to resist any such 'de-theorising' of education. Newman suggested that professionals who had a *sole* focus on 'professional learning' would develop a narrow skill base, rather than broad knowledge-based worldviews, and he claimed that the function of the university was to promote a broad liberal rather than a solely vocational and professional education. While acknowledging issues with Newman's account, the chapter argues that universities partnered with schools should support educators to further develop their own understandings of educational practices *and* concepts; develop the knowledge and the skills necessary for conducting, comprehending and interpreting practice-based research; and form a critical attitude towards government policy and the findings and application of educational research. McAllister argues for staff in partner schools being encouraged to engage with 'liberal educational knowledge', which he takes to mean educational theory that is not explicitly derived from practice or practice-based.

Three contributors address aspects of the second question – what makes a good teacher – which falls within our second major philosophical concern, the ethical dimension of teacher preparation. Drawing on a wide range of philosophical literature, Chris Higgins argues in Chapter 4 that we need a virtue ethics of teaching: the impulse to teach is fundamentally altruistic and represents a desire to share what teachers value and to empower others. The chapter is a revised version of the Introduction to 'The Good Life of Teaching: An Ethics of Professional Practice' (Higgins, 2010a), in which he develops a substantive ethics of professional life with special reference to teaching and demonstrates the ethical importance of the flourishing of the practitioner. The chapter introduces the key idea of teaching as an existential practice, as a space for the teacher's own self-enactment, and offers a vision of education as a space of humanistic questions. Higgins sees teachers as 'organic intellectuals' and defends a view of teacher education that goes beyond learning how to teach to encompass learning how to learn through teaching. As do Biesta and Wringe, Higgins calls for a teacher education for practical wisdom, one that helps teachers enter the practice of teaching, sustain a vocational conversation and further their own self-cultivation.

In Chapter 5, Ruth Heilbronn addresses ethical questions for teacher educators, considering the ideas of playfulness and solidarity. She claims that in the current culture in many schools, pupils are not seen wholly – and in some cases not even primarily – as an end in themselves. Although enabling all children to flourish and achieve may be stated as an aim of the school curriculum, the need to reach nationally recognised targets and standards drives schools to fudge these aims and in many cases skews teaching to the achievement of good test results. This runs counter to the avowed vocational values held by most student teachers and also cannot account for the relational aspect of teaching and the pastoral care that can also be strongly evidenced in some of these same schools. The chapter argues that ethical teacher educators should do all they can to alert student teachers to the contradictory pull of the two demands on them, as well as helping to develop the student teachers' capacity to withstand these contradictions and to flourish as teachers, able to maintain good and caring relationships with their pupils. The chapter develops a view of 'solidarity' as a useful concept to illuminate the particular work of practical judgement that may enable 'good' teaching in current circumstances.

The section ends with Chapter 6, in which Damien Shortt, Paul Reynolds, Mary McAteer and Fiona Hallett report on a project to facilitate ethical deliberation with teacher educators. The authors discuss findings from a small-scale research trial which focused on the design and implementation of ethics workshops, carried out with teacher educators in 2009–2012. The findings indicate a strong demand from teacher educators for such opportunities for ethical deliberation on issues arising from practice. Significantly, discussions with participants about the way in which the workshops were run interested them almost as much as the content of the workshops themselves. The chapter explores the potential for the incorporation of such meta-discussion into workshops and other such communities of enquiry, as well as their primary function to promote and establish ethical deliberation processes and practices for teacher educators and, importantly, for teachers.

David Aldridge, Pádraig Hogan and Lorraine Foreman-Peck address the last of the book's three main philosophical areas of concern: what it means to be a teacher. In Chapter 7 David Aldridge picks up a question posed by MacAllister on the role of higher education in teacher education, but his approach is 'a reorientation towards ontology'. Both discuss the possible diminished role of higher education institutions (HEIs) in teacher education and the perceived fear of teachers becoming the mechanical agents of government policy or the reproducers of unreflective and instrumental ways of acting. However, the chapter argues that the emphasis on higher education institutions as guardians of 'theory', employed to distance teaching from a conception of it as 'craft', potentially undermines the attempt to produce an accurate description of the practice of education. Developing an ontology of teaching that draws on the work of Martin Heidegger, Aldridge argues that an emphasis on theory encourages another form of instrumentalism potentially inimical to education. The chapter argues for the importance of pre- or non-theoretical aspects of teaching such as 'tact' or 'comportment', and thus the distinction between 'profession' and 'craft' is seen not to be as clear cut as might be considered convenient. Aldridge calls for an orientation of our description of teacher education towards ontology and the ongoing becoming of both students and their teachers. Rather than defending universities as the locus of academic or theoretical input, an account needs to be made of the transformational events that HEIs can provide that cannot occur elsewhere and which enable teachers to flourish as ethically oriented professionals.

In Chapter 8 Pádraig Hogan argues for a notion of capabilities rather than competencies and explores 'venturesome environments of learning', which are hospitable to the cultivation of such capabilities among students and their teachers. He identifies four kinds of relations and the interplay between them, to capture some of the particularities of venturesome learning environments. The second part of the chapter gives an account of a long-running and ongoing research project in Ireland which has been promoting such environments in post-primary education, a project with implications for educational policy on teachers' professional development. The project seeks to call attention to what has been successful, not to make universal claims about 'what works'. This part of the chapter is centrally concerned with policy implications. It highlights the merits of drawing 'evidence-based' policy makers into the richer possibilities that are brought to the fore by examples of venturesome learning environments and by research into what can make them 'truly fruitful'.

This third section of the book ends with Chapter 9, which is entitled 'Towards a Theory of Well-Being for Teachers'. Lorraine Foreman-Peck gives an account of 'the long view' of education and argues for an expanded concept of reflection to be used in teacher education that pays due attention to the need for student teachers to become aware of their own values, needs and desires in order to develop these throughout a career in teaching. The consequence of not doing so is 'burn out' and 'drop out' or, more seriously, in Higgins' phrase (2011), 'burn in'. The chapter argues that the demanding nature of a life devoted to giving to others is only sustainable in a morally defensible way through self-development and self-determination. Drawing on concepts of well-being, the chapter makes some suggestions towards developing a theory of well-being for teachers.

Ruth Heilbronn and Lorraine Foreman-Peck

Part 1
What Do Teachers Need to Know?

1

How Does a Competent Teacher Become a Good Teacher?: On Judgement, Wisdom and Virtuosity in Teaching and Teacher Education

GERT BIESTA

THE LIMITS OF COMPETENCE-BASED TEACHER EDUCATION

The idea that teachers should be competent at what they do is difficult to contest. Perhaps this partly explains the popular appeal of competence-based approaches to teaching and teacher education, which, in recent decades, have spread rapidly across many countries around the world (for an overview and critical analysis, see Heilbronn, 2008, chapter 2). National frameworks for teacher education are increasingly being formulated in terms of competences, and even the European Commission has recently produced a set of *Common European Principles for Teacher Competences and Qualifications*,[1] meant to stimulate 'reflection about actions that can be taken at Member State level and how the European Union might support these' – as it was formulated in the 2007 document *Improving the Quality of Teacher Education*.[2] The idea of competence, however, has more than just rhetorical appeal. Its introduction marks an important shift in focus from what teachers should *know* to what they should be able to *do*, and potentially even to how they should *be*. In this regard the idea

Philosophical Perspectives on Teacher Education, First Edition. Edited by Ruth Heilbronn and Lorraine Foreman-Peck. © 2015 Ruth Heilbronn and Lorraine Foreman-Peck. Editorial Organisation © Philosophy of Education Society of Great Britain. Published 2015 by John Wiley & Sons, Ltd.

of competence represents a more practical and more holistic outlook in that it encompasses knowledge, skills and professional action, rather than seeing such action as either the application of knowledge – an idea captured in evidence-based approaches to teaching and teacher education (see Biesta, 2007, 2010a) – or the enactment of skills, an approach particularly prominent in those situations where teachers are supposed to pick up their skills 'on the shop floor', so to speak, rather than that they are thought to be in need of any proper professional education.

Yet the idea of competence is not without problems, and also not without risks (see Mulder, Weigel and Collins, 2007; Biesta and Priestley, 2013). The risks have to do with the way in which the notion of competence is defined and understood, the problems with how it is being implemented and enacted. With regard to matters of definition, competence can be seen as an integrative approach to professional action that highlights the complex combination of knowledge, skills, understandings, values and purposes (for such a definition see Deakin Crick, 2008, p. 313). In such an interpretation a competence-based approach clearly has the potential to promote the professional agency of teachers. Yet many commentators have shown that the idea of competence actually steers the field of teaching and teacher education in the opposite direction through its emphasis on performance, standards, measurement and control, thus reducing and ultimately undermining the agency of teachers (see Heilbronn 2008, pp. 21–25; see also Winch, 2000; Priestley, Robinson and Biesta, 2012).

With regard to the practical implementation of the idea of competence, particularly within the field of teacher education, there are a number of additional problems. One has to do with the fact that any attempt to describe in full everything that teachers should be competent at runs the risk of generating lists that are far too long and far too detailed. The existence of such lists can result in a situation where teacher education turns into a tick box exercise focused on establishing whether students have managed to achieve everything on the list. This may not only lead to a disjointed curriculum and an instrumental approach to the education of teachers, but also runs the risk of turning teacher education from a collective experience to a plethora of individual learning trajectories, where students are just working towards the achievement of their 'own' competencies, without a need to interact with or be exposed to fellow students.

A second major problem is that competencies are always orientated towards the past and the present. It is, after all, only possible to describe what a teacher needs to be competent at in relation to situations that are already known. Yet teaching is in a very fundamental sense always open towards the future. There is a danger, therefore, that a competence-based curriculum for teacher education ties students too much to the current situation – or to a particular interpretation of the current situation – rather than preparing them sufficiently for meaningful action in an unknown future. This, as I will argue in more detail below, is not meant as an argument that teachers need flexible skills but as an argument for the central role of judgement in teaching.

All this feeds into what is perhaps the most important problem with and limitation of a competence-based approach to teacher education, which is the fact that good teachers do not simply need to be able to do all kinds of things – in this regard it is true that they need to be competent (and *being* competent is a better formulation than *having* competences) – but they also need to be able to judge which competences should be utilised in the always concrete situations in which teachers work. If competences in a sense provide teachers with a repertoire of possibilities, there is still the challenge to judge which of those possibilities should be actualised in order to realise good and meaningful teaching. This is why I wish to suggest that while the possession of competences may be a *necessary* condition for good teaching, it can never be a *sufficient* condition. And the reason for this lies in the fact that good teaching requires *judgement* about what an educationally desirable course of action is in *this* concrete situation with *these* concrete students at *this* particular stage in their educational trajectory.

In its shortest formula we might say, therefore, that '*good teaching = competences + judgement*'. But this raises a number of further questions. One is: 'Why do we need judgement in teaching?' A second is: 'What kinds of judgement do we need in teaching?' And a third is: 'How might we help teachers to become capable of such judgements?' – which is the question of teacher education. In what follows I aim to provide an answer to these questions. Through this I will articulate a conception of teacher education that can be seen as an alternative to competence-based approaches. This conception focuses on the ways in which, through teacher education, teachers can enhance their ability for making situated judgements about what is educationally desirable, with regard to both the 'ends' and the 'means' of education.[3]

As I will explain in more detail below, I refer to this approach as a *virtue-based approach* (see also Biesta, 2013), which is the reason why I will emphasise the need for teachers to develop educational virtuosity. I will preface my discussion with an exploration of the particular nature of teaching and education more generally.

ON THE 'NATURE' OF EDUCATION: TELEOLOGY AND THE THREE DOMAINS OF EDUCATIONAL PURPOSE

In order to understand why there is a need for judgement in teaching, we need to begin by looking more closely at the particular nature of educational processes and practices. In recent years it has become fashionable to do so with the help of the language of learning. Yet, as I have argued elsewhere in more detail (see particularly Biesta, 2004, 2006, 2010b), the language of learning is a very limited and to a certain degree even inadequate language to capture what education is about. Perhaps the quickest way to highlight what the problem is, is to say that the point of education is *not* that students learn, but that they learn *something*, that they learn it for particular *reasons* and that they learn it *from someone*. Questions of *content, purpose and relationships* are precisely what distinguishes (a general discussion about) learning from (a concrete discussion about) education. Education, to put it differently, is not designed so that children and young people might learn – which they can anywhere – but so that they might learn particular things (in the broad sense of the word) within particular relationships and for particular reasons.

The latter dimension – which concerns the question of purpose – is the most central and most fundamental one, because it is only once we have articulated what we want our educational arrangements and efforts to bring about that we can make decisions about relevant content and about the kind of relationships that are most conducive for this. Without a sense of purpose, there may be learning but not education. This is why we might adopt the stronger claim that education is not simply a practice that is *characterised* by the presence of purposes, but one that is actually a practice *constituted* by purpose(s) (see Biesta, 2010a, 2010b). In philosophical language, education can therefore be seen as a *teleological* practice, that is, a practice constituted by a *telos*. This already provides us with one important reason why judgement is needed in education, as we need to come to some kind of understanding of what the purpose of our educational activities should be. (It is useful here to follow the distinction suggested by Richard Peters between the purpose of an activity, which refers to the reason for it, and the aims of an activity, which concern the concrete targets one wishes to achieve; see Peters, 1973, p. 13.)

But here we encounter an additional reason why judgement is needed in education, which has to do with the fact that in education the question of purpose is a *multidimensional question*. This means that there is not one single purpose of education but that there are a number of different domains of educational purpose (on this thesis see particularly Biesta, 2009a, 2010b). The idea here is a simple one, but it has some profound implications for understanding the role of judgements in education. One way to understand the multidimensional nature of educational purpose is to start from the question how education *functions*, that is, what our educational actions and activities effect. One important function of education lies in the domain of *qualification*. Here education is concerned with the transmission and acquisition of knowledge, skills, dispositions and understandings that qualify children and young people for doing certain things. Such doing can either be understood in a narrow sense, for example becoming qualified to perform a certain task or job, or it can be understood in a much wider sense, such as that education qualifies children and young people to live life in modern, complex societies.

Some would say that this is the only dimension in which education functions, that is, that education is basically about getting knowledge and skills. Others would highlight, however, that education is not just about qualification but also about *socialisation*, that is, about initiating children and young people into existing traditions, cultures, ways of doing and ways of being. Education partly does this deliberately, for example in the form of professional socialisation, or socialisation into the culture of democracy. The idea of the hidden curriculum (Giroux and Purple, 1983) suggests, however, that socialisation also happens behind the back of teachers and students, thus reproducing existing traditions, cultures, ways of doing and being often, though not necessarily, in ways that benefit some more than others, thus contributing to the reproduction of material and social inequalities. In addition to qualification and socialisation I wish to argue – and have argued elsewhere (Biesta, 2009a, 2010b) – that any educational activity or effort always also impacts on the person, that is, on the qualities of the person and on personal qualities. Here we can think, for example, of the ways in which through the acquisition of knowledge and understanding individuals become empowered. Or how, through adopting particular culture patterns, they become disempowered. This is a domain where we can find such qualities as autonomy, criticality, empathy or compassion, which all are potential 'effects' of education. I have suggested referring to this third dimension as *subjectification*, as it concerns processes of being/becoming a human subject. (For the particular reason for using the notion of 'subject' rather than, for example, the notion of 'person' or 'identity', see particularly Biesta, 2010b, chapter 4; see also Biesta, 2006, 2014.)

If it is granted that qualification, socialisation and subjectification are three domains or dimensions in which education *functions* – which means nothing more than when we teach we always have some impact in each of these three domains – then it could be argued that as educators we also need to take responsibility for the impact of our educational actions in relation to these three domains. That is why the distinction between qualification, socialisation and subjectification cannot only be used in an analytical way – that is, to analyse the 'impact' of particular educational arrangements – but also in a programmatic sense – that is, to articulate what one wishes to achieve or bring about through one's educational efforts. That is why they can also been seen as three purposes of education. Given that within each domain there can actually be significantly different views, for example, about what knowledge is, what tradition or culture or, or what it means to be a human subject, I prefer to refer to them as three *domains of educational purpose*. And the suggestion here is that those who have a responsibility for education – be they teachers, policy makers, politicians, or students themselves – need to articulate and justify what they seek to achieve in relation to each of these domains.

WHY DO WE NEED JUDGEMENT IN TEACHING? PURPOSE, FORM, BALANCE, TRADE-OFFS AND PRAGMATISM

Against this background we are now in a position to answer the question why judgement is needed in education. The answer to this question is threefold. We first need judgement in relation to the question of what the *purpose* of our educational arrangements and activities is to be – and this question, as mentioned, poses itself as a multidimensional question, so that we need to give an answer to what it is we wish to achieve and what we wish our students to achieve in relation to each of the three domains of educational purpose, a task that also requires that we answer the question *why* it is that we want to achieve this, which is a matter of justification. The reason that we need judgement here is because any answer to this question is not a matter of stating facts, but involves values and hence normative preferences. Science and research can therefore never provide an answer to the question what education ought to be *for* in relation to the three domains of educational purpose. What it can do, at most, is provide information that might be relevant for understanding what is possible and feasible in each of the domains. Hence already at the very start of any educational endeavour we find a need for judgement. But it is not only that we need to come to a judgement about the purpose of our educational endeavours before we engage with them. The question of what it is we seek to achieve returns again and again as a very concrete question that needs to be answered in relation to concrete and, in a certain sense, always unique individual students, in concrete and, in a certain sense, unique situations. It is therefore a question that lies at the heart of teaching and of what it means to be a teacher.

A second 'moment' of judgement has to do with the ways in which we organise and enact education, that is, with regard to the *forms* of educational action. This has to do with another characteristic that makes education different from many other human fields and practices, namely the fact that in education there is an internal relationship between means and ends. The means of education – the ways in which we act; the things we say and how we say them; the ways in which we relate to our students and let them relate to each other – can never be thought of as mere instruments that should just effectively bring about certain 'outcomes'. The reason for this lies in the fact that students not only learn from what we say but also, and often more so, from how we say it and from what we do. This means that our ways of 'doing' in education do not just need to be effective (and sometimes that is not even a relevant criterion at all; see below); we always also need to judge whether they are educationally appropriate – which requires that we reflect on what our students might learn or pick up from the ways in which we do things and the ways in which we organise and arrange education. This is not to suggest that questions about how our educational actions might 'impact' in the different domains in which education functions are not relevant. On the contrary, there are important judgements to be made about that as well (I return to this in the next section). But there is always the additional question whether our means, our ways of being and doing, are educationally appropriate, that is, whether the messages they convey – implicitly or explicitly – are indeed the messages we seek to convey (which, ideally, should be a matter of congruency, but practically should at least be a matter where the means do not contradict or obstruct the ends we seek to achieve). In addition to a technical judgement about the effectiveness of our actions and arrangements, there is therefore always a need for a judgement about the educational desirability of our actions and arrangements.

The third 'moment' of judgement in education follows directly from the multidimensional nature of educational purpose, because although there are interconnections between the three domains and there are, therefore, possibilities for synergy – to understand something can, as suggested, contribute to empowerment and agency – the three domains are not seamlessly connected, so that, in addition to opportunities for synergy, there is also a real chance for tension and conflict. The three domains of educational purpose pull us as educators in slightly (and sometimes significantly) different directions. Think, for example, of the potentially damaging effects in the domain of subjectification of a constant high pressure in the domain of qualification, that is, a constant high pressure to 'perform' in the sphere of knowledge and skills. That is why in each educational situation – both at the general level of educational design and programming and at the concrete level of the encounter with each individual student – on the one hand, a judgement is needed about what an educationally appropriate *balance* between the three domains might be, and on the other hand, a judgement is needed about the inevitable *trade-offs* between what can be achieved in the three domains. It is, after all, possible to achieve highly in each of the domains, but this often comes at a cost for what can be achieved in the other domains. Think again of the 'price' of a single emphasis on qualification with regard to both the domain of subjectification and the domain of socialisation (with regard to the latter it means, for example, that we initiate our students into a culture of competition rather than one of collaboration).

The final point I wish to make is that, given the teleological character of education, any judgements we make about *how* to proceed – that is, any judgements about the form and content of education – once we have come to an understanding of what a desirable and justifiable set of purposes for our educational endeavours is, have to be understood as entirely *pragmatic*. I mean pragmatic here in the technical sense of the word, that is, where we judge the desirability of an educational arrangement or course of action in function of what the arrangement or course of action is supposed to bring about. Pragmatic judgements are therefore different from principled judgements, where we judge the desirability of an arrangement or course of action just on the qualities of the arrangement or course of action itself. While there is some room for principled judgements about the form and content of education in that we do not want them to be in any way unethical or immoral, apart from this any decision we make about how to proceed in education always needs to be taken in light of what it is we have judged to be a desirable set of purposes for our activities.

What I have in mind here is very practical and down to earth, but nonetheless very important and often overlooked in educational discussions, particularly when a new fashion emerges – sometimes from the field of practice, sometimes from the field of policy, sometimes from the field of theory and research – and those working in education feel forced or compelled to adopt this fashion, without asking what it might be good for. That our judgements ought to be pragmatic means, therefore, that in education nothing – no arrangement, no course of action, not even any content or curriculum – is desirable in itself; it all depends on what we seek to achieve (and, of course, on how we envisage that a particular arrangement or course of action might contribute to the purposes set). Concretely, it means that whether education should, for example, be flexible or inflexible, whether it should be personalised or general, whether it should be student-led or curriculum-led, whether the aims should be transparent and visible for the student, or not transparent and invisible, whether education should be easy and nice or difficult and strict, and perhaps even whether education should be effective or not, is not something we can decide in an abstract sense, but only in relation to what it is we seek to achieve. Pragmatic thinking can help us, on the one hand, to make a sound educational judgement about any new idea or suggestion that enters the educational domain – and notions such as flexibility, personalisation, transparency and visibility are currently definitely amongst the more fashionable ones – and, on the other hand, to see the value of ways of educational doing that are all too quickly discredited as a result of certain educational fashions. It can help us, in other words, to develop progressive arguments for what, from the perspective of fashion and a fetish for the new, might be seen as conservative ideas (for an attempt to reclaim the idea of teaching for education, see Biesta, 2012).

WHAT KINDS OF JUDGEMENT DO WE NEED IN TEACHING? PRACTICAL KNOWLEDGE AND PRACTICAL WISDOM

If the previous section has established a case for why judgement is needed in teaching by indicating those aspects of the practice of teaching where a judgement is called for, the question I wish to explore in this section is at a slightly higher level of abstraction and has to do with the *kinds* of judgement we need in teaching.[4] My guide in this section will be Aristotle (1980), and the reason for turning to his work is twofold. First, he provides a compelling and useful set of concepts for understanding the role of judgement in teaching. Second, he provides some interesting and original suggestions for teacher education through his ideas about the way in which we develop our ability for judgement. I will turn to the latter question in the next section and will focus here on Aristotle's views about judgement.

While in the previous section I have tried to indicate the different aspects and 'moments' of teaching where judgement is needed, one may still ask why judgement is actually needed in teaching. Couldn't it be the case, so a critic might suggest, that we only need judgement as long as there are aspects of teaching where we lack sufficient knowledge but that, with the advancement of the science of teaching, we will eventually reach a point where we no longer need judgement but can proceed with certainty? One argument against the idea of the sufficiency of a science of teaching – that is, of a conception of research that seeks to cover all the possible aspects of teaching – can be found in the work of William James who, in his *Talks to Teachers*, made the point in the following way:

> Psychology is a science, and teaching is an art; and sciences never generate arts directly out of themselves. An intermediary inventive mind must make the application, by using its originality.
>
> The most such sciences can do is to help us to catch ourselves up and check ourselves, if we start to reason or to behave wrongly; and to criticize ourselves more articulately after we have made mistakes.
>
> To know psychology, therefore, is absolutely no guarantee that we shall be good teachers. To advance to that result, we must have an additional endowment altogether, a happy tact and ingenuity to tell us what definite things to say and do when the pupil is before us. That ingenuity in meeting and pursuing the pupil, that tact for the concrete situation, though they are the alpha and omega of the teacher's art, are things to which psychology cannot help us in the least. (James, 1899, pp. 14–15)

The point James makes here could be characterised as an *epistemological* point, as he indicates the gap between the general knowledge the science of psychology can generate and the specific knowledge the teacher needs in each concrete situation. Looking at it in this way, we could say that the knowledge science can generate about teaching is never sufficient. Or, looking at it from the other side, such knowledge can never tell teachers what they should do, but can at most inform their judgements. Whereas this line of thought leaves open the possibility that a science of teaching might be possible – and in a sense only makes the point that scientific knowledge and practical knowledge are of a different category – Aristotle goes one step further by arguing that there is a fundamental difference between what he refers to as the theoretical life (the *bios theoretikos*) and the practical life (the *bios praktikos*). This suggests that his argument is not epistemological but *ontological*, as it asks what kind of reality teaching is or, to be more precise, in what kind of reality teaching takes place.

Aristotle conceives of the theoretical life as having to do with 'the necessary and the eternal' (Aristotle, 1980, p. 140), that is, with those parts of reality that do not change. He refers to the knowledge that is at stake here as 'episteme', which is often translated as 'science' (although the translation is a bit misleading as it suggests that science is an epistemological category – an idea well refuted by authors such as Karl Popper, Stephen Toulmin, Thomas Kuhn and Bruno Latour). We can think of *episteme* as representational knowledge about an unchanging world 'out there' and the connection Aristotle makes between *episteme* and the eternal suggests that it is, in principle, possible to generate knowledge that is 100 per cent certain and true, simply because its object is in the domain of the necessary and the eternal. Teaching, however, is not something that takes place in this domain. It rather belongs to the practical life, which Aristotle refers to as the domain of the 'variable' (p. 142), that is, the domain of change and possibility. It is the world in which we act and in which our actions make a difference. What is interesting about Aristotle's ideas about our activities in the domain of the variable is that he makes a distinction between two 'modes' of acting (and hence two forms or kinds of judgement; see below), one to which he refers as *poiesis* and one to which he refers as *praxis* or, in Carr's (1987) translation, 'making action' and 'doing action'. Both modes of action require judgement, but the kind of judgement needed is radically different, and this is an important insight for the art of education.

Poiesis is about the production or fabrication of things – such as, for example, a saddle or a ship – although I prefer to think of it slightly more widely, that is, as action that brings something into existence (see below). It is, as Aristotle puts it, about 'how something may come into being which is capable of either being or not being' (which means that it is about the variable, not about what is eternal and necessary), and about things 'whose origin is in the maker and not in the thing made' (which distinguishes *poiesis* from biological phenomena such as growth and development) (Aristotle, 1980, p. 141). *Poiesis* is, in short, about the creation of something that did not exist before. The kind of knowledge we need for *poiesis* is *techne* (usually translated as 'art,' although this translation is a little misleading and unhelpful as it is actually about the kind of knowledge and judgement we need in the domain of *poiesis*). Unlike *episteme,* which is knowledge about what is and how it is, *techne* is 'knowledge of how to make things' (p. 141). *Techne* thus is about finding the means that will bring about what one seeks to bring about or bring into existence. It encompasses knowledge about the materials we work with and about the techniques we can apply to work with those materials. But making something, such as a saddle, is never about simply following a recipe. It involves making judgements about the application of our general knowledge to *this* piece of leather, for *this* horse and for *this* person riding the horse. So we make judgements about application, production and effectiveness in our attempts to bring something into existence.

The domain of the variable is, however, not confined to the world of things, but also includes the social world – the world of human action and interaction. It is here that a second art is called for – the art of *praxis.* The orientation here is not towards the production of things but towards the promotion of human flourishing (*eudamonia*). *Praxis,* Aristotle writes, is 'about what sort of things conduce to the good life in general' (p. 142). We could say that *praxis* is about good action, but good action is here not to be understood as a means for bringing about something else – that is the domain of *poiesis,* which 'has an end other than itself' (p. 143). 'Good action,' on the other hand, 'itself is its end' (p. 143). The kind of judgement we need here is therefore not about *how* things should be done. We rather need judgement 'about *what is to be done*' (p. 143; emphasis added). Aristotle refers to this kind of judgement as *phronesis,* which is usually translated as practical wisdom. Aristotle gives the following, more precise definition of *phronesis* as a 'reasoned and true state of capacity to act with regard to human goods' (p. 143).

Aristotle's reflections on the domain of the variable and the different modes of action within it are important for understanding the role of judgement in education in a more precise manner. The first, and perhaps most important, point to make in relation to this is to say that we should never think of education *just* in terms of *poiesis* but always also in terms of *praxis*. While education is clearly located in the domain of the variable, it is concerned with the interaction between human beings, not the interaction between human beings and the material world. Our students are never simply objects, but are always to be seen and treated as human beings in their own right, as subjects. Yet this does not mean that we should exclude the idea of *poiesis* from our educational thinking. (I am responding here to authors in the educational literature who tend to overemphasise *phronesis* and underemphasise – or in some cases even reject – *techne* as being educationally relevant; see, for example, Heilbronn, 2008, chapter 5; Hillier, 2012, chapter 1.) After all, we do want our teaching and our curricula to have effect and be effective and we do want our students to achieve, both in the domain of qualification and in the domain of socialisation. But that should never be the be-all and end-all of education, because we also want our students to flourish as human beings – which is the question of *praxis* – which is perhaps an interest first of all located in the domain of subjectification, although we could also say that this is precisely where the interest in subjectification intersects with both qualification and socialisation (for example, in the difference between what we might call subjectivity-reducing and subjectivity-promoting qualification and subjectivity-reducing and subjectivity-promoting socialisation).

The second point that follows from these considerations is that with Aristotle we can now identify the two different kinds or modes of judgement that are needed in education. On the one hand, judgement plays a role in the domain of *poiesis*, the domain concerned with bringing something into existence – and I have carefully used the phrase 'bringing something into existence', rather than the cruder notion of production or technology, because I wish to highlight that *poiesis* is not to be understood in terms of mechanical or even mechanistic and machine-like production, but rather as a creative act and an act of creation where we do aim to bring 'things' into existence that did not exist before (see also Biesta, 2014, chapter 1). The judgements we need here are *judgements about how to do things*, and we have to acknowledge that these are indeed judgements because, in the domain of the variable, we are working with unpredictable 'material', which means that the results of our activities here will always *and necessarily* have a degree of uncertainty. This is not an uncertainty that at some point in time can be overcome once we have enough knowledge of all factors and dimensions of education. It is an uncertainty that stems from the very fact that education, as an interaction between living human beings, is in a fundamental sense open towards the future (which means that the only way to reduce this radical openness is by taking the 'human factor' out of education). In addition to judgements about how to do things, we need *judgements about what is to be done*, as the ultimate orientation of all education should be to the well-being and flourishing of our students, not in some kind of narrow, instrumental way – for example, orientated towards making our students 'happy' or 'satisfied' – but by contributing to the possibility of leading a worthy, meaningful human life (on the notion of worthiness, see Gur-Ze'ev, 2010, pp. 11–28). Both forms of judgement can be called 'practical', as they are both concerned with acting in the domain of the variable. Perhaps the first could be called *practical knowledge*, as it is knowledge about how to operate effectively in the domain of the variable, whereas the second can be called *practical wisdom* (which is the common translation of the word *phronesis*), as it is about the ability to judge what is to be done in a given situation, which is the question of educational purpose(s) as discussed above.

HOW CAN TEACHERS BECOME CAPABLE OF EDUCATIONAL JUDGEMENT?

In the previous sections I have tried to make clear why we need judgement in education, where we need judgement in education, and what kinds of judgement we need in education. I have, following Aristotle, argued that education has both *poiesis* and *praxis* dimensions, so that we need both judgement about how to do things (*techne*) and judgement about what is to be done (*phronesis*). I have also argued that because of the teleological nature of education, that is, the fact that education is constituted by purposes – and precisely here education is different from learning – all our educational actions and activities are ultimately 'framed' by our considered views about what education is for. And this question is not only an abstract question at the level of education policy or curriculum theory, but also a concrete question that returns again and again in every concrete moment of teaching. It is one of the reasons why all our judgements in education ultimately need to be pragmatic – that is, connected to the question what the activity is for. And, given that the purpose of education is multidimensional, questions about balance, tensions and trade-offs between the three domains of educational purpose are also always raised. All this means that the ability to judge and to do so in an educational way – which means to ask with everything we do whether it is educationally desirable – is absolutely central for good teaching. This is why it also should have a central role in teacher education. But how should we understand the 'ability' to make educational judgements? And how can we support teachers in 'developing' this 'ability'? It is here that I will turn once more to Aristotle.[5]

While practical knowledge (*techne*) plays an important role in teaching, all judgements we make in relation to how we should proceed are ultimately framed by judgements about what is to be done, which is the domain of practical wisdom (*phronesis*). While it is important for teachers to develop their ability for judgement with regard to the question how to act, the underlying need – which precisely marks the difference between a competent teacher and a good teacher – has to do with the ability to make judgements about what is educationally desirable. For this teachers need practical wisdom (*phronesis*). While some try to suggest that practical wisdom is itself a competence – that is, something a teacher can acquire and then possess – Aristotle argues, and this is the lead I will follow here, that practical wisdom should be understood as a quality or excellence of the person. It is therefore in the domain of *being*, not the domain of *having*. The question for teacher education, therefore, is not a question of how a student can *acquire* practical wisdom; rather it is a question of how the student can become educationally wise. Or, in Aristotle's terms: the question is not how the teacher can acquire *phronesis*, but how the teacher can become a *phronimos*, a practically (and educationally) wise person (on this distinction see also Biesta, 2013). What we are talking about here is what in Greek is called *arete* and in English is often translated as *virtue* or *character*. While both words have problematic sides – and the notion of 'character' particularly has, through discussions on character education, been made into an aim for rather strict and reproductive socialisation – what we have with the idea of ἀρετή is not a skill or cognitive faculty, but rather something that *characterises* the way of being and acting of a person. It is a quality that permeates how the person is and acts, which means that, in more modern terms, it is a holistic and embodied quality. So how can student teachers become educationally wise? Aristotle makes two interesting points in relation to this question. The first is his observation 'that a young man of practical wisdom cannot be found' (Aristotle, 1980, p. 148), which suggests that practical wisdom comes with age or, to be more precise, that it comes with *experience*. The second is that Aristotle does not provide abstract definitions of what practical wisdom looks like, but rather tries to make this clear through examples, referring to those who exemplify *phronesis* in a particular domain. Taking all this together, I would like to conclude with three 'reference points' for teacher education: a focus on the formation of character or educational virtuosity; a focus on practising judgement; and a focus on engagement with examples of educational virtuosity.

The first point is that teacher education should be understood as a process of the formation of the person – not, that is, the individual person, but the person as professional. This means that in terms of the three domains of educational purpose, we should not confine teacher education merely to the domain of qualification – to just providing teachers with the knowledge and skills they need – nor to the domain of socialisation – that is, just initiating them into the (existing) professional culture. While such paths may bring about teachers who are competent, they may not result in teachers who are good, precisely because they may lack the embodied ability to place their knowledge, skills and ways of doing within the wider context of the question of what is to be done, the question of what is educationally desirable. To make that question the centre of one's professional action as a teacher requires that this question – and the ability to engage with it in a meaningful way – permeates everything one does. We could say therefore, that teacher education should focus on the formation of educational character. However, given potentially problematic connotations of that word, I prefer to describe the approach I have been outlining here as a *virtue-based approach*, that is, an approach aimed at the formation of educationally virtuous professionals. To play a little with the word 'virtue', we could rephrase this as a concern for the education of professionals whose ways of acting exemplify *educational virtuosity*, that is, embodied educational wisdom: the embodied ability to make wise educational judgements about what is to be done, about what is educationally desirable. As I have tried to make clear throughout this chapter, such a virtue-based approach is significantly different both from a competence-based approach and an evidence-based approach. When we think of how musicians develop their virtuosity we can see two other important dimensions of a virtue-based approach, which give us the other two reference points for teacher education.

The second reference point is that we can only develop our virtuosity for educational wisdom by practising such judgement, that is, by being engaged in the practice of judgement from the very start of our formation as teachers. The question as to what is educationally desirable is, to put it differently, not a question that should come at the very end of teacher education, once all the knowledge, skills and competences have been acquired, but should be there from day one – perhaps on the simple principle that if you want to learn to play the piano there is no point in starting on a flute; you have to engage with the piano, its challenges, complexities and difficulties, from day one if you want to become a good piano player. It is perhaps important to emphasise that this is not an argument for training on the job. It is only an argument for saying that if our ultimate aim is the formation of educational wisdom, of educationally wise teachers, this needs to permeate the teacher education curriculum from the very start.

The third reference point that follows from my considerations is the importance of developing educational virtuosity through examples – through studying the virtuosity of others – precisely because we are not talking about an abstract skill, but an embodied and situated way of doing, which therefore requires careful study of those who we might see as good (or, for that matter, bad) examples of having become educationally wise. Again, this is not an argument for training on the shop floor, and also not for the fashionable idea of peer learning. It is precisely the difficult task of studying the virtuosity of experienced educators, trying to see how it functions, how it is embodied, where it is done explicitly, where it is held back precisely for educational reasons, and so on. Such a trajectory of study requires careful attention to detail, and thus requires time and deepening, because what we may be able to see the first time we look may be very different from what we might be able to see the second time we look, and so on.

CONCLUDING COMMENTS

In this chapter I have tried to answer the question of how a competent teacher might become a good teacher. I have suggested that the difference between a competent and a good teacher lies in the ability to bring judgement to the task of teaching. I have, on the one hand, tried to indicate why and where teaching needs judgement, and, on the other, tried to make clear what kinds of judgement teachers need. Against this background I have made a case for a virtue-based rather than a competence-based or evidence-based conception of teaching and teacher education and have, in relation to the latter domain, highlighted the importance of working on educational virtuosity in order for teachers to become educationally wise. Initial teacher education has an important and unique role to play in this, and I have provided a number of reference points for such forms of teacher education. I believe that teachers can continue to grow in their educational wisdom, and in this regard the question of what is educationally desirable is one that should remain central throughout their teaching career.

NOTES

1 www.atee1.org/uploads/EUpolicies/common_eur_principles_en.pdf (accessed 18 October 2014).

2 http://europa.eu/legislation_summaries/education_training_youth/lifelong_learning/c11101_en.htm (accessed 18 October 2014).

3 As I will try to make clear throughout this chapter, my ambition is not to specify what an educationally desirable course of action is, but to highlight the fact that in education the question about what is educationally desirable – both with regard to the aims and ends (the purpose of education) and with regard to the ways of proceeding (the 'means' of education) – is

inevitable. What I seek to do is to highlight the dimensions of this question, but it is up to educators in concrete situations to engage with the question of what is desirable and formulate and justify their situated answers, in dialogue with other 'stakeholders' in the process. My aim is to ensure that such deliberations and justifications play a central role in teaching and hence also have a central position in the education of teachers.

4 The argument I am developing in this chapter focuses on how we might understand teaching and what such an understanding implies for the role of the teacher. The understanding I put forward focuses on the role of judgement in teaching, and thus highlights the crucial importance of teachers' judgement. My focus is on the implications of this understanding for teacher education. There is a further question that falls outside of the scope of this chapter, which is the extent to which teachers are able to exercise the judgements that, in my view, are crucial for any educationally meaningful teaching. This question partly has to do with the self-understanding teachers have of their own profession and professional scope for action, but is of course also highly influenced by the concrete environments in which teachers work – environments that nowadays often offer little scope for teacher judgement.

5 In what follows I provide a particular interpretation of Aristotle that I find useful for the point I wish to make about teacher education. For this I focus on *phronesis* and the idea of virtue in Aristotle. The question I leave aside in this discussion is about the status of *techne* and the extent to which this does or does not belong to the intellectual virtues. In some places Aristotle does include it, yet in other places he does not – which raises further questions about (the different interpretations of) the distinction between *episteme* and *techne* in Aristotle's work. For a helpful discussion, see Parry (2008).

2
Learning to Teach and Becoming a Teacher: *Techne* and *Phronesis*

COLIN WRINGE

It will be readily acknowledged that before entering upon any occupational role, one needs a certain preparation. This chapter argues that such preparation requires not only that the person concerned knows and does the various things the role entails and does them well, but that some roles, notably that of the teacher, also involve becoming the kind of person the occupant of the role needs to be. To further the discussion it is proposed to divide occupational preparation into three categories, which, though scarcely hard and fast, will suffice for the purposes of discussion: these three elements of preparation may be seen as the learning of procedures, the acquisition of skills and, for want of a better word, education. It will also be evident that though a modicum of all three of these modes of preparation may be necessary for all occupational roles, their proportion and importance may vary widely from one occupation to another. These distinctions are important for two good reasons. First, these elements are acquired under different circumstances and in radically different ways. Second, it is important to avoid the error of supposing that if we have given a great deal of attention to one or other of these elements, the whole task of preparation for the role in question has been achieved.

Philosophical Perspectives on Teacher Education, First Edition. Edited by Ruth Heilbronn and Lorraine Foreman-Peck. © 2015 Ruth Heilbronn and Lorraine Foreman-Peck. Editorial Organisation © Philosophy of Education Society of Great Britain. Published 2015 by John Wiley & Sons, Ltd.

PROCEDURES

These are prescribed ways of carrying out parts of an occupation or job that are relatively invariant and that, if deviated from, may require some special explanation or further action. They may be very simple, but not necessarily so: 'When a customer books in at this hotel, you take her name and credit card details, ask how long she intends to stay, ask if breakfast or other meals will be required, assign a room and issue the key.' 'When carrying out a surgical operation the surgeon must ensure that the consent form has been signed, wash her hands thoroughly, ensure that the necessary instruments are to hand, check the relevant clinical data, and so on.' Procedures are valuable in ensuring the smooth and efficient running of busy institutions, especially large ones, by enabling people to rely on colleagues doing or not doing certain things, thus avoiding the need for ad hoc decisions, consultation or close supervision by high-level staff. They are particularly important in institutions performing highly replicable activities such as chains of retail outlets, hotels or snack bars but also in hospitals, police forces and armies. Unnotified deviations from procedure may justify a presumption of fault and require excuse or explanation. On the other hand, the fact that correct procedure has been followed may protect the employee or member of staff in the event of mishap. If procedures are to serve their purpose effectively they need to be explicitly communicated or drilled in training to the point of becoming second nature.

PROCEDURES AND SKILL

It is important to distinguish procedures from skills, albeit in much discussion of both labour markets and vocational training the two are often conflated and described as skills when they are in fact procedures. Preparation for many occupations, including some that require significant periods of training, is in fact heavily loaded with procedures. Typically much instruction for such occupations will be highly specific as to what is to be done, and how. The procedures may be highly complex and have to be got right on pain of disasters that may prove fatal. Considerable practice may in some cases be necessary if they are to be performed with the necessary manual or mental dexterity. Arguably, much of the extensive body of knowledge required in many occupations, from those of doctors, lawyers and engineers to computer technicians and London taxi-drivers, should be considered part of the procedures of the occupation. The facts are as they are and must be correctly applied with relatively little scope for variation. Procedures, unlike skill, which is typically acquired with experience over a period, have to be got right from day one.

The difference between procedures and skills will be apparent if we consider that the characteristic mode of appraisal of a skill is not purely one of whether or not it has been performed properly, but whether it has been done well. The accolade of 'skilful' is something more than that of competence, which is not to say that competence should be sneezed at, especially if the task is complex or important. The skilful joiner is not only able to produce a serviceable table of standard design from new timber but is also able to make good use of material that is, perhaps, slightly flawed or produce a specialised piece of furniture for a particular individual purpose. A skilled pilot not only lands our plane safely when the sun is shining but also in dangerously difficult conditions, with our hearts still in our chests and not in our mouths. To have become skilled is not merely to have mastered the procedures but to have learned enough about the medium of one's occupation – about wood in the case of the joiner, about weather conditions and the limits and mode of performance of one's plane's controls in the case of the pilot – to go creatively beyond the limits of procedure. This is not learned by instruction or demonstration, but as a result of experience and intelligent observation as well as supportive coaching and guidance. The acquisition of skill also necessarily involves an underlying cognitive component.

Even joiners are likely to become skilful more readily if they have some prior expectation of how wood, or particular kinds of wood, are likely to behave or some knowledge of the range of joints and fixings that others in the trade have developed over time. Even if not delivered to apprentices in formal lectures on the Theory of Wood Technology, joiners who are to become skilful will have acquired this knowledge either through their own interest or from colleagues over time, or will have imaginatively created their own informal body of theory by which they make sense of their practice to themselves. Despite the contempt in which theory is held by some practical people, no practical activity can be rationally carried on at all without some theory regarding the activity's goals or the empirical conditions of its successful performance, even if this is no more than the simple, unsophisticated kind of theory that a relatively inarticulate craftsman might use to guide his own actions or explain what he is doing. Skill involves not the mere performance of procedures, but the making of choices – judgements of better or worse among a range of available options – and can only be judged to have been successfully acquired in the light of actual outcomes.

EDUCATION AND SKILL

We need not add a further definition of education to the many that have already been suggested by philosophers. It suffices here to say that we may readily imagine expert engineers, lawyers, surgeons or classical scholars who, despite their undoubted knowledge and even skill in their specialised fields, strike us as profoundly uneducated, even ignorant, in the narrowness of their knowledge or interest in other matters, dismissive of the achievements, values or priorities of other occupations or ways of life and unsympathetic or unaware of the misfortunes of others, for education is a matter of attitude, of openness and generosity of mind, as much as of knowledge.

If a civil engineer is dismissive of environmental concern for the landscape through which she is engaged in building a by-pass, or a joiner is unconcerned about the aesthetic appearance of an otherwise perfectly serviceable table, this may be a matter of relatively contingent though not necessarily inconsiderable concern. To certain other occupations, however, qualities of flexibility, understanding and empathy produced by education would seem to be inherently necessary. These are essentially occupations that involve work with other human beings which may importantly affect their well-being or destinies. Typically these might include the law, work in social service institutions for the care of vulnerable individuals, young, old, physically or mentally sick, many kinds of social administration and, notably, teaching. Children of school age are a prime example of dependent and vulnerable human beings whose well-being and, in many cases, whose destinies and future lives may be significantly influenced by the actions, words and judgements of those who teach them. In such occupations mere crude efficiency in pursuing the ostensible goals of their employment is inadequate. Obtusely inhumane psychiatric nurses, policemen, prison governors or orphanage directors may meet the express efficiency criteria of their employment but in human terms they are the stuff of nightmares. Their obtuse inhumanity may not necessarily be seen as a purely ethical failure. They may be people of sterling moral character, unflinching in their determination to serve their employers or authorities to the best of their abilities and even committed to what they see as or have been led to believe is in the best interest of those in their care. The failure is not one of moral intention but of perception of where duty lies. No doubt this is the reason why recruitment to such occupations usually requires some minimal general education, which may be thought to ensure some breadth of perspective through, for example, some elementary study of life in other countries or other times, a humbling awareness of the complexities of the physical universe or views of human life as seen through the eyes of serious writers.

LEARNING TO TEACH: DELIVERING THE CURRICULUM EFFECTIVELY

Such procedures as teachers are strictly required to follow – how and when new stationery may be obtained, the collection of dinner money and absence notes, the completion of end of term reports; what to do in cases of accident or sudden illness, and so on – are rather marginal to teachers' actual educational role. In this respect the preparation of teachers differs markedly from that of certain other occupations such as medicine, engineering or the training of air crew. Certain things in school may be assumed, such as that boards will be left clean or equipment put away, but these things are rarely made explicit, at least until their neglect inconveniences others or gives rise to problems. It is true that these days teachers are expected to plan lessons with relevance to national curricula and departmental schemes of work, and no doubt the efficient transmission of curricular content might be increased if all teachers, not just those in training, were required to identify and record specific learning objectives in advance, as well as listing materials and activities to be used, approximate timings for different parts of the lesson, modes of formal or informal assessment to be employed and observations as to whether successful learning appears to have taken place. Possibly something of the kind may increasingly form part of many teachers' procedural repertoire, but all too often these things may be done in a somewhat loose and informal way and the manner of their performance or even occasional omission may be seen as a matter of individual style, to a degree that would be unacceptable in many other occupations.

While teaching is relatively light on procedures, success depends heavily on skill. In this it differs sharply from the work of nurses, doctors, electricians or architects who, provided they keep strictly within the accepted rules and procedures of their occupations, are to some extent protected against too evident failure in their professional work, even if they show relatively little intelligence or flair. A teacher, by contrast, may regularly devote due time to the preparation of her lesson, giving attention to relevant parts of the National Curriculum and the department's scheme of work; identify the objectives of the lesson beforehand and even write them on the board; make use of perfectly standard teaching materials or an approved textbook; present the content clearly; set some perfectly normal learning activities and an adequate assessment exercise, which she takes in, marks and promptly returns next morning. But this is no guarantee of a successful or even an acceptable lesson if it leaves the learners glassy-eyed, bored with the subject or with education generally, with little understanding of the point of what is being taught, or if the classroom ends up in a state of chaos or noisy insurrection. Of course, a teacher who follows the above procedures meticulously and is fiercely authoritarian may achieve good examination results and be thought of as highly competent, even if her pupils end up with little understanding or liking for the subject and are happy to forget everything about it as soon as the examination is over.

Though we might regard it as a procedural requirement that a teacher should explicitly identify lesson objectives, plan specific learning activities and build in assessment activities, what is important is not that these things should be done, but that the teacher should identify *appropriate* objectives, choose *stimulating* materials, *motivating* activities and *searching* assessment tasks. To do these things is not a matter of simple compliance but of skill, implying as it does choices based on qualitative judgements. This can, in principle, not be learned by instruction but only acquired in a period of practical experience. Experience alone, however, is far from being the best and most efficient manner of acquiring skill.

There is no sure-fire standard procedure for teaching the past tense in a foreign language, simultaneous equations or Ohm's law. Skilful teachers interpret curricula in ways that will engage their classes; calibrate their objectives to the level of their abilities and existing conceptual structure; judge how explicitly and to what extent to reveal their objectives; carry their classes with them, controlling them closely or loosely as is most expedient, weighing from moment to moment what learning and assessment activities to set, and are shrewd in their interpretation of assessment tasks. They have acquired the ability to do this because of their understanding and commitment to the broader aims of their profession, coupled with an understanding of what is truly involved in the topic of the present lesson and above all the interests and abilities of the pupils they are presently teaching.

It would be surprising if the acquisition of skill in teaching were not enhanced by some general acquaintance with such theories of learning as behaviourism, gestalt theories of perception, constructivism and so on, or some understanding of the processes of social learning or the motivations, values and use of language of learners from different social backgrounds. It is true that in the staffrooms of the past one often met grand old characters whose experience and skills were praised by pupils and colleagues alike but to whom the very word 'theory' was like a red rag to a bull. Such individuals, however, were not without theory or theories of their own, self-generated and backed up by years of survival in the classroom. However simplistic such theories may have been, they were theories nonetheless. Theory that facilitates the acquisition of skills should not be seen as a set of prescriptions. This mistake is often made by its detractors. Skill itself can only be acquired in practice, background understanding simply serving to point the way and explain why some approaches are likely to be more helpful than others or, perhaps, helping to puncture time-honoured nostrums that inhibit the range of strategies that the practitioner perceives as open to her. Essentially, the knowledge involved in becoming a skilful teacher is not simply 'knowledge that' or even 'knowledge how' but 'knowledge by acquaintance' of the complex conditions of the classroom.

BECOMING A TEACHER: BEYOND PROCEDURES AND SKILL

So much for simply learning to teach. Might this not be sufficient: that the teacher be sufficiently well qualified in her subject to articulate its content accurately, punctilious in the performance of procedures necessary to the smooth running of a school and satisfactory coverage of the curriculum, as well as being sufficiently skilled, with all that implies for background understanding of learners and the process of learning, to manage a class properly and transmit her knowledge at a level appropriate to her particular pupils by means of skilfully chosen materials and activities? That at least would be a start. But in itself it is woefully inadequate and represents a crudely technicist model of education. If all that was required of young people at the end of schooling was that they should possess eight or so lists of useful pieces of information or sets of procedures or routines, the above model would be fine. Efficiency in transmission would be the paramount – indeed the sole – requirement. And it sometimes seems that this crude conception of education, the successful achievement of which is signalled by a list of good examination scores, is not only widely but even officially held.

If education is conceived of as instruction in a number of separate academic subjects, then the teacher herself needs to have received such instruction to a reasonably high level. That much is generally agreed within the current policy orthodoxy. To teach English literature you need a degree in English literature; the better the degree, the better it is. Similar remarks apply to the teaching of other school subjects. But does the only professional benefit of having studied English literature for two years in the sixth form and three years at university lie in the teacher's having sufficient material to pass on to her pupils?

A more educationally reputable justification for pupils' studying literature – to stay with our current example – is not that one will know a certain number of facts about certain novels, plays or poems and their authors and be able to expound these in an account that is accurate, coherent, concise, grammatical and correctly spelt. This is, of course, a valuable transferable skill, useful to an employer and possibly sufficient to pass most English literature examinations. But what is more important from an educational point of view is the fact that literary works usually present a range of characters and human predicaments, and insights regarding them. Various points of view regarding characters, predicaments and outcomes may be plausible and worthy of discussion. Works as a whole may exhibit qualities of style and rhetoric that merit appreciation or criticism over and above the content of what is said, and comments both within and about literary works may be couched in terms that are nuanced, often ambivalent or hypothetical and not infrequently ironic.

Educated teachers of history, geography, foreign languages and the mathematical and physical sciences will be able to demonstrate the wider educational benefits of their own subjects beyond those accruing directly from the mere possession of their content. To study any subject seriously and in depth is necessarily to become aware of a number of further things. First, it is to become aware that any body of knowledge is an artefact of human creation, not just there to be confidently read off from the universe or handed down authoritatively from one generation to another but brought into existence by the work of countless individuals over innumerable generations, not simply methodically or routinely but often in the heat of controversy and strife. Nor does our present state of knowledge, as we are inclined to call it, represent arrival at some ultimate destination, for we know that the next generation, including our pupils, will see things differently. Those of our current views that are not actually proved mistaken or misguided may be seen in a different light and given a radically different degree of importance.

Second, as the study of a subject advances we cannot, unless we are extraordinarily insensitive, fail to become aware of its implications and seriousness. The physical sciences and the technologies to which they give rise explain much that we see around us in the modern world.

We are obliged to see their deliverances as both reassuring and threatening. The study of history engenders senses of both pride and obligation, giving rise to pleasure in what has been achieved and making us uncomfortably aware of the transitory nature of the present. Third, to understand science, history, literature and the arts, and so on is not only to know the facts that constitute those subjects but to come to an understanding of the nature of those subjects and the nature of the claims that they comprise. Statements in relation to science, history, a literary work or mathematics may all be true but they are true for radically different reasons, so that utterances in different fields may be made with varying degrees of confidence. In the absence of such understandings learners cannot autonomously pursue their own intellectual development after the end of their formal schooling and are, even if they know the literal meaning of the words, still to an extent in the position of Dearden's (1972) pupils, who can state that the centre of the earth is igneous but do not fully understand the significance of what they say.

That which is learned needs to coalesce in a coherent picture of the world into which the individual can enter with more freedom, safety, confidence and enjoyment than if she had been untaught. What is learned not only has to be known and understood in its own internal complexity; it has to be applied to the real external world and its significance grasped by the learner in relation to her own subjective experience of the world and possible or envisioned purposes and aspirations. It also has to have significance in relation to the bodies of knowledge encountered in other areas of school learning. For pupils to grasp all this in the course of Lesson 3 on Tuesday afternoon would be a bit much to expect, but if some such reflections do not rub off on pupils in relation to some of their school learnings, little has been done to promote their educated understanding.

The teacher who is herself educated rather than a mere instructor will not miss opportunities to correct such assumptions as that the age and origins of the universe are known for certain, that statements about literary works and their authors may be established by reference to authorities rather than the text, that certain grammatical forms in a language are used 'because there is a rule' or that certain rulers in the past were unequivocally good or bad. This is one of the reasons why teachers need to be educated beyond a mere content knowledge of their subject, simply trained in the procedures of school and classroom and skilled in the narrow crafts of presentation and motivation. If learners are to be educated rather than merely competent and knowledgeable, their teachers must be so before them.

A further reason why teachers need to be educated and not merely skilled is that theirs is a profession that deals with human beings who are both vulnerable and dependent, being at a formative stage in their development, which is supposedly influenced – if by no means determined for good or ill – by those who teach them. One can scarcely be seriously involved in the business of teaching without caring about the future destinies of those one teaches. Teaching is not a job for someone, however knowledgeable and skilled, who is arrogantly or uncritically convinced of the importance or incontestability of their own limited field of expertise or their own point of view. Pupils these days not only come from more varied backgrounds than may previously have been the case, bringing with them a more varied set of values and aspirations than in the past; they also have open to them a more varied range of futures. Whether or not social mobility is increasing or decreasing, pupils nowadays may aspire to a greater range of occupations than formerly. Also, as a society we no longer embrace a single value system or single conception of the good or worthwhile life. This is not to say that relativism rules. No one wants to see young people embrace a life of drug addiction, fecklessness or petty crime, but there are, nevertheless, a range of acceptable aspirations that may form the focus of a good or flourishing life: the life of religious observance, duty and respectability, the life of social, professional or economic ambition, the life of scholarship, artistic creativity or performance, or, for both men and women, the traditional life of marriage and devotion to family. Privately we may find some of these options more admirable than others but legitimate options they are, even if they are rarely expressed explicitly. It would be a teacher ill versed in the possibilities of a flourishing life who felt it incumbent upon herself to pressurise learners in one direction or another. The positive, humane and ultimately reasonable affirmation of the diversity of others is the natural fruit of a good all-round education. Such attitudes and qualities can only be passed on by teachers who possess them themselves.

EDUCATION AND PHILOSOPHY

We might be inclined to say that teachers whose own education had led them to reflect in this way about the nature and status of knowledge or the nature and diversity of human life and human aspiration had, albeit unwittingly, already made a start on philosophy of education and had gone beyond what he or she had been told to teach by the curriculum or examination board. Such claims are, of course, deeply resented by the members of other disciplines who may see them as imperialistic claims to authority in what they see as their own territory. Nevertheless, the existence of such substantial and respected bodies of work as philosophy of science, philosophy of the social sciences, philosophy of mathematics, philosophy of law, political philosophy and so on gives support to the claim that philosophy may contribute to the understanding of other modes of enquiry or other curriculum subjects. To many of the actual practitioners of other disciplines – physicists, historians, medical practitioners and so on – the philosophy of their subject may seem relatively marginal to the expertise they employ in their day-to-day work. If, however, one is using one's subject as a teacher in the education of others, this cannot be the case, for to simply transmit the content of one's subject is to risk producing a generation of well informed zombies with little understanding of what they purport to know. This suggests the highly contentious claim that the educational element of what is taught – getting to the bottom of things about the nature of knowledge, human nature, human destiny and so on – just is what is educational, and that the rest is mere content; that the relationship between education and philosophy is not just guiding or directive, but is more intimately constitutive. One cannot take a rounded or 'educated' view of what one learns without reflecting upon it in a partly philosophical way. Whatever one may ultimately think of Hirst's (1965) so-called 'forms of knowledge', one cannot fail to see the educational value of pupils, and therefore of teachers, coming to reflect upon what is involved in making an assertion in physics, history or the study of literature. More recent postmodernist and phenomenological studies have also played their part in drawing attention to the problematic nature of many of our knowledge claims, the finite nature of individual and cultural perspectives and the ultimate foundation of both in individual subjectivities.

It is true that some philosophers of education (Carr, 2000; Winch, 2010) have argued that philosophy should form an important element in the preparation of future teachers because they are often faced with ethical and epistemological or curricular decisions. Winch adds that this applies not only to those teachers who will spend the majority of their careers in the classroom, but especially to those who will progress to positions of authority and influence in the profession. While this may be perfectly true, the decisions that teachers have to make are not of this kind and such arguments suggest that philosophy has a mere external or contingent contribution to make to the performative competence of teachers, rather than making a profounder contribution to enabling the teacher to become the kind of educated person a teacher ideally needs to be. Philosophy is not simply a body of technical knowledge to which teachers may refer in deciding between two or more particular courses of action. Unlike the members of some other professions, such as doctors deciding between surgery and medication, architects calculating the thickness of a beam required to support a particular structure or lawyers advising clients whether or not they have a legal claim, teachers are not, as part of their everyday work, required to make single one-off decisions depending on rigorous technical or theoretical justification. A teacher may occasionally need to offer a student advice on a future course of study or decide between noticing a potentially serious misdemeanour or looking the other way, but these are mostly matters of professional prudence and a shrewd judgement of likely consequences rather than genuinely philosophical issues. It is not the role of teachers to determine the overall aims of education; nor is it that of school authorities, curriculum planners or, for that matter, governments. The practice of teaching embodies traditions that predate modern institutions and structures by centuries, if not millennia. In this regard, one must profoundly disagree with the claim that little useful educational planning can be undertaken until the overall aims of education have been established (White, 1990). The practical reason that needs to guide the *praxis* of teachers is of an altogether different order. Their day-to-day work contributes to many valid educational goals and teachers do not need to make permanent or systematic choices between them. Choices to be made by the classroom teacher relate to what it is in the interests of this child or this group to help them to achieve here and now. The answer will vary from individual to individual and may change from moment to moment, even if clarity in regard to the issues involved, and a grasp of the range of options available and legitimate, may have an obvious part to play in the making of judicious choices in particular situations.

The major doctrines of ethics have sometimes played an important part in the professional education of teachers and an acquaintance with these is no doubt helpful in the reasoned appraisal of both individual choices and policies at school and wider levels. An acquaintance with ethical theories, however, does not provide formulaic solutions to particular dilemmas, though it may serve to mitigate more peremptory conclusions and lead to more nuanced, wiser and more educationally informed outcomes. The well-established analytic tradition of subjecting topical educational slogans and fashionable educational panaceas to scrutiny in terms of meaning, justification and implications remains an essential discipline in the professional education of teachers while, as with the more epistemological strand of philosophy of education, recent post-analytical developments have also had the positive educational effect of moderating many of our over-confident value assumptions.

The contribution of philosophy to the preparation of teachers lies not in the conclusions of any particular philosopher or philosophical doctrine but in the general attitude it engenders and in its insistence on returning to fundamentals rather than relying too heavily on tradition, received wisdom, current fashions in 'common sense' or religious and political ideology. Though teachers may not have to decide to what extent induction is a valid form of argument or whether we can truly have knowledge of other minds, an awareness of these issues may influence the tone of finality with which a science teacher links evidence to generalisation in presenting a scientific law, or contribute to the tentativeness and sensitivity with which a literary work or historical event is presented or interpreted.

Crucial to the present discussion is the fact that education is neither an industrial process nor a *techne* or craft requiring merely the execution of set procedures or the exercise of technical skills for its successful performance. It is not a *techne* but a *praxis* (Luby, 2006). The content of education is not a set of finite, unambiguous messages to be imprinted on units of material differing only in their ability to take up the print. The decisive reason why the craft model of teacher education is inappropriate lies in the nature of human beings. In learning a craft the future practitioner has to learn both the accepted procedures of her craft and the skills that will enable her to bring about what are in most cases more or less pre-specifiable outcomes. The object of a craft remains strictly that, an object. It does not participate in the work of the craftsman and does not have aspirations of its own that it is free to pursue after the work has been completed. It is true that some skilled occupations – beauticians, chiropodists, hairdressers, surgeons, solicitors – do not work on inanimate objects, though eyebrows, corns, gall bladders and the like are objects of a kind. This is why practitioners who do work in this close manner with their human clients require a modicum of education, because those for whom they work may vary in their interests, priorities and aspirations. Nevertheless, the outcomes of their services remain fairly closely pre-scribed and are, as it were, handed over to the client rather than set at liberty to enjoy an autonomous existence of their own. To this degree the notion of schools 'producing' a certain kind of 'material' to meet the needs of society or government, to say nothing of employers, is morally grotesque. Teachers do not and cannot determine, and there-fore cannot ultimately be held responsible for, the eventual outcomes of their professional activity. They may influence the actions and development of their pupils but they do not determine what they even-tually do or become, for human beings are not material objects or even trainable animals but the initiators of their own actions (Arendt, 1958), agents of their own futures, within the unforeseeable situations into which they are 'thrown' (Heidegger, 1927) by circumstance, even if some part of the future to which they aspire may have been prepared by what they have been taught. Educated human beings do not resem-ble artefacts to be produced, however intricate or aesthetically noble, nor are they patients to be cured of their maladies, or clients to have aspects of their appearance enhanced or even their material interests protected at law. The mode of practical reason appropriate to the guid-ance of teachers is not *techne* but *phronesis* (Dunne, 1993) and it requires no mere briefing in procedures or even training in the skill of achieving pre-specified objectives but the wisdom, imagination and flexibility that results from their own education, clarified and enlight-ened by philosophical reflection.

3
The Idea of a University and School Partnership

JAMES McALLISTER

This chapter considers whether or not the idea of university and school partnerships is a good one for teacher education, with particular focus on what the role of the university ought to be in any such partnership. If the recent proposals for teacher education reform in England and Scotland respectively come to pass, there is a danger that some partnerships in England may increasingly train teachers to think about education in rather narrow and instrumental terms. J.H. Newman's *The Idea of a University* (originally published 1852/1858) is examined in the chapter. While Newman's liberal disciplines model of the university may not value profession-based learning nearly enough, I claim here that exclusively school-based models for teacher education are in danger of going too far in the other direction of not valuing enough any knowledge that is not directly derived from professional practice. With reference to Alfred North Whitehead (1967) and Paul Hirst (1965, 1983), I contend that university staff involved in teacher education should still draw upon the disciplines of education, but in ways that encourage new and qualified teachers to *both* develop the practical skills they need to teach competently *and* think broadly, deeply and imaginatively about education.

Philosophical Perspectives on Teacher Education, First Edition. Edited by Ruth Heilbronn and
Lorraine Foreman-Peck. © 2015 Ruth Heilbronn and Lorraine Foreman-Peck. Editorial Organisation
© Philosophy of Education Society of Great Britain. Published 2015 by John Wiley & Sons, Ltd.

WHAT SPACE FOR EXPLORATION OF 'THEORY' IN UK TEACHER EDUCATION OF THE FUTURE?

Recent policy development in the UK (DfE, 2010; SG, 2011) indicates that substantial and imminent changes are afoot in regard to how teachers ought to be trained and developed in their roles. Central to the reforms are new partnerships between schools and universities. In England the White Paper *The Importance of Teaching* declared the government's intention to establish a new framework of 'teaching schools', as well as some 'university training schools' (DfE, 2010, p. 23). A network of up to 500 teaching schools was planned to be established by 2014 (DfE, 2012a). The *National Teaching Schools Prospectus* declares that all teaching schools must be 'centres of excellence for ITT', adding that each teaching school must 'ensure that demonstrably excellent practitioners take responsibility for and lead each trainee teacher's training programme' (NCL, 2011, p. 18). The institution overseeing the new framework of teaching schools in England, the National College for School Leadership and Children's Services (NCL),[1] also has an 'expectation that university tutors will participate in professional development activities undertaken in the network (in schools), and that network staff (from schools) will contribute to university-based elements of teacher training and development' (NCL, 2011, p. 18). While it is expected that teaching schools will take a lead role in any liaison with HEI (higher education institution) providers (DfE, 2012a), the new partnerships in England appear to favour more joint working of university staff in schools and school staff in universities than in the past, with demonstrably excellent (whatever that might mean) staff in schools being given increased levels of responsibility for the mentoring and professional learning of student teachers.[2]

Meanwhile, the recent review of teacher education in Scotland similarly urges reform and greater collaboration via the establishment of 'hub schools' that are characterised by a 'strong and meaningful partnership with a university to support their work' (SG, 2011, p. 111). The proposed reforms in England and Scotland therefore appear to share an emphasis on partnership. However, the *nature* of the partnership models advocated, as well as the suggested *knowledge content* of teacher training courses respectively endorsed in each country, are markedly at variance. This divergence becomes especially apparent when consideration is given to the different degree of space afforded for exploration of educational theory in the proposals for teacher education reform in England and Scotland. In Scotland, room has traditionally been found for a significant 'intellectual and academic dimension' within initial teacher education (SG, 2011, p. 31) and it appears that this trend will continue, and perhaps even be extended.[3] *Teaching Scotland's Future* explains that 'while the BEd degree is generally seen as a good preparation for the classroom ... its specificity of purpose can lead to an over-emphasis on technical and craft skills at the expense of broader and more academically challenging areas of study' (SG, 2011, p. 39).

The review therefore recommends that 'exploration of theory through practice should be central to all placement experiences' (p. 42), while theory should also be 'developed through practice' (p. 7). In view of this, it seems plausible to suppose that student teachers in Scotland may be exposed to educational theory in two possible ways in the future: through academic study of a given educational theory outside the classroom prior to exploration of that theory in the classroom, and through the development of educational theory through practice itself. In England, however, theory is conspicuous by its absence. The English reforms, we are instead told, will focus on helping student teachers acquire 'what is really important', namely 'the key skills that they need as teachers, for example the teaching of systematic synthetic phonics as the proven best way to teach early reading, and the management of poor behaviour in the classroom' (DfE, 2010, pp. 22–23). Crucially, as far I can see, no mention whatsoever is made of the value of, or need for, teacher exploration of educational *theory* in either the *Importance of Teaching* White Paper or the *National Teaching Schools* prospectus. Educational theory does not, it seems, fall under the category of 'what is really important' for teachers in England to think about or become acquainted with. But is the apparent lack of explicit space for exploration of educational theory in the proposals for teacher education in England important?

The position taken in this chapter is that this omission of theory is important and importantly regrettable, because the knowledge base of the competent – let alone excellent – teacher is not wholly practical; teacher knowledge rather involves a combination and fusion of both the theoretical and the practical. In short, it is my view that any teacher education that focuses only on technical know-how and does not invite teachers to consider educational theory will only provide teachers with an incomplete knowledge base from which to make practical educational judgements. The argument in this chapter proceeds in three steps. First, it is contended that a central function of universities in the UK has traditionally been a liberal one, namely the initiation of students into a broad range of knowledge forms, rather than merely instrumental training for a professional role. Second, it is claimed that the foundation disciplines of education (the history of education, the philosophy of education, the psychology of education and the sociology of education) that were central to teacher education in the UK in the 1960s and 1970s represented, at least in part, such a liberal body of educational knowledge; and further, that some sort of engagement with a range of different educational disciplines, concepts, ideas and research may continue to be valuable in teacher education, because such engagement can provide a broad base of knowledge and understanding from which teachers can make sound practical judgements. In this section I hope it will become clear that while the traditional disciplines of education did not and could not represent the sum of all things that new teachers needed to consider regarding education and teaching, the disciplines nonetheless invited teachers to think deeply and from different perspectives (from a philosophical, sociological, psychological and historical perspective at least) about education. Third, I provide a brief historical overview of school and university partnerships, with a particular focus on the English context where the disciplines of education – indeed, all educational theory – seem under very real threat of extinction. I conclude that the idea of school and university partnerships as a model for teacher education may have much to commend it, but only if neophyte and qualified teachers are supported both to develop the practical skills they need to teach competently *and* to think broadly, deeply and imaginatively about education. Before we look to the future, though, what has been the function of the university, and the school of education, in the past?

THE IDEA OF A UNIVERSITY

In *The Idea of a University*, Newman argued that the function of the university was *not* to generate new knowledge through research. Rather, it was pedagogical, and specifically the promotion of a broad liberal and intellectual – rather than a solely professional – education. Newman reasoned that if university students focused only on 'professional learning', they would develop a narrow, skill-based rather than a broad, knowledge-based worldview. He stated that though 'the intellect may be devoted to some specific profession ... I do not call *this* the culture of the intellect' (Newman, 1996, p. 197). His view was that the inculcation of professional or scientific knowledge in students is not a sufficient end for the university. The end of the university should rather be a cultured and unified intellect, but such student development could for Newman only be brought about through a thorough engagement with a range of different forms of liberal knowledge. As Alasdair MacIntyre puts it, in Newman's scheme 'we all of us ... need to be schooled in a number of disciplines' (MacIntyre, 2009, p. 353). Liberal knowledge for Newman could be contrasted with servile knowledge, but the more essential distinction is perhaps 'between the instrumental and the non-instrumental: an activity is liberal when, pursued for no external end, it is rather, its own end' (Dunne, 2006, p. 423). David Carr agrees that the liberal conception of university education of the sort advanced by Newman was based upon the premise that students ought to be initiated into a range of forms of knowledge, pursued for their own sake, where such initiation avoids narrow specialisation and 'assists learners to grasp meaningful connections between diverse forms of knowledge' (Carr, 2009, p. 3). While I am generally in favour of the principle that universities should support students to think in broad and unified rather than narrow ways through exposure to different disciplines of knowledge, there are profound difficulties with Newman's framework too.

For one, few in our age would be inclined to accept Newman's suggestion that theology can unify the other disciplines (MacIntyre, 2009; Collini, 2012). Nor would it seem feasible to deny that a core function of today's university is the generation of new knowledge through research (MacIntyre, 2009). Furthermore, widening access to university education was of no concern to Newman – a view very much out of kilter with today (Dunne, 2006; Collini, 2012). To add to this, since the influential Robbins Report of 1963 at least, UK universities have increasingly had both liberal and vocational functions – of not only developing the general powers of the mind, but also instructing in vocational skills[4] (Anderson, 2009). While there may well, then, be significant substance to Joseph Dunne (2006) and Stefan Collini's (2012) observation that Newman endorsed an unduly restrictive notion of liberal knowledge that excluded anything that was instrumentally beneficial, professional learning at university was not entirely ruled out by Newman. After all, he states that 'in saying that Law or Medicine is not the end of a university course, I do not mean to imply that the university does not teach Law or Medicine. What indeed can it teach at all, if it does not teach something particular? It teaches *all* knowledge by teaching all *branches* of knowledge, and in no other way' (Newman, 1996, p. 118). The notion that a university can teach *all* knowledge seems entirely untenable today and it is doubtful that this was ever possible. However, Newman appears to defend the merit of a university curriculum founded upon a range of liberal disciplines precisely because student engagement with different ways of thinking could, for him, prevent the narrowing of mind, judgement and vision that would otherwise follow from a solely vocational university education (MacIntyre, 2009). MacIntyre (2009) and Dunne (2006) both suggest, in fact, that a liberal education of the type advanced by Newman may have the benefit of improving the practical judgement of those students who receive it. While the problems in Newman's concept should not be glossed over then, perhaps the general principle of valuing distinctively liberal learning may yet still provide insight into some of the problems encountered in contemporary universities and schools. Indeed, I think Newman's concept of liberal learning brings into sharp relief the extent to which some school partnership models evolving in England seem to be embracing an instrumentalist and 'production model' (Dunne, 2006) of teaching and learning, where knowledge is generated for largely instrumental reasons, which in turn tends to encourage largely instrumental and technical thinking in students.

Newman, of course, is not the only person to have written about the purposes that should underpin higher education; nor was his vision of the university the only one that flourished in the nineteenth century. The concept of the modern university was initially formed in diverse but related ways by, amongst others, Kant, Scheller, Humbolt and Newman (Peters, 2010). While Kant and Newman both thought universities ought to promote culture and the search for truth, the account of the university offered by the German idealist tradition differed from Newman's in a vital aspect: the truly modern university in Germany would search for truth and promote culture via teaching *and* research (Peters, 2010). Whitehead, too, agreed that modern universities ought to be places of education and research (Whitehead, 1967). In his essay 'Universities and Their Function' Whitehead maintained that the 'proper function of a university is the imaginative acquisition of knowledge ... A university is imaginative or it is nothing – at least nothing useful' (Whitehead, 1967, p. 96). For Whitehead the primary reason for the existence of universities is to provide opportunity for university scholars and students to come into imaginative contact with each other so that knowledge could be imparted and created anew in ways that provide lasting social benefit. Notably, Whitehead indicates that universities should have a special function in the preparation of professionals: namely, to promote the 'imaginative consideration of the various general principles underlying that career' (ibid.). For Whitehead, a professional university education should entail a prior engagement with general principles pertaining to a given career, followed by a 'period of technical apprenticeship' where the more practical and routine aspects of the profession are learned, but in a manner that is illuminated by the more general principles first studied.[5] While it is unhelpful to construe educational principles and practices as necessarily distinct from each other, as either liberal or technical/ useful, I do think that teacher education should systematically enable university staff and education students/practitioners to be in contact with each other, so that educational ideas, research and practices can be imaginatively and broadly considered and in ways that seek to improve current practice. To what extent, though, have schools of education encouraged thoughtful educational practice? How, moreover, has educational theory been conceived and its value explained?

THE FOUNDATION DISCIPLINES OF EDUCATION

It has been well documented that in the 1960s and 1970s the foundation disciplines of education (namely, philosophy, history, psychology and sociology) were thought to provide student teachers with a base of academic content that could in theory provide knowledge of and insight into educational practice (see, for example, Pring, 2007; Standish, 2007; Lawn and Furlong, 2009; Oancea and Bridges, 2009; Biesta, 2011). As Paul Standish explains, the disciplinary approach was founded on 'the view that Education as an academic study cannot be a discipline in its own right because it does not have its own characteristic mode of enquiry' (Standish, 2007, p. 160).[6] What student teachers needed instead was a broad initiation into a range of disciplines of education each of which could offer different insights into the nature and purpose of education. Thus, in my view, the disciplines of education when taken together embodied, at least in part, a distinctively liberal vision for teacher education in so far as the disciplines exposed student teachers to a range of different ways in which to think about education. Indeed, Martin Lawn and John Furlong suggest that the coming together of the disciplines of education in the 1960s constituted the collective school of education response to the Robbins Report, which was, they say, 'probably the UK's last expression of liberal higher education' (Lawn and Furlong, 2009, p. 542). There is substance to this view. The Robbins Report did, after all, stress that universities should instruct in skills but also develop general powers of the mind (Anderson, 2009). Lawn and Furlong go on to explain that the 'search for degree worthiness' ensured the disciplines 'came to the fore' in teacher education post-Robbins (Lawn and Furlong, 2009, p. 542). However, it has been equally well documented that in the last 20 years the influence of the disciplines of education has steadily been eroded (see, for example, Standish, 2007; Lawn and Furlong, 2009; Oancea and Bridges, 2009; Biesta, 2011), while there has been a related increase in more technical means–end thinking about education generally, and teaching and learning specifically (Carr, 1992; Dunne, 1993; Furlong *et al.*, 2006; Pring, 2007).

But do the disciplines of education have any meaningful perspective to offer in terms of future teacher education? MacIntyre (2009),

Standish (2007), Carr (1992) and Lawn and Furlong (2009) all seem to think they can and should. Carr opines that the proper task of academic study in schools of education is 'not that of training technicians to perform routine functions' (Carr, 1992, p. 247). Instead he emphasises the distinctively liberal value of the disciplines. Teaching, he implies, entails a human rather than technical association between teacher and pupil, and the disciplines offer student teachers a foundation in humanistic thinking. Standish also thinks the 'disciplinary approach needs to be restored and strengthened' (Standish, 2007, p. 162), with a particular focus on the philosophy of education – this because teachers ought to be supported in their training and continuing professional development to think more clearly about the real ethical and practical problems that confront them in the classroom (Standish, 2007). Lawn and Furlong (2009) claim that the disciplines of education have in the past played the vital role of breaking practical and public problems down, so that logical actions to meet those problems may result. Indeed, 30 years ago Hirst, in *Educational Theory and Its Foundation Disciplines*, expressed the view that rational educational practice 'must start from a consideration of current practice … and the knowledge, beliefs and principles that the practitioner employ in both characterising that practice and deciding what ought to be done' (Hirst, 1983, p. 16). Hirst adds, however, that it is the job of the disciplines 'to provide a context of ever more rationally defensible beliefs and values' (p. 19) so as to inform the formation of practical educational principles. Though history, philosophy, sociology and psychology do seem like bodies of knowledge that could still help teachers to think deeply, imaginatively and practically about education, they are far from the only ones that could do this. Indeed, Lawn and Furlong (2009) have recently added economics, geography and comparative and international education to the traditional disciplines in the hope of awakening debate about the potential future value of the disciplines of education.

Furthermore, it is probably the case that the traditional disciplines of education have all evolved considerably since the 1960s too. For example, while the philosophy of education in the 1960s and 1970s was, in the UK at least, rather dominated by the analytic tradition, earlier philosophical thinking on education from sources as diverse as

Plato (1987), Aristotle (1981), Kant (2003) and Dewey (2008) suggests that the philosophy of education involves much more than mere analysis. Indeed, the philosophy of education now draws upon a much more diverse range of philosophical traditions than in the 1960s and 1970s, including, for example, existentialism, deconstruction, virtue ethics, epistemology, pragmatism, as well as the analytic – and the list could go on.[7] Overall, this suggests to me that the bodies of knowledge used to stimulate disciplined thinking about education should not be conceived of as being permanent in form – they should rather be continually subject to review and revision in light of the changes that invariably occur in educational systems. While I do not want, then, to suggest that future educators need only, or necessarily, study the traditional disciplines of education, it is my position that teacher education should aim to develop thoughtful practitioners – ones, that is, who think deeply about their practice and at times use educational theory and research to do so. To this end I think that different educational ideas, theories, disciplines of knowledge and empirical research may all serve to illuminate teacher practice and make it more thoughtful. Indeed, it seems to me that the general idea of engaging practitioners in dialogue about both their *practical challenges* and *wider educational ideas* is a most sound one – an idea, moreover, that I think ought to centrally animate teacher education in any university and school partnerships of the future. With this in mind, it may be the case that the disciplines can retain some future value for teacher education if they are not perceived as fixed in nature but rather as malleable enough to be made anew through the sort of imaginative contact between scholar and student teacher generally advocated by Whitehead.

This is not to say that teacher education must begin with or involve the disciplines of education – far from it. Indeed it is probably most often the case that deeper teacher thinking about education generally evolves out of practical educational situations. As Ruth Heilbronn (2008) argues, processes of teacher reflection upon practice can lead to the articulation of theoretical knowledge about the practice of teaching. While there is an important sense, then, in which the capacity for sound teacher judgement may be most directly developed in practice, it would be a mistake to think the practical learning of teachers should be thought of as being invariably devoid of theory or deep thought. As Newman generally implied when discussing professional learning, and as Heilbronn (2008) suggests, practical teacher judgement is probably neither wholly theoretical, nor wholly practical, but rather involves aspects of each. This brings me to the nub of my argument on the future value of teacher engagement with the disciplines of education and other educational theory and research – that such engagement can be valuable when it provides a broad background of knowledge and understanding from which teachers can draw when thinking about education generally and in practical teaching situations specifically.[8] For example, while promoting positive pupil behaviour in schools is no doubt something that must be centrally learned in practice, I also think that the more traditional disciplines of education may still provide educators with importantly different perspectives and insight into the perennial challenges of fostering pupil discipline in schools. Teacher engagement with the work on school discipline by (for example) R.S. Peters (1974) and P.S. Wilson (1971) (both the philosophy of education) or Durkheim (1961) and Furlong (1985) (both the sociology of education) may lead to more sagacious teacher judgements about specific pupil disciplinary issues, as well as greater background understanding of how to arrange school discipline generally in a more educational and morally formative manner. However, how have school and university partnerships evolved to date, and how likely is it that future partnership arrangements in the UK will provide a platform for the teacher exploration of both practical problems *and* wider educational ideas and research?

THE IDEA OF UNIVERSITY AND SCHOOL PARTNERSHIP

The idea of university and school partnership is far from new. In England, partnership was an important recommendation of the 1944 McNair Report, even though it was not until 1992 that the government formally required teacher training to be delivered via school and university partnerships (Furlong *et al.*, 2006). Furlong *et al.* (2006) maintain that in the 1990s teacher training partnerships in England tended to be led by HEIs and that at this time partnership was an organisational concept that retained important epistemological dimensions. They explain that universities both synthesised the student experience and provided access to 'knowledge based on theory ... Schools on the other hand gave access to knowledge based on direct practical experience itself' (Furlong *et al.*, 2006, pp. 33–34). The Oxford University model of teacher education was an example of a university-led partnership with schools that involved educational theory and sought to encourage student teachers to think deeply about their practice. This model saw student teachers collaborating with mentor teachers and university tutors in two different phases of professional learning, predicated on the assumption that student teachers ought to be supported to work out for themselves how best to teach (MacIntyre and Hagger, 1992). In phase one, the student teacher would be asked to modify their teaching as need be, so as to ensure they developed the skills and habits necessary for competent teaching. In phase two, however, the student teacher would control the agenda of their professional development more, and be expected to articulate their own criteria for their teaching.

However, the establishment of the National Partnership Programme (NPP) in 2001 signified an important shift towards a less HEI-based approach to teacher training through the expansion of school-based routes into the profession such as School Centred Initial Teacher Training (SCITT) and Teach First (Furlong *et al.*, 2006). Such schemes, managed by the schools themselves, continue to be promoted by the government, this 'despite the low rating of many of them by Ofsted' (Furlong *et al.*, 2006, p. 35). The *Importance of Teaching*, after all, specifies a more holistic move towards 'improving and expanding the best of the current school-based routes into teaching – school-centred initial teaching training and the graduate teacher programme' (DfE, 2010, p. 23). However, in their empirical review into teacher education in England, Furlong *et al.* suggest that the important epistemological dimension of teacher education is becoming diminished in school-based routes and especially in the case of partnerships between schools that do not involve universities. As they put it: 'partnership arrangements are no longer predicated on the complex task of bringing together partners who provide access to different conceptions of professional knowledge ... when schools offer their own mentor training – in a competitive market ... there is a real danger of undermining the complexity of professional education' (Furlong *et al.*, 2006, p. 41).

Given the lack of explicit mention of educational theory or different conceptions of professional knowledge within the recent proposals regarding teaching schools, and bearing in mind the declared intention to further expand school-based teacher education, there is ample reason to be gloomy about the prospect of new teachers in England being generally encouraged to think deeply for themselves about the complexities of their role. This is not, of course, to say such thinking will not be possible in more school-based approaches – far from it. But it is to say that the structural arrangements that have been evolving over the last 10 years (and that look set to continue) may not be the best ones to support broad and imaginative thinking about education.

There appear to be grounds for more optimism about how the structures in Scotland may serve to promote a broad education of teachers rather than a merely narrow training. Indeed, there is a possibility that undergraduate student teachers in Scotland may in the future receive an even more liberal education, as *Teaching Scotland's Future* specifically champions the merit of a broader concurrent degree, where student teachers study a range of disciplines of knowledge and in faculties outside of education. Given the prior noted requirement that student teachers be encouraged to explore theory through practice, I think the Scottish context may have greater potential to offer student teachers and practitioners the opportunity to collaboratively consider both their practical educational problems and wider educational ideas. I am not suggesting that the concurrent degree model must necessarily and always be better than the more exclusively school-based routes that have been evolving in England (although the former would seem to provide a more balanced education rather than training). Indeed, it may well be the case that those working within the Scottish and English models of partnership can learn from each other. In England, for example, there is perhaps some hope to be found in the notion that 'the teaching school model will ... provide opportunities for ... members of staff to reflect on and develop their own practice' (NCL, 2011, p. 7). Teachers clearly do need a broad range of practical skills to both encourage learning in others and extend their own, and it is probably true to say that the English system (with its proliferation of academies and federations) is much more advanced than the Scottish one in terms of sharing 'good' (again, whatever this may mean) practice across schools. In this respect, it would seem foolish to deny that there are many practices and rules of thumb that experienced teachers can pass on to colleagues and trainee teachers in ways that can help them to become more competent in their roles. However, a fear persists that too many beginning teachers in England will in the future be encouraged to uncritically adopt the practices of others, rather than systematically develop and improve their own, unless educational theory, ideas and research are still valued as possible sources of insight. While Newman's model of the university explored earlier may not have valued profession-based learning nearly enough, more exclusively school-based models for teacher education are in danger of going too far in the other direction: of not valuing enough knowledge that is not directly derived from professional practice.

So, is the idea of university and school partnerships a good one? The view taken here is that the idea is probably, in and of itself, neither good nor bad. On the one hand, the heightened opportunity that partnerships seem to provide for practitioners to collaborate with each other to think about common-sense solutions to practical problems would seem to be worthy. On the other hand, if partnerships result in a general promotion of teacher preparation that involves more instrumental training and less broad education, the idea of partnership becomes much less defensible. However, if partnerships can facilitate forums for school and university staff to work together to think imaginatively and deeply about both practical educational problems and educational theory, disciplines and research, then I think the idea becomes a more promising way forward for teacher education.[9] This process may start with groups of teachers paying careful attention to the particularities of the classroom and school context (Standish, 1995), or with student or experienced teachers reading and discussing texts that encourage them to consider the wider purposes of education. This process may also, for some, begin with an exploration of disciplinary knowledge in university through lectures or seminars about education. Importantly, I think the role of university staff should not be to present educational theory, research and concepts to teachers in a way that makes them seem final or complete in themselves – the value of the disciplines of education, for example, would seem to invariably reside in teachers being asked to imaginatively draw on them in ways that promote context-specific and practically wise educational judgements. It may well be desirable for university staff to pay attention to the particularities of school contexts too so that they can identify and mediate the content of 'theory' likely to resonate with the specific experiences of teachers and, in turn, challenge their thinking. What seems important, though, is for teachers to be routinely invited to consider the complexity of the teaching and learning process and systematically expected to explore ways in which their teaching can promote an attitude to learning in school pupils that transcends the instrumental.

In conclusion, it has been argued here that an element of disciplined and imaginative study of educational ideas, research and concepts should be preserved in teacher education because such study may have potential to stimulate broad rather than narrow teacher knowledge, understanding and thinking about education. Academic staff in universities might encourage beginning and qualified teachers to think through the complexities of their role in a range of other ways too. They may, for example, help school staff to acquire the knowledge and skills necessary for conducting, comprehending and interpreting practice-based research.[10] This may also in turn lead to practitioners being better able to form a critical attitude towards government policy and the findings of educational research and how they ought to be translated (if at all) into practice. It is my view, though, that a central role of any university partnered with a school is to ensure that teachers are encouraged to think broadly about education, learning and teaching. My claim then is not that the disciplines of education ought to be reinserted back into teacher education in the manner of before, and presented again as the foundation pillars of all student teacher learning; instead it is that some form or other of disciplined and imaginative teacher engagement with different educational ideas, research and bodies of knowledge are all important ways in which instrumental thinking about education has been, and can still yet be, resisted.

NOTES

1 This body merged with the Teaching Agency in 2013 to become the National College for Teaching and Leadership (NCTL).

2 For a review of how some teaching schools have been evolving in practice, see NCL (2012, 2013).

3 There is no doubt an element of political rhetoric attached to this claim. However, it is true that the model of teacher education in Scotland has not yet diversified to include the less theoretical and more practical school-based approaches now being witnessed in England (SG, 2011).

4 It is arguable that even the ancient universities embraced vocational functions much earlier than this. Whitehead (1967), after all, points out that as early as 1316 a college was formed at Cambridge tasked with providing clerks for the king's service.

5 For further discussion on Whitehead's views on education, see MacAllister (2012b).

6 Gert Biesta (2011) has pointed out that in the German-speaking world education has emerged as a discipline in its own right, while Semel (2010) indicates that in the United States history, politics, sociology and philosophy make up the foundation disciplines.

7 For examples of discussions that consider the educational implications of these traditions, see Kakkori and Huttunen (2012) (existentialism), Biesta (2009b) (deconstruction), Carr and Steutel (1999) (virtue ethics), MacAllister (2012a) (epistemology), Dewey (2008) (pragmatism) and Hirst (1965) (analytic).

8 Though I am emphasising here how educational theory may support the development of enhanced teacher judgement in practice, I do also think that the notion of teachers studying more theoretical aspects of education for its own sake should be considered as valuable too.

9 It is interesting to note that there is some empirical evidence to support the general argument that engagement with theory in teacher education improves educational practice. Chris Holligan's (1997) study of student teachers in Scotland, for example, found that those judged to have a better comprehension of the university-led education studies course were also those judged to be more effective in the classroom. Hobson is probably right, though, to observe that we 'should be wary of assuming a causal connection on such a complex issue' (2003, pp. 258–259).

10 It is, after all, indicated that teaching schools (DfE, 2010) and hub schools (SG, 2011) should be sites of educational research as well as teacher education. The point here, though, would seem to be that university staff ought to support school staff to conduct and/or use educational research for more than instrumental purposes.

Part 2
What Makes a Good Teacher?

4
Why We Need a Virtue Ethics of Teaching

CHRIS HIGGINS

This is a revised version of the Introduction to *The Good Life of Teaching: An Ethics of Professional Practice* (Higgins, 2010a, 2011), in which I develop a substantive ethics of professional life with special reference to teaching. In that book, I build on the revival of virtue ethics (drawing on Bernard Williams, Charles Taylor and Alasdair MacIntyre) and the recovery of practical philosophy (featuring Michael Oakeshott, Hannah Arendt, John Dewey and Hans-Georg Gadamer) to challenge the narrowness of modern moral philosophy and the application approach to professional ethics. At the heart of my project is the desire to demonstrate the ethical importance of the flourishing of the practitioner. Far from constituting an exception, I argue, this is especially true in so-called 'helping professions' such as teaching, in which the teacher's own, ongoing self-cultivation is crucial to successful practice. In *The Good Life of Teaching*, I explore teaching as an existential practice, as a space for the teacher's own self-enactment. I offer a vision of education as a space of humanistic questions – and our putative answers to those questions in theory and practice – and of the teacher as an organic intellectual. And I defend a conception of teacher education that goes beyond learning how to teach to encompass learning how to learn through teaching. I call for a teacher education for practical wisdom, one that helps teachers enter

Philosophical Perspectives on Teacher Education, First Edition. Edited by Ruth Heilbronn and Lorraine Foreman-Peck. © 2015 Ruth Heilbronn and Lorraine Foreman-Peck. Editorial Organisation © Philosophy of Education Society of Great Britain. Published 2015 by John Wiley & Sons, Ltd.

the practice of teaching, sustain a vocational conversation and further their own self-cultivation.

> I believe the impulse to teach is fundamentally altruistic and represents a desire to share what you value and to empower others. Of course, all teachers are not altruistic. Some people teach in order to dominate others or to support work they'd rather do or simply to earn a living. But I am not talking about the job of teaching so much as the calling to teach. Most teachers I know, even the most demoralized ones, who drag themselves to oppressive and mean schools where their work is not respected and their presence not welcome, have felt that calling at some time in their lives (Kohl, 1984, p. 7).

SAINTS AND SCOUNDRELS

Open any text on teaching and you are likely to find the same formula. It is nicely captured in the passage above from Herb Kohl's well-known work *Growing Minds: On Becoming a Teacher*, but there is no shortage of examples. Kohl tells us that teaching is altruistic, fundamentally so. If we find a non-altruist in the classroom then we have discovered an imposter to the role. From the point of view of working teachers, we all know there are days when we live up to our ideals, and days that fall depressingly short of those hopes, and days that seem to dwell uncertainly in between. Yet in representations of teaching, we find instead a stark contrast of motivations: teachers are either serving students or using them. In the helping professions, it seems, one must not 'help oneself'. As one teacher recruitment campaign succinctly put it: 'You've made your own dreams come true. Isn't it time you started on someone else's?'[1] In the educational imagination – from posters to policies, from monographs to movies – we find more and less restrained versions of the same Noh drama. Enter stage left – the selfless saints, devoted to nothing but the welfare of their students and martyred for the cause. Enter stage right – the selfish scoundrels: narcissists, lechers, and petty dictators of their classroom worlds. What seems clear is that these two characters and, correspondingly, the two main discourses about teacher motivation – the inspirational and the suspicious – are but two sides of the same coin.[2] Inspirational accounts tend to focus on the role of teacher, holding out an image of teaching as a noble service.[3] These accounts suggest that a teacher's personal interests and needs more or less harmonise with the demands of their role, and when they do not, that those needs can and should be addressed outside of work. Suspicious accounts turn to the person in the role in an attempt to reveal the hidden springs of self-interest and debunk this idea of the altruistic teacher.[4] These accounts aim to show that such a division between personal and professional is impossible to maintain, and that trappings of the role become a cover for teachers who really want to feel smart, revisit their youth, vent their aggression, and so on. What is striking is that neither discourse seems capable of helping us understand how teaching might be the expression of the person who teaches. For in the second sort of story, there is no real teacher; in the first, there is no real person.

What these seeming rivals share is their attachment to the stark opposition between a lofty altruism and a base self-interest; neither lends itself to a believable portrait of teaching. Inspirational accounts ring hollow when they gloss over the immense difficulties and frustrations inherent in the life of a schoolteacher. They portray teachers as having *no* personal agenda, conveniently wanting only what students need, and needing only to give that. However, they tend to assume that teachers have *only* a personal agenda, which they merely disguise with their talk of educational aims and student needs.

In contrast, my study asks how teaching might be the *expression* of one's personal ambitions and deepest motivations. It probes the reasons for our dichotomous tendency to imagine teachers as either selfless saints or selfish scoundrels and challenges the very idea of a 'helping profession'. It sets out instead to imagine the fate of the teacher struggling to be *self-full* in the midst of a task that is overwhelming, an environment that can be deadening, and a professional culture that secretly prizes self-abnegation. In showing the resources the practice of teaching offers for self-cultivation, without minimising its very real challenges and constraints, we move closer to a humane, sustainable ethic of teaching.

A BRIEF FOR TEACHERLY SELF-CULTIVATION

Teaching is a helping profession, where caring teachers assist active learners. At the same time, education contains an ineliminable feature that pushes us past such dichotomous thinking. The feature, simply put, is that selfhood is contagious. In order to cultivate selfhood in students, teachers must bring to the table their own achieved self-cultivation, their commitment to ongoing growth, and their various practices, styles and tricks for combating the many forces that deaden the self and distract us from our task of becoming. In this stubborn refusal to be sorted into a duty or an inclination, an act of altruism or of self-interest, the practice of teaching proves a rich ground for exploring one of the central human dilemmas and oldest ethical problems. How do we reconcile self-regard and concern for others? Can we live with the demands of human self-hood, that each of us exists for ourselves and for others, or will we allow the quest for individuation to collapse? Will we settle for so many semi-selves propping each other up: actors and facilitators, saints and scoundrels, 'mermaids and minotaurs'? (Dinnerstein, 1991 [1976]).

In teaching and other helping professions, such questions come to a sharp point. Here we encounter a powerful drive to sort ourselves into subject and object, for-oneself and for-others. The flourishing of the teacher sounds like an oxymoron. And yet, the logic of selfhood, emulation and development pushes back against this tendency. Consider, if you will, the following argument for teacherly self-cultivation as a pressing practical and rich ethical issue (I first state the propositions in bare form and then discuss each further below):

1   Education, no matter what else it involves, involves self-cultivation.
2   Achieved and ongoing self-cultivation on the part of the teacher is a necessary (though not sufficient) condition for fostering self-cultivation in students.
3   (from 1 and 2) Teacherly self-cultivation is a necessary condition of education.
4   Poor working conditions and the intense needs of students conspire to make such self-cultivation exceedingly difficult; the life of a teacher, it must be admitted, may be miseducative as often as it is educative.

5   Rather than recognise the teacher's self-forgetfulness and self-sacrifice as a threat to teaching itself, we rationalise them with the rhetoric of service; we hail them as the call of duty and very mark of a teacher.

6   (from 3) But teaching is not a 'helping profession', if this is taken to mean that one helps others *rather* than oneself.

7   (from 4–6) Therefore, teaching should be understood precisely as one of the human practices that most clearly forces us to confront a fundamental existential tension: we exist for ourselves and for others, and while these two dimensions of life rarely fit together easily, neither do they work well alone.

The first proposition will strike some readers as patent and others as wildly utopian. This is not surprising if Philip Jackson is right that education has long been torn between two fundamentally different outlooks: the mimetic (or transmissive) and the transformative (Jackson, 1986).[5] While the educational aim of self-cultivation is the very premise of the transformative outlook on teaching, it has come to seem largely out of place in K–12 schooling with the 'gradual ascendance of the mimetic tradition' (p. 133). Two features of the current climate make it much easier to understand education as transmission of detachable skills and discrete knowledge. According to current wisdom, nothing exists that can't be measured and nothing can be measured that can't be measured by a standardised test. Since it is quite difficult to measure transformations and self-formation, this constitutes a distinct advantage for the mimetic model. The transformational model also runs up against our faith in liberal neutrality expressed in our belief that government-run schools in a liberal democracy can and should remain neutral on questions of the good life. Personal transformation as an educational aim cannot help but set off the Establishment Clause alarm system.[6] An education based in putatively neutral, transmissible skills and knowledge is a much easier sell.

Still, for thousands of years before this brave new world, the dominant assumption, whatever the specifics, was that education was self-formation. Such an education could be oriented around ideals of civic virtue, aesthetic sensitivity or intellectual acuity. The educated person could be understood in terms of Cicero's oratory, Pico's dignity or

Austen's amiability. But if an education does not help you at all to answer the question, 'What sort of person are you going to become?', you should ask for your money back. I will close this brief defence of the first proposition with the rousing words of one of the relatively late defenders of (one very particular version of) education as self-cultivation, Friedrich Nietzsche:

> Your true educators and molders reveal to you the true original meaning and basic stuff of your nature, something absolutely incapable of being educated and molded, but in any case something fettered and paralyzed and difficult of access. Your teachers can be nobody but your liberators. And that is the secret of all education; it does not provide artificial limbs, wax noses, or corrective lenses – on the contrary, what might provide such things is merely a parody of education. Education is rather liberation, the clearing away of all weeds, rubble, and vermin that might harm the delicate shoots, a radiance of light and warmth, the kind rustling fall of rain at night; it is imitation and adoration of nature where nature is maternal and mercifully minded; it is perfection of nature when it prevents nature's fits of cruelty and mercilessness and converts them to good, when it throws a veil over nature's stepmotherly disposition and sad incomprehension. (Nietzsche, 1990 [1874], p. 166)

If the truth of the first proposition has tended to be marginalised or rejected, the truth of the second has tended to be trivialised as much as accepted. The difficulty here lies not so much in proving this premise as in rescuing it from its status as a truism: we learn by example, we teach who we are, and so forth. That something is a commonplace does not mean that we truly affirm it. Truisms are in fact a canny strategy for resisting ideas. After all, if you hide or oppose an idea, someone will dig it up or come to its defence. However, if you embalm a claim in a cliché, its truth can be acknowledged in an empty gesture, one that calls for no action on our part. Thus, the truism seems to fit the logic of disavowal as famously described by the French psychoanalyst Octave Mannoni: 'I know very well, but all the same ...' (Mannoni, 2003 [1969]).

To rescue a living thought from such a fate requires putting the idea back into play, and this calls for the special kind of seriousness known as irony. It also requires awareness that no truism is an island. In this case, shoring up the clichés that we learn by example and teach who we are is a whole supporting cast of truisms: (1) everyone is a person; (2) everyone is unique; (3) we are grateful for the examples set by others. The ironist is not cowed by these sweet-sounding notions, but is willing to deal with the embarrassing, all-too-human exceptions to these rules, such as: (1) full-fledged personhood is difficult and rare and most of us get stuck somewhere not very far along the way; (2) we are often threatened by the influence of others and haunted by the feeling that the influence of others runs so deep that we cannot be sure what if anything in us is truly our own; and, (3) when we do finally find the way toward ourselves, we may well turn off the road, choosing the comfort of habit and the crowd over freedom, which in fact we fear as much as desire. What is needed, then, is work on influence that does not shy away from such human frailties and paradoxes.[7] With at least some of this coating of obviousness now worn away, I would like to call the following witnesses to offer testimony on behalf of premise 2:

Philip Jackson: 'Of the many attributes associated with transformative teaching, the most crucial ones seem to concern the teacher as a person. For it is essential to success within that tradition that teachers who are trying to bring about transformative changes personify the very qualities they seek to engender in their students. To the best of their abilities, they must be living exemplars of certain virtues or values or attitudes. The fulfillment of that requirement reaches its apex in great historical figures, like Socrates and Christ, who epitomize such a personal model; but most teachers already know that no attitude, interest, or value can be taught except by a teacher who himself or herself believes in, cares for, or cherishes whatever it is that he or she holds out for emulation.' (Jackson, 1986, p. 124)

Maxine Greene: 'A teacher in search of his/her own freedom may be the only kind of teacher who can arouse young persons to go in search of their own.' (Greene, 1988, p. 14)

Bob Dylan: 'He not busy being born is busy dying.' (Dylan, 1965)

William Arrowsmith: 'And this freedom, this ripeness of self, is the indispensable element in all true teaching, simply because it speaks so compellingly to those who hunger to be free – that is presumably to all.' (Arrowsmith, 1971, p. 12)

The teacher's achieved self-cultivation is the catalyst in the educative process. But, as these witnesses also testify, educators cannot simply rest on their laurels, producing accomplishments from the past like dusty old trophies. It is the teacher's present and active search for freedom, Greene says, that communicates to students what freedom might mean. The teacher must be 'busy being born' if she is to give students a sense of what living is about. Past insights and growth quickly spoil if self-cultivation is not ongoing. It is the other's self-in-process, or 'ripeness' as Arrowsmith puts it, that moves us. In their own way, sardonic movies about teachers offer further testimony on this point. Certainly, such movies rely on stock characters and cheap sight gags: teachers whose underwear is showing, whose power lunch is peanut butter, jelly and chalk dust, who can't operate the rudimentary technology in their classrooms, who drive up to school in battered second-hand cars, who have no love life or social skills (for a wonderful distillation of this motif, see the opening montage in Pressman, 1994).[8] Ultimately, though, what these movies intend is more than comic effect. There is a pathos here, one that echoes the testimony above. Whether or not one finds such images funny, they express, I contend, a powerful and understandable thirst on the part of young people for examples of why it is worth 'growing up'.

As the third proposition indicates, the conclusion we must draw on the basis of this testimony about the importance of the teacher's own existential exemplarity – given our earlier conclusion that education fundamentally involves self-cultivation – is that the achieved and ongoing self-cultivation of teachers is a necessary condition of education.

We turn now to the fourth premise. That teaching centrally involves helping students prepare for, launch and enrich their own life projects often distracts teachers from the fact that teaching is their project. Even those teachers determined to make their practice into a vehicle for their own ongoing growth will find this difficult given typical working conditions. Indeed, the very term 'teacher' suggests such deprivations. Consider the social distinction we make between 'teachers' and 'professors'. The distinction does not seem to be fully explainable by the age of the students each educates, the amount of knowledge each possesses, or even by the fact that professors engage in both teaching and scholarship. Ultimately, this distinction seems to serve as a rationalisation for the fact that society does not have, or is not willing to commit, enough resources for all of its teachers to work, as professors do, in conditions compatible with self-renewal, conditions such as teaching fewer courses (on topics and via methods of their own choosing) with fewer students (who are genuinely interested in taking the class), and leaving time for reading, writing and open-ended discussion with colleagues (not to mention the chance to take a sabbatical). Where is the high school or middle school or kindergarten teacher who would not choose these terms instead, and flourish under them?[9]

What is at stake here is precisely whether an occupation is able to pass John Dewey's cardinal test, of 'balancing the distinctive capacity of an individual with his social service' (Dewey, 1916, p. 308). Occupations with this quality are often marked by a characteristic rhythm between withdrawal and engagement, and characteristic patterns of planning, pursuit and completion followed by intervals of rest and reflection. Such rhythms are not some optional perk. They speak to the basic link between work and flourishing. G. W. F. Hegel brings this out with his concept of practical *Bildung*. According to Hans-Georg Gadamer's reading of Hegel, *Bildung* is a process of development or self-formation whose 'basic movement ... consists ... in returning to itself from what is other' (Gadamer, 2004 [1960], p. 13).[10] The essence of *Bildung*, Gadamer explains, 'is clearly not alienation as such, but the return to oneself – which presupposes alienation, to be sure' (ibid.). How is such a process of alienation and return educative and what does it have to do with work?

When we work we subordinate our private whims and fancies to a public discipline and an objective set of materials. To make a table, for example, the carpenter must undergo a process of alienation, or, if you will, 'unselfing'.[11] He cannot merely stay rooted in his consciousness, dreaming up how the table could or should be. He must leave this cosy, subjective place for the rigors of technique and the realities of wood, grain and gravity. If he has successfully transcended his particularity to make something universal, a table, and allowed himself to become alienated from his subjectivity into the objective realm of chestnut and chisel, then he will stand before the finished work. It will be an independently existing thing, with its legs on the ground of the objective world. And yet, it will also be his table, with him in it. As the carpenter takes in the completed work, he takes in the structure, the complexity, the culture of the made thing. He returns to himself, but he returns with more, and as more, than when he set out.[12] In this way, work is a basic modality of *Bildung*.

What do we find when we return to the practice of teaching with such thoughts in mind? First, if *Bildung* requires a dialectic of solitude and relation, a rhythm of withdrawal and engagement, then teachers have a problem. For, as Maxine Greene nicely puts it:

> The problems are inescapable, wherever the teacher is assigned to teach, because he is asked to function as a self-conscious, autonomous, and authentic person in a public space where the pressures multiply. Unlike an artist or a scholar or a research scientist, he cannot withdraw to studio, study, or laboratory and still remain a practitioner. He is involved with students, colleagues, school board members, and parents whenever and wherever he pursues his fundamental project; he cannot work alone. (Greene, 1973, p. 290)

Most teachers do not even have an office, let alone a true studio space and the time to explore and renew their craft. Add to this the fact, noted by many, that teaching currently lacks a true career path, so that 'moving up' typically means moving out of teaching into administration or research.[13] The continuity of the teacher's work is also threatened on the day-to-day level: fractured by the rapid change of classes, compressed (Jackson, 1966, p. 14, reports that 'the teacher typically changes the focus of his concern about 1000 times daily'), and complicated by the fact the teacher hesitates to say of the well-educated pupil what the carpenter says of his completed table: look what I have made. Teachers instead want to say to their students: look what you have done, what you have made. And yet, teachers must not forget that launching students on their quests and helping them find their projects is their own quest, their own project.

If, after a thorough consideration of the teacher's world and work, our conclusion is that teachers are prone to self-forgetfulness and even self-sacrifice, that their bid to make their practice nourish them is often squelched by the harsh conditions of their labour, then we should be quite alarmed. But as I suggest above, the alarming conclusion of proposition 4 is typically met with the rationalisation of proposition 5, that self-sacrifice is the mark of a true teacher. However, the argument of premises 1–3 should now help us to see through this rationalisation. When we hear of someone sacrificing their self in order to teach, this should sound something like: the soccer game will proceed as planned even though we have not been able to locate a ball; the lead singer has lost her voice, but the show must go on; or, go ahead and show me your tango routine, we don't have time to wait for your partner. That is, while collapses of the delicate balance between self-regard and care for students may be inevitable, they are worrisome. And this is where the rhetoric of service comes in. In the so-called helping professions, deprivation can become a badge of honour.

Actually the rhetoric of service is only the second line of defence, cleaning up any mess left over after education's pervasive kitsch has done its job. Rather than confront the reality that many teachers grow old even as they tend to the young, educational discourse offers here as elsewhere a simplified and sweetened version of reality. Then, in so far as we even acknowledge our failures to support self-full (as opposed to both selfish and selfless) teaching, education's nagging asceticism is there to redeem such failures as moral victories.

But as point 6 makes clear, the implication of point 3 is that teaching is not a helping profession, at least not if this means, as it typically does in implication if not inspiration, that one helps others *rather* than helping oneself. After all, architects and lawyers and veterinarians all help their clients too, and all experience so-called 'intrinsic rewards'. And yet in these cases this does not exclude their receiving ample 'extrinsic' rewards of money, autonomy and recognition; nor are we tempted to call them 'helping professions'. Thus, what leads us to label teaching, nursing and social work as 'helping professions' does not seem to be that they offer help to others but that they refuse to help themselves in the process.

Indeed, we can offer a fairly precise sociological definition of the 'helping' professions: they are those forms of work, historically associated with women, combining difficult working conditions and a caring attention to the client's whole person. As such, the helping professions admit of Jessica Benjamin's paradox that precisely here where the essence of the work is a kind of intersubjectivity, we find the most intense desire to split the participants into subjects and objects, agents and helpers, self-interest and altruism.

Thus, in point 7, I conclude that teaching forces us to confront the inevitable tensions arising when subjects meet and each retains his or her agency. The question of the flourishing of the teacher turns out to test our mettle as to whether we really care about self-cultivation at all. The stakes go far beyond the fate of individual teachers. For education is one of the primary cultural sites where we wrestle with the fundamental challenge of personhood. Subjectivity emerges in the matrix of intersubjectivity, in relationships where we successfully maintain the complex tensions between self-assertion and recognition, independence and dependence, separation and connection. This task is extremely difficult, however, and we are constantly on the lookout for ways to ease this tension. Indeed, we are prone to act out on a cultural scale our wishful fantasies that pure agency might be met by pure facilitation. Everywhere we look we find masters and servants, talkers and listeners, doers and facilitators. We find divisions of a labour that cannot be divided, attempts to escape the fundamental burden of personhood: that each of us must work out, for ourselves and with others, how we can exist for ourselves and for others.

FROM THE TERRAIN OF TEACHING TO THE DEFINITION OF PROFESSIONAL ETHICS

My project, then, concerns the interplay of altruism and self-interest in the practice of teaching; it is a philosophical exploration of teacher motivation, identity and development. To see that such questions are not the exclusive province of psychologists and sociologists, we need simply rephrase the familiar question 'Why teach?' as 'Why is the practice of teaching worth putting at the centre of one's life?' It then turns out that we are dealing with one of the central questions of professional ethics, or so I argue, building on Bernard Williams' distinction between ethics and morality.

Along with Alasdair MacIntyre, Charles Taylor and others, Williams has led the charge in showing the limits of modern morality and in recovering an older, broader tradition of ethical reflection.[14] Such reflection will often touch on moral considerations – impartial deliberations about duty, right action, and the needs of others – but it begins and ends with first-personal questioning, in thick evaluative terms, about the shape of one's life as a whole. Ethics is rooted in the perpetual practical question 'What should I do next?' and flowers, in our more contemplative moments, into questions like 'What do I want to become?', 'What does it mean to be fully human?' and 'What would make my life meaningful, excellent, or rich?'

Professional ethics, then, should be distinguished from what I call 'moral professionalism', which deals with codes of professional conduct and our role-specific obligations to others.[15] In contrast, the ethics of teaching, as I propose it here, will probe the relation between the teaching life and the good life, connecting the question 'Why teach?' with the question 'How should I live?' It considers what draws us to the practice of teaching and what sustains us there in the face of difficulty. The ethics of teaching involves questions like these: What constitutes human flourishing, and how does tending to the growth of others nourish my own growth? What do I prize most, and how does teaching put me in touch with such goods?

Restoring to its central place the question of the flourishing of the practitioner is the first step in constructing a virtue ethics of teaching. However, I argue that we must go even further if we want a truly virtue-theoretic professional ethics. Following MacIntyre (2007), I show that virtue ethics implies not only that different types of normative considerations will be applied to practice, but also that the very notion of application must be rethought. What MacIntyre reveals is that ethics is practical in a much more fundamental way. Practices are in fact our ethical sources: they are the sites where aspects of the good are disclosed to us as well as the primary scenes of our ethical education. Thus, if applied ethics carries findings worked out in the philosophy seminar to the various practices, practical ethics turns to practices themselves to learn about goods and virtues, in their variety, as they are disclosed through the particular terms and problematics of each practice. Virtue ethics therefore needs teaching as much as teaching needs virtue ethics.

Thus, I pursue long-standing philosophical problems – about self-interest and altruism, personal freedom and social roles, and practical wisdom and personhood – on the terrain of teaching. The aim is not only, as I said at the outset, to provide a more realistic and liveable account of the moral psychology of teaching, but also through this process to shed light on these basic philosophical problems. Put another way, my project:

- advances discussions of teacher motivation, identity and development, using the resources of virtue ethics to avoid the dichotomisation of duty and interest that has plagued many treatments of teaching;
- sheds light on fundamental questions in ethics and philosophical anthropology, considering the particular form these questions take in the context of the practice of teaching;
- contributes to the development of a more substantive professional ethics, showing the full implications of the contemporary retrieval of *arête* (excellence, virtue) and *eudaimonia* (flourishing, happiness, well-being) for a philosophy of work.

NOTES

1 NYC Teaching Fellows advertisement, posted in New York City subway, 2002.
2 There are, of course, several happy exceptions to this rule: the idea of teaching as an existential project has been a consistent theme in the work of Maxine Greene (see, for example, Greene, 1973, 1978, 1987). Margaret Buchmann (1988) describes teaching as a 'given form of the good life'. David Blacker (1997) explores teaching as a bid for immortality. For a rich portrait of how one high school art teacher shaped himself and others through his teaching, see Barone (2001).
3 There are countless examples of works in what I am calling the inspirational mode. Indeed, we can identify three genres here: self-help books on reflection and renewal; literature on teaching as a noble calling; and first-personal narratives of trial and triumph. And indeed, teaching may be reflective, noble, even triumphant; but, such celebrations of the teaching life ultimately demean it when they fall prey to simplification and sentimentality. Too many

works in this mode substitute bullet points for argument and analysis, clichés and jargon for thinking through something in a fresh way. Meanwhile, rhapsodies on the rewards of teaching ring hollow when they fail to acknowledge how difficult it is for teachers to make their practice a vehicle for their own self-cultivation. The self-help genre does acknowledge the problem but then typically treats the symptoms in a superficial way. One book offers teachers tips on: alternatives to antibiotics, calming the inner critic, headlice, meditation, snacking, and on 'taking time to: breathe, celebrate success, collaborate, communicate, declutter, drink water, eat, exercise …' (Holmes, 2005, p. 194, bulleted in original). Another counters with this list of 'antidepressants': Sunlight/Conversations about good books and films/Cheerful students/A baby's face/Dark chocolate and excellent coffee/Ocean views …' (Casanave and Sosa, 2007, p. 47).

There are also books that invite teachers to attend to themselves in a deeper way (from Waller, 1932, especially part 5; through Jersild, 1955; to Palmer, 1998). In *Letters to a Young Teacher*, Jonathan Kozol (2007) creates a discursive space (in his literary recreation of his actual correspondence with a teacher) that is anything but simplistic or sentimental. And yet there is always the risk that even a work like this will be swallowed up by the pervasive kitsch that plagues education. For example, the cover of the Kozol volume describes it in this way: 'the author … gently guides a first-year teacher into "the joys and challenges and passionate rewards of a beautiful profession"' (it is not clear who or what the jacket is quoting, but it does not seem to be Kozol himself). A work like Kozol's is genuinely inspiring because it resists at every turn the urge to inflate and sweeten, modelling how someone combines deep ideals with a keen eye for the real. On the whole, though, the inspirational mode too often gives in to the urge to buoy up the spirits of teachers with literal or rhetorical antidepressants. Whether it is chocolate or a sweet narrative about how a teacher beat all the odds to change her students' lives forever, there is always a crash after a sugar rush, triggering a craving for an even sweeter confection.

There are, of course, works on teacher calling whose idealism is more than cheerleading and narratives by teachers whose hopefulness is more than Pollyanna optimism. In his portrait of a transformational teacher called Franklin Lears (who, it is worth remarking, left teaching after one year), Mark Edmundson makes a point of noting:

> Frank Lears was a remarkably good man, though it took me some time to see it. Lears' goodness was of a peculiar sort. He was always doing something for himself as well as for you. In the process of working his best deeds, he didn't mind affronting what you might call his spiritual enemies. Lears' goodness, like that of almost all great teachers, always had an edge to it. (Edmundson, 2003, p. 7)

Two teacher autobiographies that also get at this 'peculiar' sort of goodness are Rose (2005 [1990]) and Inchausti (1993); for a typology and sympathetic discussion of this genre, see Preskill (1998).

4 It is difficult to illustrate a pervasive, informal discourse concisely. Suspicion of teacher motives seems to be the default assumption of many in educational circles. Here are three (constructed) examples of the kind of debunking of idealistic takes on teacher motivation one

hears. Readers may judge for themselves whether the italicised lines below, those of the cynical character B, are familiar.

EXCHANGE 1

A: Teachers have a calling.

B: *You mean they feel called to have summers off.*

A: That's too cynical.

B: *Perhaps, but this talk of personal calling is still mystification. What we have here is social striving. Given the class position of certain families, teaching is an acceptable compromise between trades and out-of-reach, high-status professions.*

EXCHANGE 2

A: Teachers want to help their students gain the knowledge to succeed.

B: *Hogwash! Teachers construct students as ignorant in order to feel smart themselves. And we can go further and say that maintaining this gap helps teachers maintain their authority, feeding what is ultimately a kind of power trip.*

EXCHANGE 3

A: Teachers need to master techniques of classroom management in order to maintain an orderly learning environment.

B: *I'm afraid you have it backwards: the supposed need for order to teach the official curriculum is the very enactment of the true, if hidden, curriculum. Schools are designed to breed docile citizens and compliant workers.*

A: But, on that theory, teachers are pawns in a larger social agenda rather than driven by a hidden personal agenda.

B: *True, but consider that those who choose to teach, and thus to make young people sit still and fill in worksheets, are themselves survivors of this very process. So we could see teaching as a selection process for those who have a high tolerance for the kind of boredom and compliance built into schooling.*

A: If schooling is really as bleak as you suggest, I don't think anyone would naturally thrive in that world.

B: *Ok, maybe no one naturally likes seeing the world divided into multiple choice, short answers. So perhaps the best explanation for teacher motivation is what Freud called 'fort-da': one way to deal with suffering something unpleasant is to turn around and do the same thing to someone else. So teaching is a kind of educational 'Stockholm syndrome'.*

We can find examples of suspicion of the teacher's motives as early as Willard Waller (1932) who, for example, speculates at one point that teachers may be drawn to the profession out of a desire to control others, 'an inherent need of the personality for being in some sort of managerial position' (p. 379), adding sympathetically that educators may become autocratic because they are working in a low status profession and feel threatened by the constant encroachment of parents, politicians and other groups on their autonomy (pp. 10–11). (Thanks to Darryl DeMarzio for pointing me to these two passages, and reminding me of the Delpit passage I quote below.) To pick one strand of a more recent literature, that of critical pedagogy, we observe two stages of suspicion of the teacher's agenda. First, there is the idea that traditional teachers secretly want to perpetuate an unjust society, taking delight in the sonority of their own speech and construction of themselves as rich in knowledge ready to be banked into students. I refer of course to Paulo Freire who taught us that and how educational 'generosity' can be 'malefic' (see, for example, Freire, 2000 [1973], pp. 44–45, 60, and *passim*). Even as this inspired a generation of critical pedagogues, it also inspired a second wave of suspicion of these supposedly liberatory intentions. The most famous of these is Elizabeth Ellsworth's critique of the notion of dialogue in critical pedagogy (Ellsworth, 1989). Or consider Lisa Delpit's equally famous intervention, calling the 'good intentions' of progressive educators (specifically white educators who dogmatically insist that students of colour need to be protected from direct instruction in hegemonic Anglo culture) 'conscious delusions about their unconscious motives', suggesting (second hand but seemingly with approval) that white teachers must really be wanting to ensure for their own children 'sole access to the dwindling pool of American jobs' and that at least 'black folks *know* when they're lying!' (Delpit, 1995, p. 27; emphasis in original). To pick one final example, almost at random, Swiffen, following Jones, suggests that while dialogical teachers may appear to want subaltern students to come to voice, what is really at work is 'the fantasy or romance about access to and unity with the other' (Jones, 2004, p. 62; quoted in Swiffen, 2009, p. 57) and 'the desire to be recognised as eliciting oppressed voices' (Swiffen, 2009, p. 60).

5 Since Jackson acknowledges the central role of 'personal modelling' in transformative teaching, it seems clearer to call his two outlooks 'transformative' and 'transmissive', noting that mimesis is at work in both traditions in different ways. Jackson is far from alone in diagnosing this educational schizophrenia. For example, Zvi Lamm sees education conflicted over aims of socialisation/enculturation and self-actualisation (Lamm, 1976; quoted in Egan, 2008, pp. 9–10); Richard Rorty sees education confused over how to pursue both 'socialization' and 'individualization' (Rorty, 1999); and Kieran Egan sees education as an unworkable marriage of 'socialization, Plato's academic idea, and Rousseau's developmental idea' (Egan, 2008, p. 9).

6 The Establishment clause of the First Amendment to the Constitution of the United States reads: 'Congress shall make no law respecting an establishment of religion'. Church/state issues are different in each national context and many liberal democracies have no such formal separation. And, of course, de facto and de jure separation, as recent US history testifies, are often different matters. Still, the question of the neutrality of government-run schools arises in some form in many liberal democracies.

7 For a theory of influence that foregrounds our dread and disavowal of duplication, see any of Harold Bloom's 'revisionist' works (beginning with Bloom, 1973); for two classic explorations of originality and influence, see Emerson (1985 [1841]) and Nietzsche (1990 [1874]); for two recent studies of pedagogical imitation and apprenticeship, Steiner (2005) and Warnick (2008).

8 This episode is available online at http://www.imdb.com/title/tt0654963/

9 Of course, it has always been a relatively small percentage of college instructors who have enjoyed such working conditions. Many college instructors are part-time or work in ironi- cally named 'teaching colleges', where they have 4/4 or 5/5 teaching loads and no support for scholarship. Indeed, given the rapidly changing face of higher education, we may not need to worry much longer about this two-tier system. According to a new US Department of Education study, tenured or tenure-track faculty members now constitute only one quar- ter of US college instructors, down from 57 per cent in 1975 (reported in Wilson, 2010). And this is only one symptom of a more general trend toward corporatisation of the univer- sity, vocationalisation of higher education and commercialisation of campus life. Here I refer less to the historical entwinement of the 'multiversity' with the military-industrial complex (see, for example, Washburn, 2006; Giroux, 2007), or to the equally alarming recent rise of for-profit universities (see, for example, Ruch, 2003; Tierney, 2007), or even to the current dismantling of the public university (Newfield, 2008; Morphew and Eckel, 2009; Folbre, 2010), but primarily to the increasing commodification (within a wide variety of colleges and universities) of teaching, learning and scholarship. This new 'university of excellence' (Readings, 1996, chapter 2) seems to have less and less interest in person, pro- cess and pedagogy in its adoption of an entrepreneurial, product delivery, customer satisfac- tion model. In this model, students are viewed as 'instructional units', faculty described as 'full-time equivalents', and scholarship assessed by grant dollars and publication poundage (for a sample of the growing list of portraits and political economies of this new university, see Kirp, 2003; Slaughter and Rhoades, 2004; Waters, 2004; Bousquet, 2008; Donoghue, 2008; Chan and Fisher, 2009; Tuchman, 2009).

10 For a history that traces the development of *Bildung* through nineteenth-century German culture, especially literature, see Bruford (1975). On how the Hegelian concept of *Bildung* is taken up and transformed by Dewey, see the recent work by Jim Garrison and James Good (Garrison, 1995; Good, 2006; Garrison and Good, 2010). For explorations of how the quin- tessentially modern concept of *Bildung* might continue to have life in postmodernity, see the recent special issues of *Educational Philosophy and Theory* (Bauer, 2003) and the *Journal of Philosophy of Education* (reprinted as Løvlie, Mortensen and Nordenbo, 2003). Arcilla (2010) shows how to be a post '68 Marxian humanist through his powerful rehabilitation of aesthetic *Bildung* in which he defends the project of existentialist, liberal learning through encounters with modernist artworks (those which stress their medium). (For some other recent discussions of *Bildung*, see Thompson, 2005; 2006; Vinterbo-Hohr and Hohr, 2006; Hammershøj, 2009.)

11 Thanks to Richard Smith for suggesting this term. For a recent defence of manual work as 'soulcraft', including a description of just this sort of unselfing, see Crawford (2009, pp. 90–100).

12 There is another aspect to practical *Bildung*, namely the way in which a vocation enables one to claim a space in the network of social relations and seek the recognition of others. As Garrison and Good explain, for Hegel self-development depends on fulfilling the universal norms of a determinate social function, thereby achieving social recognition: '[A] human being must be *somebody* [*etwas*]. … he must belong to a particular estate [*Stand*, a place, a

standing in society]; for being somebody means that he has substantial being. A human being with no estate [*Stand*] is a merely a private person, and does not possess actual universality.' We seek confirmation of our self-worth through the recognition of other self-conscious agents like ourselves (Garrison and Good, 2010, pp. 59–60, quoting Hegel, *Philosophy of Right*, §207).

13 See, for example, Johnson (1990, pp. 6 and 282–284).

14 See, for example, MacIntyre (2007 [1981]), Williams (1985) and Taylor (1989). Such work in the 1980s was made possible by the groundbreaking work of G.E.M. Anscombe, Iris Murdoch and Philippa Foot. See, for example, Anscombe (1958), Murdoch (1985 [1970]) and Foot (1978).

15 There is a growing literature linking the revival of virtue ethics to professional ethics, but all of it tends toward a fairly narrow, moral interpretation of virtue (see, for example, Oakley and Cocking, 2001; and Walker and Ivanhoe, 2007). Martin (2000) promises to rethink professional ethics in the spirit of Williams, but even he largely ignores the question of the flourishing of the practitioner. Two recent books extend MacIntyre's theory of a practice to a specific occupation, one for journalism and the other for business (see Borden, 2007; Painter-Morland, 2008). For a religiously inflected and suggestive, if unsystematic, look at the aspirational aspects of the professions, see Shaffer (1987). The best virtue-theoretic treatments of teaching are Sockett (1993), Hare (1993), Hostetler (1997) and D. Carr (2000, 2005, 2006). On the whole, though, these works tend toward a moral (rather than ethical) interpretation of virtue, failing to foreground the flourishing of the teacher or counter the asceticism implicit in the discourse around teaching. Hostetler's (1997) edited collection, though focused on practical wisdom, remains tied to moral dilemmas. Sockett (1993) explicitly disparages a 'what's in it for me?' approach to teaching (p. 130), illustrating his discussion of the service ideal with references to Gandhi and Christ (p. 132), explaining that there is a spectrum of teacherly idealism from cynical, 'pandering' teachers to 'the saints and heroes like Jessica Siegel who struggle along in circumstances of considerable deprivation' (p. 139). What Sockett does not mention is that Siegel, the focus of Samuel Freedman's *Small Victories* (1990), burns out and leaves the profession. On the other hand, Sockett makes a point of saying that teachers need care and thus must be allowed to show the private person in the public role so that their students may see and appreciate them for who they are (Sockett, 1993, pp. 142–143). And Hare concludes with the notion that the virtues of teachers are not only to be valued as a means to enhance student growth but also, in their own right, as part of the teacher's own development into 'an educated individual and admirable person' (Hare, 1993, p. 161). In a previous work (Higgins, 2003, p. 138), I faulted Carr for neglecting the flourishing of the teacher in his virtue-ethical account of teacher professionalism; he has since replied, offering a thoughtful and helpful critique of my own position (see D. Carr, 2006, pp. 178–180).

5
Wigs, Disguises and Child's Play: Solidarity in Education

RUTH HEILBRONN

INTRODUCTION

Sources of tension and difficulty reside in teachers' daily work when it is situated in what is widely acknowledged to be an audit culture. In many education systems worldwide, the aims of education are predominantly subsumed to economic ends, related to gaining skills, qualifications and employment in a global economy (Ball, 2001; Apple, 2004, 2005). In such systems, pupils are routinely audited to ensure they achieve these skills, as are teachers, to monitor their 'effectiveness' in curricular 'delivery'. As a powerful director of school action, this culture may undermine other educational principles promoted in these same curricula, which can create tension for teachers. In England, for example, teachers may try to balance the principle of inclusion with a target- and test-led curriculum. The statutory national curriculum takes a principled stand on the value of inclusion, stating that 'teachers should aim to give every pupil the opportunity to experience success in learning and to achieve as high a standard as possible' (DfE, 2011a). However, the drive to achieve high ranking in league tables often entails tightly prescribed teaching practices (Korthagen, 1999; Crocco and Costigan, 2007), which may militate against the principle of inclusion. An illustration of this clash of principles comes from guidance accompanying a policy on 'personalisation of learning'.

Philosophical Perspectives on Teacher Education, First Edition. Edited by Ruth Heilbronn and
Lorraine Foreman-Peck. © 2015 Ruth Heilbronn and Lorraine Foreman-Peck. Editorial Organisation
© Philosophy of Education Society of Great Britain. Published 2015 by John Wiley & Sons, Ltd.

Personalisation is promoted as a means to enable each individual pupil to learn. This may seem familiar to many teachers, who have their own tried and trusted means to differentiate teaching in order to tailor their lessons to individual pupils. The guidance states that 'the key to manageability is the layering of targets in order to provide a clear route from the numerical target to the curricular target for the group or individual pupil' (DCSF, 2008, p.16). It is apparent then that 'personalisation of learning' is conceived within an audit paradigm, for if individual flourishing were the primary aim of the strategy, the means to attend to pupils individually would not be so technically prescribed. It is a short step from here to claiming that pupils in this paradigm of education are primarily conceived as a means to an end of higher test results and not as an end in themselves (Fielding, 2008). Dialogical practice and the primacy of relationships in teaching are, by definition, not a feature of *techne*. However, the term 'personalisation' seems to suggest attending to individuals' learning, and this eliding of meaning can be a source of tension and confusion for teachers.

Teachers' difficulties in trying to attend to all students, particularly in large classes, are exacerbated when they are expected to plan lessons from a prescriptive work scheme. These generally contain specified outcomes for lessons and technical guidance on learning objectives, outcomes and assessment opportunities. Much of the advice underlying the lesson planning may be sound, such as pupils being clear about what they are learning and why. However, the language in which these pedagogical principles are couched is often a technical one of inputs and outcomes, which does not foster a reflective attitude to lesson planning, nor a classroom in which a teacher may take time to reflect. The scheme of work's time frame is an instrument that drives individual lessons and weighs against being able to pick up on spontaneous and teachable moments or return to something unfinished and unplanned. Teacher judgement is often overridden by having to 'move on', and lack of time to engage with pupils' concerns and questions in the normal 'flow' can be difficult for teachers, knowing that some may be 'left behind' in the rush. This may seem a technical matter, resolvable by better teaching methods or resources, for example, but this is not so, because the tensions experienced by teachers in these cases cannot be easily dissipated since they are rooted in beliefs and values.

TEACHER BELIEFS AND VALUES

There is strong evidence that most teachers see teaching predominantly as a vocation (Huebner, 1987; Rogers and Webb, 1991; Hansen, 1994, 1995; Schwarz, 1998; Estola, Erikkilä and Syrjälä, 2003) and demonstrate what Aloni has called 'the fundamental commitments of educators' (Aloni, 2008). Individual teacher narratives are evidence of a 'teacher's vocation as a moral voice and its manifestation in the form of caring' (Estola *et al.*, 2003, p. 239). Examples can be found in accounts commonly written at the beginning of pre-service training to establish their starting point in teaching. These refer predominantly to the establishment of relationships and to the qualities and dispositions they remember in their 'best' teachers and wish to cultivate themselves, and they frequently make points about social justice, in the sense of 'wanting to make a difference'. They do not write in an effectiveness discourse. Some career change teachers talk about returning to education to escape the values of their previous careers, which they have experienced as lacking in orientation towards social ends (Heilbronn, 2011). Pupils generally hold similar views and describe good teachers as those who listen to them and help them, and not in technical terms of achievement of targets and results (ESRC, 1997; Wiedmaier *et al.*, 2007; Wang and Holcombe, 2010). When teachers set out at the beginning of their careers they see teaching as essentially a relational practice, in the sense defined by Dunne (2003) and Noddings (2003), so we might question why they often appear to collude with being constrained into the technically rational activity dictated by an audit paradigm (Davis, 1999, 2008; Stobart, 2007). Teachers rarely step outside their own curriculum paradigm and this could be because of what is at stake, for to ask fundamental questions of one's daily work could lead to a loss of faith in that work, in the sense of removing the ladder one is standing on. It is not surprising that teachers rarely question that the predominant aim of education is pupils' employability and not education as an initiation into 'worthwhile activities' and morally defensible forms of enquiry and experience (Peters, 1965).

One source of tension in the economic educational paradigm lies in a possible confusion between two senses of vocational education: one as educating students to achieve autonomy through the ability to find satisfying work, which most teachers would support as an end of education, and the other, more narrow, view of training in skills to serve the needs of industry or the economy. Teachers may be critical of the narrow definition but find it difficult to challenge. Possible further confusion between two senses of 'vocational' relates to differences in use of the word 'vocation'. One sense is close to its Latin origin in '*vocare*', 'to call', signifying work as a calling with all the dimensions of moral responsibility that 'to be called' originally had in a religious context. Having a vocation in this sense means holding an ethic of care, having vocational values. The other, more modern use, usually traced back to the turn of the last century (Parsons, 1909), focuses on developing skills for employment. The question of values is not foregrounded in this second sense, although the individual gaining the skills may need to embrace a professional code of conduct. Teachers with strong vocational values of the first kind, who find these values compromised by what 'schooling' for narrow vocational aims may demand, are at risk of the kind of emotional and psychological difficulty described by Bateson (1972) as being in 'a double bind'. Bateson used the term to name the traumatic experience of receiving contradictory messages that demand two different responses or actions that cannot both be completed. People experiencing these contradictory messages suffer intense emotional pressure that makes normal functioning difficult or impossible. It is not surprising that many teachers with strong vocational values do seem to comply with practices which seem to strain and even contradict their deeply held beliefs and values (Hartley, 1994). Prescriptive modes of curriculum delivery may offer a security blanket, a discourse of certainty of inputs and outcomes, supported by 'a regime of rituals', such as inspections and audits (Ball, 2001), whereas to question is to open oneself to the possibility of risk. The audit culture is risk averse, driven by what Dewey has called 'the quest for certainty' (1960), symptomatic of 'the obsession with effectiveness [that] leads to an ideal of minimising or effacing risk' by 'limiting educational goals to those that can be achieved fully' (Papastephanou, 2006, p. 51). Yet, without an opening to risk, teachers are not open to the particularities of individual encounters with pupils, which is characterised by an existential openness to the possibility of uncertainty and of fallibility. In the next section, I focus on the implications of the discussion for teacher educators.

SOLIDARITY AS A TEACHER EDUCATOR

It is a premise of this chapter that educators have an ethical responsibility to those they teach which encompasses not misleading them and, in the case of teacher educators, not misrepresenting or ignoring the tensions and difficulties of the practice, in order to prepare them 'to understand the moral and ethical complexities of their role and thus enable them to reflect ethical actions and decisions in their professional practice' (Campbell, 1997, p. 255). Importantly, too, teachers' practice 'inevitably has a strong influence on the moral lessons students directly and indirectly acquire in the classroom' (*ibid.*). This responsibility entails an injunction on teachers, as Kitchner points out, to 'affirm their ethical values throughout the curriculum', since it is the case that 'implicit attitudes and explicit behaviour of faculty communicate as much as course content about being ethical' (Kitchner, 1992, p. 190).

To affirm these ethical values in relationship with others is to demonstrate solidarity with others. To argue this claim I first examine the concept of solidarity as applied to the teacher educators in this context, taking the meaning of solidarity with its obvious connection with 'solidity' meaning 'solid, not flimsy', which resonates with the need for situational competence, a quality that is necessary for teachers in the lived circumstances of the practice. But 'solidarity' has a more widely used connotation as meaning 'solid with another': the term carries a socially embedded meaning. Being 'double bound' by the exigencies of technical rationality and vocational ideals sets up a conflict in many practitioners. To resist the demands of technical rationality requires strategic competence. If people are to survive and thrive in repressive situations, they need to cope with these situations without losing agency. Since these situations are social situations, solidarity with others is fundamental to coping and resistance since it is highly unlikely that the socially atomised individual could develop successful modes of engagement with their situation. Teachers are socially and culturally bound, and not isolated agents. Resistance to difficult and oppressive situations needs engagement with others who are 'solid' with the resistors, which means solid in an existential sense and solid with the values upheld. This implies that teacher educators should support the development of certain capacities and capabilities in their students. Camus (1962) has characterised a choice to be made between two existential positions: one can be 'solidaire ou solitaire', either solid with another or alone. The resonances with the vocabulary around 'solidarity' accord with English common usage of the word 'solid' as an adjective (first recorded in English in the fifteenth century, from Old French *solide* meaning 'firm, dense, compact', and, originally from Latin, *solidus* meaning 'firm, whole, entire'). 'Solitary', meaning 'on one's own', has resonances with the word 'isolated', from the Latin *insulatus*, meaning 'made into an island' (OED, 2046–7), a meaning that Donne finessed in his meditation in 1624, using a geographical metaphor to say that an individual does not exist on her own, like an island, but is joined to a whole continent of others: 'No man is an Iland, intire of it selfe; every man is a peece of the Continent, a part of the maine' (Donne, 1975).

Freire powerfully used the concept of solidarity as applied in education in his book *Pedagogy of the Oppressed* (1970). For Freire, the concept forms part of a liberation project in the particular class and ethnic circumstances in which he was teaching and writing. It has been claimed that the political aspect of Freire's book negates its function as a text about education (Stern, 2009). More profoundly, Freire's concept has been challenged on ontological grounds: solidarity is an impossibility, the Other is not 'knowable' in the sense taken by Freire. As Margonis (2007) reminds us, for Levinas

> the relationship with the other is not an idyllic and harmonious relationship of communion, or a sympathy through which we put ourselves in the other's place; we recognize the other as resembling us, but exterior to us; the relationship with the other is a relationship with a Mystery. More basic than any posited unity stands the radical difference of the other (Levinas, 1987, p. 75–76).

In this account of solidarity as 'solid with' I make no ontological claim that might be open to Levinas's criticism and do not imply that 'being solid with' must lead inevitably to a radical pedagogy. I refer back in fact to its original coinage, in the entry in the Enlightenment project of the *Encylopédie*, to mean 'mutual responsibility'. The *Encyclopaedia* entry forged the new word from *'solidaire'*, meaning 'interdependent, complete, entire', derived from *'solide'*. Mutuality and communality are important ideas here. For teacher educators, 'being solid with' entails two strong ethical demands. The first is the responsibility to prepare teachers to manage the process and practices of schools and schooling in an environment where much of a technical nature needs to be learnt. The second is to demonstrate 'solidarity' as 'being solid with' these teachers, which means not glossing over, burying, avoiding, nor yet confronting for the sake of contestation, the dilemmas generated by their sense of teaching as a vocation, a calling to be with others, in audit-driven times. This second injunction entails living with contradiction and inducting student teachers into the practice of living in the space of contradictory demands, seeing such 'double-bindedness' for what it is, being able to articulate dilemmas and understand the sometimes painful existential position of living with them. Ethical teacher educators should help those they teach to develop ways of living with contradictions, so that they do not become paralysing.

Part of the role of teacher educators may also involve assessment, leading to accreditation, as gatekeepers to teaching. Where this accreditation is based primarily and narrowly on standards and competences it may seem as if this role does oblige compliance with practices that border on the unethical. The reasons for this lie in the widely discussed objections to standards assessment for teachers (Thompson, 1992; Carr, 1993; Lum, 1999, 2003). Ethical teacher educators need to enable student teachers to develop strategic competence and capability, the ability to work within the confines of the curriculum and the culture and also keep their own agency, which includes the ability to exercise their professional judgement and their critical faculties.

Developing strategic competence and capability can be helped by engaging in practices that promote solidarity – as 'being solid with' – and do no harm to others, such as pupils. Strategic competence and capability are demonstrated in the exercise of practical judgement (Heilbronn, 2008). In *The Practice of Everyday Life*, de Certeau introduces a useful concept that can explicate some of the aspects of solidarity that I am advocating here. De Certeau develops the French idiomatic expression *la perruque*, used to refer to activities or tasks undertaken for personal reasons, under the pretence of legitimate, paid work. *La perruque* literally means *wig* and, according to de Certeau, its origins lie in an ancient tradition of 'duping the master'. *'La perruque'* may be as simple a matter as a secretary's writing a love letter on 'company time' or as complex as a cabinetmaker's 'borrowing' a lathe to make a piece of furniture for his living room (de Certeau, 1984, p. 25). The significant factor about engaging in *'la perruque'* for my current argument is not the material diversion of an employer's resources to the employee's own ends, but the carving out in the working day of personal time. Is time borrowing unethical? Is it unethical to write a personal letter in the boss's time, or shop online using office-supported equipment? Engaging in *la perruque* differs from pilfering in that nothing of material value is stolen. It differs from absenteeism in that the worker is officially present at work. 'The worker who indulges in *la perruque* actually diverts time (not goods, since he uses only scraps)' (*ibid.*). This personal time becomes a space for an action related to human ends and not the ends of the factory, the workshop, the production line, and, I am suggesting in this case, the classroom. And once this personal time-space exists it poses the possibility of action outside these other-manufactured exigencies. One engages in *la perruque* 'for work that is free, creative, and precisely not directed toward profit' (*ibid.*). De Certeau rightly asserts that successful exercise of the practice relies on the worker's wit and ingenuity, and as such represents autonomous acting and experiencing, within the confines of what might otherwise be monotonous work – work undertaken merely for the wage it represents and not for any intrinsic value to the worker. He is at pains to point out that nothing material is stolen and there is no implication that engagement in *'la perruque'* entails incompetence or inefficiency.

De Certeau's discussion is situated within the specific context of contemporary consumer society. In this context *la perruque* should be valued as a strategy to support survival and flourishing in any institution designed for ends not related to human flourishing. The worker who engages in *la perruque* exercises desirable qualities in a situation of constraint, and at times, servitude: 'In the very place where the machine he must serve reigns supreme, he cunningly takes pleasure in finding a way to create gratuitous products whose sole purpose is to signify his own capabilities through his work' (de Certeau, 1984, p. 3). Consumer products in a market economy rely on the profit motive and the good of individual consumers and producers. De Certeau situates his interpretation of '*la perruque*' within the discourse of communal shared values. For de Certeau the worker engaging in '*la perruque*' asserts a different ethic to the dominant ethic of the market and does so only 'with the complicity of other workers (who thus defeat the competition the factory tries to instil among them), he succeeds in "putting one over" on the established order on its home ground' (pp. 25–26). The worker confirms his solidarity with other workers or his family 'through spending his time in this way' (p. 25).

Wiggery (a translation I will use for '*la perruque*') is aligned to playfulness rather than unethical behaviour. Wit and ingenuity in being a good wiggery player are qualities that support resilience, as the persistence of a genre of 'gallows humour' suggests. These human qualities are related to playfulness: they enable us to stand back from an otherwise engulfing situation, to see it with some sense of perspective, and in the exercise of our own playfulness we are put back in charge of our actions. When we act playfully we create our own meanings in a situation. Good wiggery players manage to keep their own creative sense of playfulness, as opposed to absorbing the dominant orthodoxy, and this in turn keeps the possibility for rational reflection alive. Playfulness enables and announces that alternative viewpoints exist, even if these alternative viewpoints are not fully rationalised. The possibility of resistance is announced through witty responses in restrictive situations. The concept of wiggery carries more than mere wit and ingenuity since it also implies not coming headlong against authority, acting at all times in a non-confrontational manner. The concept is applicable in all the relationships under discussion here, teacher educator with student teacher and student teacher with pupil, as is further developed in the next section.

SOLIDARITY WITH PUPILS AND PLAY

Student teachers and teacher educators frequently notice 'wiggery' in the classroom when they observe pupils in lessons. In this section I shift focus from the relationship between the teacher educator and her student teacher to those relationships that teachers develop with their pupils, and I wish to suggest that charity towards 'off task' behaviour might be a step towards reconciling conflicting demands of those teachers' own practice. Why should teachers in general, which includes student teachers in particular, turn a blind eye to 'off task' behaviour in the classroom? Does encouraging playfulness and 'wiggery' undermine teacher authority? Does ignoring 'off task behaviour' act against the pupils' best interest? Can an ethical teacher educator invite student teachers to turn a blind eye to such behaviour? To answer some of these questions I want to think about the transition – I might even say the translation – of the infant child into the school child. In England this takes place at the age of five, or in the school year in which she becomes five, but generally it ranges from ages five to seven in most education systems. A number of reasons and stories about going to school might be offered to her. From the perspective of the state, the child is enrolled in a social institution in which she will begin her education as a future citizen of that state, so the entry into school is in some sense a call-up for compulsory school service. In an English school context she will begin her work on the first Key Stage of the National Curriculum very soon after entry. At the end of the Key Stage her educational achievements are audited and counted with the schools' targets and achievements in the published league tables of schools' results, according to the market model discussed earlier. In this climate both junior and infant pupils routinely undergo the kind of educational experience that was once common to 16–18-year-olds, when school examinations took place predominantly and only at this age. 'Cramming' for examinations was a feature of the education of this age group and the institutions engaging in it were often called 'sausage machines'. This kind of learning experience equates to de Certeau's account of being a factory worker, 'on the boss's time', which we could contrast with a pedagogy based on enquiry and exploration advocated by educationalists such as Rousseau, Dewey, Bruner, Piaget, Vygotsky, Froebel and Montessori, who, while differing in theoretical detail, all based their pedagogy on the primacy of experience in the child's development of knowledge and understanding.

It is not disputed that play is of foundational importance to the psychological, emotional and cognitive development of children (Isenberg and Quisenberry, 1988; Fromberg, 1998, 2002; Jenkinson, 2001; McCune and Zanes, 2001). Indeed, at one time in England the primacy of play to children's development was recognised as a foundational aspect of curriculum design in the primary school. Following the 1967 Plowden Report, play and experiential learning became central to the primary curriculum in England, a curriculum that was changed after the 1988 Education Reform Act established a statutory National Curriculum and testing regime from ages 5–16 (DfE, 1988). Plowden had stated specifically that we should not assume that only what is measurable is valuable (1967). In the current context, when student teachers are able to be charitable to pupils' playfulness in class they are at the same time acknowledging children's right and need to play, and in so doing enabling those children to create a space for play, in a non-confrontational manner. From the children's perspective, they have to survive in school without getting into head-on clashes with authority. Children who are unable to dissimulate and disguise non-compliance often get into difficulties that may lead to exclusion from school and other adverse circumstances. These can lead to a career of disadvantage and confrontation. Children who are good natural 'wiggery players' have some survival and developmental advantages in the school system. With an ability to sometimes 'do their own thing', they may develop a number of dispositions that are important to leading a good life, such as tactfulness and diplomacy, attentiveness, situational alertness, creativity, independence, solidarity. Children have to respond with tact to teachers if they are to avoid confrontation. They need to notice what is going on around them, otherwise they may be caught out. They need to be aware of their classmates and know how to draw on friendships: their wiggery needs to fit in with interests beyond their own, otherwise it would soon be revealed. Therefore teachers who understand and appreciate the benefits of wiggery would stand in solidarity with their pupils in their pupils' daily encounter with schooling.

SOLID WITH AND SOLID AGAINST?

How does this discussion about children and wiggery relate to the central argument of the chapter, that teacher educators need to stand in solidarity with their student teachers and those on courses of professional development? I suggest that noticing and understanding playful wiggery in their pupils can remind teachers of the space and time that can be created for activity related to human ends; it can help foster a humane approach to their pupils, and a situational alertness and competence which they and their pupils require to cope with the tensions and contradictions of school life, helping to keep open a pedagogic space of thoughtfulness, a space for what Van Manen has called 'tactful teaching' (1991). Unless teachers are able to understand and resist the technicist demands of their working situations, they risk, in their turn, acting unethically, by treating the children as means to an end, that of better test results and higher targets, rather than people in their own right, 'an end in themselves' with entitlements to exist in their own liminal space.

De Certeau thinks of '*la perruque*' as the tactics of the weak. In the current school situation student teachers and teachers in general have very little chance to exercise their own judgement on curricular matters and even on relational matters in many cases.[1] In celebrating '*la perruque*' de Certeau expresses how the practice might benefit us within an institution led by managerial, rather than humanistic aims. He tells us that:

> we can divert the time owed to the institution; we can make textual objects that signify an art and solidarities; we can play the game of free exchange, even if it is penalized by bosses and colleagues when they are not willing to 'turn a blind eye' on it; we can create networks of connivances and sleights of hand; we can exchange gifts; and in these ways we can subvert the law that, in the scientific factory, put work at the service of the machine, and, by a similar logic, progressively destroys the requirement of creation and the 'obligation to give' (de Certeau, 1984, p. 149).

So this resistance is not passive, and not confrontational. It is the resistance embedded in relationships. 'It relies for its success, or at least for its continuation and avoidance of destruction, on the connivance of others in some form' (de Certeau, 1984, p. 14.). It relies on other people tacitly agreeing not to 'inform' that 'shirking' is taking place, that someone may be avoiding their duty, or their obligations to an authority. It relies on 'camaraderie', or 'comradeship'. 'Comrade' has a political connotation for English speakers and here again it is useful to decouple the sense of the word from its twentieth-century associations and reclaim an early recorded use as 'one who shares the same room', in a similar move to that around 'solid with' and 'solitary'. The French word *camarade* as used in the sixteenth century is still used today to mean 'friend'. 'Camaraderie' is friendship of a certain kind; there is also the French word *amitié*, which is more related to a personal friendship, having its origin in the word for 'love'. 'Camaraderie' refers to the kind of relationship of a shared social space, a *camera* (Latin for 'a room'), a classroom, for example. The language of solidarity and comradeship might be usefully reclaimed for education from its predominantly political context to help to focus a sense of communality in the service of countering the orthodoxy that schools need to be run on economic aims and not primarily for human flourishing.

CONCLUSION

Teacher educators have a fundamental pastoral responsibility to their student teachers, and this implies being solid with them in all circumstances. Unconditional solidarity does not mean uncritical acceptance of all they say and do. It is an existential and not a cognitive injunction, and does not entail agreeing with their choices and behaviour in all circumstances. In the current specific context outlined at the beginning of the chapter and referred to as an audit culture, 'being solid with' means both preparing student teachers with the applied technical knowledge and 'sharing their burdens', the tensions and contradictions of teacher existence.

NOTE

1 An example is a nationally adopted policy on managing pupil behaviour in England, known as 'Behaviour for Learning', which gives particular advice of a mechanistic, behaviourist kind.

6

To Believe, to Think, to Know – to Teach?: Ethical Deliberation in Teacher Education

DAMIEN SHORTT, PAUL REYNOLDS,
MARY McATEER AND FIONA HALLETT

Our interest in ethical deliberation in teacher education goes back a number of years to around 2009, when the organisation then responsible for teachers' personal and professional conduct in England, the General Teaching Council of England (GTCE), was in the process of preparing a new Code of Conduct. At the time, the GTCE had provoked something of a controversy in England, when various interested parties debated the prospect of a quasi-autonomous non-government agency (that is, a 'quango') like the GTCE apparently attempting to extend its powers (with its new Code of Conduct) from controlling the professional conduct of teachers to also exerting an element of control over their private lives as well. Our interest, at that time, was in investigating how teachers were being prepared (if at all) during their training and education to engage in debates like this, and, perhaps more importantly, how they were being prepared to deliberate over the multitude of moral and ethical dilemmas with which teachers are faced on an almost daily basis. As Elizabeth Campbell puts it:

> Concerted efforts within individual school communities and professional organizations more broadly to augment ethical knowledge

Philosophical Perspectives on Teacher Education, First Edition. Edited by Ruth Heilbronn and Lorraine Foreman-Peck. © 2015 Ruth Heilbronn and Lorraine Foreman-Peck. Editorial Organisation © Philosophy of Education Society of Great Britain. Published 2015 by John Wiley & Sons, Ltd.

may provoke the kind of discussion and debate needed to highlight teaching as a moral pursuit. This, in turn, may lend support to the lone teacher struggling to cope without much guidance with the dilemmas and tensions that unavoidably surface when one is engaged in the moral domain. (Campbell, 2003, pp. 138–139)

The topicality of our research focus was greatly enhanced in 2010 when a new government came to power in England promising to change radically the entire teaching profession. One of the ways it set out to do this was to abolish the GTCE and to reassume the powers that had previously been devolved to that quango from central government. As part of this new policy, and in a bid to improve the standard of teaching in England, a new performance management regime would come into force and teacher training would be completely overhauled. A key way in which this would happen would be through the establishment of a new set of *Teachers' Standards* (2012b) against which practising teachers would be continually assessed and around which trainee teachers would have their education and training built. Unlike all previous incarnations of official teaching standards in England (1992, 1998, 2002 and 2008), these new standards also included a section covering personal and professional conduct, meaning that the teaching and facilitation of ethical deliberation in teacher education has arguably become more important than it has ever been before. For example, teachers would now be assessed, throughout their careers (from the first day of training until they leave the profession), according to their ability to 'respect the rights of others' and not to undermine 'fundamental British values, including democracy, the rule of law, individual liberty'. All of these (rights, values, democracy, law and liberty) are weighty philosophical concepts about which, we argue, almost all trainees, teachers and teacher educators would benefit from having some education and a space in which they could discuss and debate what they actually mean for the teacher in the classroom.

It is this government policy landscape that provides the background for our interest in the promotion of ethical deliberation in teacher training and why we feel it is becoming an increasingly important area of education studies. We hope, given the apparent ubiquity of teaching standards and codes of conduct in many education systems around the world, that international readers will be able to see the applicability of what we discuss in the remainder of this chapter to their own situation. It is our belief that teaching is a practice, irrespective of geographical location, that is fundamentally about making ethical choices and about helping children and young adults to navigate their way through the various dilemmas with which they will be faced in life. In our work with teachers and teacher educators, we have found that there is a tension, to different degrees, with which we all appear to live: when it comes to decisions about right and wrong, good and bad, worthwhile and worthless, we seem to experience significant discomfort in moving from what we believe to what we think, from what we think to what we feel we know, and onwards to what and how we teach that which we think we know. This discomfort, it seems, stems at least in no small part from our desire to be able to provide a rationale for this movement from belief, onwards through thought and knowledge, to teaching. When it comes to matters of ethics and morality in the teaching profession, it seems, it is widely considered important to be able to rationalise one's moral position.

Additionally, there appear to be many levels of ethical deliberation in which teachers very commonly engage and that range from the 'big' abstract questions about whether or not that which we teach is inherently good, through the practical questions of whether or not the methods that we employ are good or bad, down to the seemingly trivial questions about everyday issues like whether or not it is right to 'shush' children in class (see, for example, Thornberg, 2006). In essence, then, our interest in this area is in assisting those who are involved in teaching to acquire the confidence and skills that will enable them to reflect upon their own value judgements and the way in which these affect their everyday practice. Through this, we hope, they will be better able (and more likely) to discuss with those they teach how and why they have arrived at particular judgements; again, as Campbell argues: 'There is no one uniform or generic model of the ethical teacher who comes in many forms, reflective of the uniqueness of individuals. However, ethical teachers do share a similar sense of moral agency and purpose framed by a deep regard for core moral and ethical principles' (Campbell, 2003, p. 140). The acknowledgement of and deliberation over these similarities between teachers, we believe, will improve the relationship not only between practitioners but also between teachers and their students, and, as a consequence, improve the quality of education achieved. Before expanding upon this, however, we would first like to scope the field of research and writing that is particularly concerned with teaching as a moral profession – ethical deliberation, and the facilitation of such deliberation.

TEACHING AS A MORAL PROFESSION

In writing this chapter, we are very much aware that there are a number of assumptions which we are asking our readers to accept for the sake of brevity, and one of the key assumptions is, as Michael Totterdell succinctly puts it, that 'the profession is ready to take seriously the possibility that education contains within itself the potential for creating an ethos amongst its members, to which beginning teachers will submit themselves for training and for which, because it is both politically and professionally acceptable, it can elicit support from the wider society' (Totterdell, 2000, p. 141). We acknowledge that this is a rather large assumption to ask of our readers. However, for teachers to assume the opposite of this, as Totterdell puts it, is akin to 'moral autism', which would be a 'clearly intolerable' quality in a teacher (p. 129). A second key assumption that we are making is the very notion that teaching is itself a profession, let alone the notion of teaching as a moral profession, since we are aware that this is a topic of much debate (see, for example, Carr, 2000; McCulloch, Helsby and Knight, 2000; Buus, 2005; Martinez, Desiderio and Papakonstantinou, 2010). Nevertheless, by way of temporarily putting forward a working definition of teaching as a profession, we concur with McCulloch *et al.*, who argue that 'the ideals of (teacher) professionalism in the English context have always been associated with the assumption that teachers control the curriculum, that is, what they teach and how they teach it' (McCulloch *et al.*, 2000, p. 13), since this definition of a profession being a practice that is controlled by practitioners runs throughout the literature on professionalism in general (this literature is voluminous; see, for example, Witz, 1992; Gunnarsson, 2009; Ronnie, 2013). Yet, we must acknowledge, as those involved in education the world over are in no doubt aware, that teachers are seldom able to exert any significant degree of control over what and how they teach.

Nevertheless, if we can, for the purposes of this discussion, assume that teaching is a profession, then we can more robustly make the case for the need for professional ethical deliberation since, as Tomlinson and Little argue: 'In any circumstances where an individual or group of individuals takes responsibility for aspects of the lives of others on the grounds of special knowledge or expertise, whether in a context of public funding or not, ethical issues arise and some form of guidance for action is required' (Tomlinson and Little, 2000, p. 147). Where this conceptualisation of teaching as a moral profession actually leads us, according to Totterdell, is to a pleasingly rich 'conception of morality that is role-centred' since 'not only does the vocabulary of virtues seem most sensible in the context of roles, the same is true of duties and rights, obligations and choice, goodness and badness, and of "ought" evaluations in general' (Totterdell, 2000, p. 135). Using this 'vocabulary of virtues', however, should not be understood as a wholesale adoption or advocacy by us of virtue ethics to the exclusion of deontological or consequentialist thinking. Indeed, as the reader will see below, ethical deliberation in action amongst teachers appears to interweave aspects of all three paradigms of ethical reasoning. The most important thing for the purposes of this research, we feel, is that by grounding ethical reasoning in the professional role it enabled us to build our discussions with teachers and teacher educators around virtues and character dispositions, which are arguably much more positively viewed by practitioners than sets of rules and the imposition of supposedly measurable outcomes (even though all teachers acknowledge that rules and outcomes are a fundamental part of our profession). First, though, we would like to move on to providing some background discussion about ethical deliberation and its facilitation.

ETHICAL DELIBERATION: WHAT IS IT?

In the context of our research, we have drawn upon a number of different academic fields in order to characterise our conceptualisation of what form ethical deliberation might take in the realm of teacher education. Generally, our model primarily involved facilitating participants to reflect upon and articulate the decision-making processes through which they pass when confronted with an ethical dilemma, in the hope that such reflection and articulation would expose both the participant's hitherto unacknowledged expertise in this process as well as the tensions that cause them personal and professional distress. More specifically, our understanding of ethical deliberation is quite succinctly articulated by Howe and Miramontes when they state that ethical deliberation is the attempt to answer the question as to what ought to be done in a given set of circumstances, all things considered. They go on to unpick this by arguing that:

> The nature of this question helps to distinguish ethical deliberation from certain other intellectual activities. For example, unlike the reasonable well-defined puzzle-solving that characterizes mathematics and physics, ethical deliberation must take into account an almost boundless array of considerations, including the facts and the law, as well as personal beliefs, attachments, feelings, and conceptions of 'the good life'. This renders ethical deliberation exceedingly complex, uncertain, and tentative. Furthermore ... everyone, not just the experts, is afforded a voice and possesses *expertise* when it comes to ethical deliberation. (Howe and Miramontes, 1991, p. 8)

In addition, Howe and Miramontes advocate the drawing-upon of ethical theory in order to '(1) explicate and systematise standards of ethical deliberation that may be used to (2) evaluate ethical choices' (p. 13).

It is this foundation of informal group deliberation upon traditional ethical theory that has largely shaped our work so far, an idea shared with Jacquelyn Kegley, who argues that:

> Rather than centring only on the 'capacity to reason' as the foundation of moral reasoning and judgment and focusing on the individual, autonomous, self-sufficient rational person, the self of ethical deliberation and action must be seen as a social, embodied, passionate, imaginative, interpretive, problem-solving being with the capacity to enter into certain kinds of relationships

with other persons, to be functional as a member of a 'moral community'. (Kegley, 2011, p. 117)

By attempting to build such a moral community we hoped to assist participants in developing the confidence to facilitate their own students in cultivating the capacity, as Nancy Matchett puts it, 'to deliberate meaningfully and responsibly about ethics' rather than 'teaching a single decision procedure or recommending a particular set of values, principles, or norms' (Matchett, 2008, p. 25). Indeed, it is a quite widely held belief amongst teacher educators who do not have a formal background in ethical theory or moral philosophy (we found) that ethical deliberation is precisely the knowledge and application of theory to situations with the intention of ensuring a wished-for outcome. It was our wish to debunk this notion and to employ ethical deliberation as a means to demonstrate to participants their own expertise in these matters.

A final point to note in our working definition of ethical deliberation is, following Cheryl Misak (2008, pp. 620–621), that we have proceeded in this research in the belief that by dint of getting involved in ethical deliberation we are assuming that our ethical beliefs can be justified to at least some degree and, further, that, through deliberation, we can improve upon them. Further, we have based our research on the belief that 'We have no option in ethics but to look to accounts of experience and acknowledge their fallible authority. If we are careful and critical in evaluating these reports, they can be the source of new and important moral insights' (p. 632). Finally in this section, before moving on to a discussion of the methodology we have adopted and the methods we have employed in our research, we wish to very briefly provide some information on what has informed our thinking with regard to how ethical deliberation might be best facilitated.

FACILITATING ETHICAL DELIBERATION

In all of the work that we have done with teacher educators, our main objective has primarily been to get people talking about moral values so that we can begin to reflect upon where these values come from, how they manifest themselves in our daily lives, and how they might be critiqued. The main way in which we have sought to achieve this objective is by the employment, in various forms, of dialectic. Used well, this method gives us, we believe, the opportunity to engage participants not only in the actual content of the sessions but also in a discussion about the very format of the sessions themselves. However, we are aware that there are many different opinions about, and variations of, the dialectic method as a means of facilitating dialogue and assisting education. Therefore, we would now like to briefly outline the style that we have adopted.

It seems reasonable to assert that Socratic dialogue is the most common dialectic method when it comes to education: a simple search of academic journal databases for the terms 'Socratic dialogue' and 'education' covering the past ten years produces over 2000 items. An important theme that emerges in academic discussions about the employment of Socratic dialogue in the classroom or seminar is that it can potentially lead to the perplexing, shaming or even humiliation of students (see, for example, Leigh, 2007; Boghossian, 2012). Our belief, when approaching this issue, was that in many of the dialogues written by Plato it is the intention of the central character to disabuse an interlocutor of an erroneous belief that they hold (see, for example, Knezic *et al.*, 2010); this, we felt, was not an appropriate approach to take in the context of working with colleagues. A further concern that we had about the traditional Socratic dialogue is articulated by Richard Smith (2011) when he warns that the Socratic dialogues of Plato are inherently textual in nature, that they are narrated by unreliable narrators, and that their meaning is consequently highly unstable.

Smith is principally concerned in his article in warning about the potential pitfalls of blithely adapting what is contained in Plato's dialogues as a ready-made, off-the-shelf method for philosophical deliberation. (He is particularly concerned about doing this when practising philosophy with children, but his argument still stands, we believe, when working with newcomers to the discipline of philosophy.) That the Socratic dialogue method is primarily textual, Smith argues, means that 'live, face to face conversation' may not have as many 'philosophical possibilities' as its uncritical adherents might think (Smith, 2011, p. 231). Sebastian Mitchell argues in a similar vein to Smith when he concludes that any facilitator of dialogue, just like Socrates himself, 'cannot ensure that his interlocutor [will follow] a particular path of thought and action once the dialogue [has] come to an end' (Mitchell, 2006, p. 194). Smith's arguments, along with Mitchell's, succinctly encapsulate our own worries about the presupposition that merely talking things out in a public forum will necessarily lead a group of interlocutors to a more insightful, or philosophically robust, view of moral values in the classroom.

Where we have engaged in the discussion of hypothetical situations followed by questions, answers and counter-questions with our participants, it has never been (as will be seen later) in the expectation that we will necessarily end up with a more enlightened understanding of the core theoretical principles. Nor have we sought to disabuse our participants of views and values that we might consider erroneous, which is one thing that the original Socratic dialogues appear to do (see the brief discussion of this 'gadfly' method of dialectic above). We therefore see our employment of dialectic as being more akin to the *maieutic* (or mid-wifely) method of Plato (in *The Sophist*) as described by Fiona Leigh:

> [The *Sophist*] can be read as designed to facilitate a dialogue of sorts between the reader and the text, taken as a whole. This dialogue would take place after the reader has already gone right through the text and is reflecting upon the theory it contains. This dialogue is, therefore, a conversation the reader has with herself (cf. 263e), in which one side of the discussion is guided and prompted by the text that has been read. It is this dialogue that brings the learner to the point of understanding, elsewhere described as giving birth (*Theaetetus* 148e–151d), and is in this sense an expression of 'mid-wifely' or *maieutic* method. (Leigh, 2007, p. 317)

This post-dialogue reflection and critique is something that became, as our research progressed, one of the most important methodological, or facilitation, discoveries that we made. In preparation for moving on to the analysis of what we discovered, we would now like to briefly outline the methodological perspective through which we approached the eclectic forms of data that we gathered over the course of our pilots and trials.

METHODOLOGY AND METHODS

Methodology

The genre of our chapter is perhaps quite different from the others that make up this collection, in that ours exists in the interstice between theoretical and empirical research. Consequently, we feel that it is appropriate to provide for our reader a brief overview at this point of the different approaches that we have taken in exploring the promotion of ethical deliberation in teacher education. We are at pains, however, to make it known that we make no claim that any of our results or recommendations are to be taken as definitively proven, nor that the trials and conclusions that we recount below are presented as if they are repeatable experiments with guaranteed identical outcomes. The very best that one can achieve in this type of research, we believe, is to recount as accurately as possible for the reader the theoretical and methodological architecture that shaped our approach to finding out more about how successfully to facilitate ethical deliberation in the hope that some will be encouraged to take up the challenge and to try it for themselves.

The core issue with which we grappled when considering how we might reliably know if our attempts to promote deliberation were successful, or not, concerned what type of data we might gather, on the one hand, and how we might convincingly analyse it, on the other. As a group, we knew from our previous teaching experiences as well as our previous research that our collective interest lay in testing whether or not certain trialled interventions would prove successful in promoting deliberation. However, at that point we could not conclusively articulate what success in such a scenario might actually look like, let alone how it might be measured. Further, we knew that we intended to trial a number of different interventions, each of which would generate different types of data, so, we needed to consider how we might synthesise our experiences and findings into one coherently communicable story.

It was this need to synthesise data of different types from a number of different sources that led us to drawing upon aspects of Grounded Theory as a way to frame this research. In brief, Colin Robson defines Grounded Theory as a research methodology aimed at finding a 'central core category which is both at a high level of abstraction and grounded in (i.e. derived from) the data you have collected and analysed' (Robson, 2011, p. 489). The basic three stages of this approach, according to Robson, are (i) to find the conceptual categories contained within the data (open coding); (ii) to find relationships between and interconnect those categories (axial coding); and, finally, (iii) to establish the core categories (selective coding) (also see Gray, 2009, pp. 502–513; David and Sutton, 2011, pp. 191–202). The overall thrust of this methodological approach is that 'it is feasible to discover concepts and come with hypotheses from the field, which can be used to generate a theory' (Robson, 2011, p. 147).

There are, of course, a number of criticisms of Grounded Theory. Most criticisms highlight this methodology's tendency to fragment and decontextualise data that was originally in narrative form and which might consequently lead to radically different interpretations. Another common criticism is that there is no firm agreement amongst adherent researchers as to what the methodology's core concepts actually mean; and a third criticism that is often made of Grounded Theory is that it is frequently more descriptive than analytical in its approach and that, as a consequence, what is generated as a result of the research is not really a theory (for these criticisms and others, see Clarke, 2007 and Bryman, 2012). In the context of our research, we merely wanted a clearly articulated approach that would allow us to coherently collate and analyse our data and that would enable us to articulate to those who shared our interests the core lessons that we learned about how best to facilitate ethical deliberation in teacher education; Grounded Theory, we believe, provides a valid and well-tested set of tools for just such an endeavour.

We remind the reader again, however, that our research and this paper are not attempting to masquerade as bona fide Grounded Theory in practice. What we have done is to employ the Grounded Theory approach to the analysis of varied qualitative data such as feedback questionnaires and interview transcripts and recordings. By immersing ourselves in this data and then gradually and systematically honing down the data through successive processes of thematic coding until we ended up with a small number of core themes, we feel that we have been able to present coherently a manageable number of well-founded observations. From these observations, we believe that we are able to make recommendations and, to some extent, predictions that will enable readers to learn from what we have experienced and that they will be able, as a result of our work, to better inform their thinking and practice should they wish to pursue a similar path.

Methods

We launched our research with an ethics day, in which we invited colleagues to attend a day of events that focused on ethics, education and teaching. The day began with a lecture given by an established external academic who had worked and published for many years in the field. The day also involved break-out sessions and a final plenary at which colleagues were invited to feed back what their groups had felt were the most pressing ethical issues with which they were regularly faced in their professional roles. Following the ethics day, and as a result of what participants had suggested in the feedback forms, we organised a series of ethics workshops. These workshops usually happened in the late afternoon, and involved a very short introductory presentation on an aspect of moral philosophy, and then a group discussion prompted by the presentation of some hypothetical scenarios in which a moral dilemma was described and participants were asked to talk through and reflect upon possible courses of action. Simultaneously with the workshops, we created an online discussion forum through which contributors could further articulate their opinions and reflections about the issues discussed at the ethics day and during the workshops. We then conducted follow-up interviews with ten participants, in which we reflected upon a wide range of topics relating both to the format of the ethics events, and also upon the part played by ethical deliberation in the lives of our participants.

Having amassed a significant amount of data about the ways in which ethics and moral philosophy influenced colleagues in their jobs, we organised an ethics weekend (in association with the Philosophy of Education Society of Great Britain). This was a residential weekend at which approximately 15 participants from the fields of teaching and teacher education came together to engage in, and reflect upon, ethical deliberation. Following the ethics weekend, we interviewed nine of the participants and discussed their opinions about both the content and format of the weekend. These interviews were conducted over the telephone, and were semi-structured in nature.

With such a variety of different types of data at our disposal, it was clear that it would serve little purpose to attempt to quantify it with a view to condensing it into some form of tabulated results. The best that we could do, it appeared, was to identify the most dominant, recurring themes that were interwoven throughout the data and, from this, to construct an overarching view (theory) about what we could see. This is where our adaptation of some of Grounded Theory's methods for data analysis played a pivotal and work-reducing role. To code such qualitative data is always going to be, at some level, subjective, and no two researchers are likely to code the same data in precisely the same way. However, the belief is that as one moves from open coding, to axial and then on to selective coding, the likelihood of significant differences occurring is lessened. Hopefully, this will be seen as we now present our core categories/themes, where the reader is unlikely to see anything that is startlingly unexpected. Put simply, what our method of data analysis does is to move beyond the simple presentation of cherry-picked quotations; instead it offers a collation and condensation of the most recurring and significant observations made by participants.

DATA PRESENTATION, ANALYSIS AND DISCUSSION

It seems reasonable to suggest, from our research, that there is indeed a demand from educators for the space and time to engage in ethical deliberation. Our initial launch event attracted almost 60 participants from four different universities in the north-west of England, and the series of follow-up ethics workshops attracted a consistent attendance of between five and ten participants each time. That so many busy colleagues were willing to give up their time to come to these events voluntarily suggests that, if they were more formally encouraged (and timetabled) to engage in this type of professional development, the engagement could have been even greater. Additionally, the responses that participants provided to us via feedback present some interesting insights into the opinions of what we consider to be a reasonably representative sample cross-section of teacher educators, which point towards a demand for such events.

For example, only one in four of our launch-day respondents declared that ethics had been a part of their formal education and training, yet three-quarters of them recognised that ethics and ethical issues impinge daily upon their day-to-day professional role, with the remaining quarter stating that they deferred to classroom conventions and institutional rules in decision making. In our follow-up interviews with ten participants, there were even stronger calls for more opportunities to engage in the study and discussion of ethics theory and to put this theory into practice. Of our ten interviews, nine participants stated that they had little or no formal training in ethics and stated that they generally relied upon past experience and personal opinions when it came to morality and values. All expressed a desire to learn more, and all could see the benefits that increased knowledge about, and practice of, ethical deliberation and decision making could bring to their professional lives.

In a separate tranche of interviews with people who had taken part in our ethics weekend, we collected several interesting insights into how best (or how best not) to facilitate such fora for ethical deliberation. The first of these insights relates to the employment of methods of group investigation that can be referred to as broadly sitting under the umbrella term 'Socratic dialogue'. In our experience, the employment of a question and answer format in which the facilitator plays the role of a probing questioner (gadfly-like) who endeavours, through pointing out tensions, flaws or contradictions in a participant's definitions of key ethical terms or their proposed resolutions to model ethical dilemmas, did not work very successfully. Our participants reported that the model dilemmas were not recognisable to everyone in the same way, and that this led to the conversation often becoming fragmentary and tangential.

In a similar vein, it was perceived in our group that there was a significant difference between taking on a Socratic role and being a facilitator. Socrates, it was felt, knew the teaching point that he wished to make, and manipulated the questions in order to lead his interlocutors to some realisation vis-à-vis that point; we, on the other hand, were involved in something that was more akin to group enquiry, in which the facilitator was as much on a learning journey as the participants: consequently, it was perhaps inappropriate for them to take on a cajoling role. Further, coming at this same issue but from an almost opposite end, participants alluded to the notion that, in common Socratic dialogue, the facilitator is necessarily distanced from the actual conversation/dialogue, and that it would be a problem in ethics fora like ours if the facilitator were the only one in the room with any type of background in ethical theory. This focus on roles was actually a theme to which participants frequently returned in our interviews.

All of our interviewees discussed the attempts that we had made in the employment of role play as a tool for prompting reflection and debate, and almost all of them commented upon one or other, or both, of two main issues. First, it was quite consistently noted that, in our workshops, too much time was spent in setting up the scenario. Participants and facilitators engaged in protracted discussions, it seemed, about the intricacies and details of situations and character traits. After a relatively short period of time, this resulted in so many variations and interpretations of the same scenario circulating amongst the group that there were too many opportunities for multiple interpretations.

Second, and as a direct result of this first issue, it was noted by interviewees that role play is necessarily about exploring the motivations and actions of characters in a fictional scenario rather than participants in the forum. To them, it seemed as though such a group of professional educators should be able to deal with issues directly, and not in an artificially distanced fashion. To situate a dilemma, one interviewee remarked, is different than role play, since it does not require one to waste time in laboriously garnering the minutiae of a particular character's profile and dispositions. In general, this group of professionals felt that there was enough experience in the room to have enabled a more direct treatment of ethics and morality in education than either traditional Socratic dialogue or role play typically allow. Indeed, it was the level of experience in our participants that appeared to generate one of the biggest tensions with which we were faced.

In all of the follow-up interviews that we undertook with participants, a core theme that emerged was related to democracy in discussion groups of different types. It became clear to us, as we facilitated the sessions, that it was getting increasingly difficult to, on the one hand, ensure that all participants had the opportunity to contribute whilst, on the other hand, ensuring that the discussion was not continually side-tracked by contributions that ignored previous contributions and which tended to shunt the discussion onto a different track. The follow-up interviews showed that participants were almost unanimous in agreement that a totally open group discussion does not necessarily equate to a more democratic or egalitarian one, since it can easily move towards the anarchic. Likewise, a structured discussion, it was felt, can help a group to achieve something by focusing the conversation on one, or a few, topics but can just as easily facilitate the domination of the group by a small number of people who are particularly strong in voicing their views. This is clearly something of a dilemma for facilitators of such fora, since it requires them to assume a role with which they may not be comfortable and which, on the face of it, might look to be the very opposite of the sort of ethical deliberation that formed the motivation to organise such an event in the first place.

The encapsulation of what we, as researchers, learned over the course of our work in this field emerged, in the end, somewhat serendipitously. In order to bring our research trials to some sort of conclusion, we asked participants on our ethics weekend to spend some time in the remaining session discussing the strengths and weaknesses of what we were doing and how we were doing it. What followed was one of the most focused and intense sessions that we had experienced over the entire exercise. Participants appeared to become fully engaged in self-reflection and criticality and, as a result, generated a number of strong suggestions as to how things might be improved. Eventually, they decided for themselves that the final exercise they would undertake would be for one of them to retell a real ethical dilemma from their past professional life. The rest of the group then engaged in a discussion with that individual about the type of dilemma it was, the contingent circumstances, the possible alternative reactions, and so on. In a short space of time, we felt that the group had covered more ground, and delved deeper, theoretically, than in any other session that we had facilitated.

In the follow-up interviews we reminded participants about this final session and, almost unanimously, they commented how it had been the most rewarding experience of the entire exercise. One participant summed up the general feeling when they said that this dialogue about dialogue (or meta-dialogue) forced the group to contemplate what it could realistically achieve in the time remaining, and forced them to prioritise what they most wanted to discuss in that time and how they wanted to discuss it. Other participants described this experience as being quite empowering for the group, since it gave them ownership over what they were doing. Without the preceding meta-dialogue, perhaps, participants would not have engaged as much in the exercise of questioning a fellow participant about some ethical dilemma from their past. It was the meta-dialogue, it seems, that motivated the group to address the gaps and questions in their own knowledge and experience.

The facilitation of this final session, in which participants first engaged in a meta-dialogue and then engaged in a deliberation exercise, was handled in such a way as to enable the participants, rather than the facilitators, to drive the session. This was achieved by facilitators simply outlining the parameters of the meta-dialogue and then stepping back to act only as session chair (calling on participants in turn, and asking each to consider the contributions of others). The final deliberation exercise was handled in much the same way, with facilitators merely chairing the discussion and ensuring that the participant who presented their dilemma to the group had sufficient time to respond to, and reflect upon, each question and contribution from the others. The session was brought to a close by opening up the discussion for more general reflections. As reported above in the follow-up interviews, participants felt that this method of facilitation encouraged the participants to contemplate the limited time available and to consider and then prioritise what could feasibly be achieved in that time. For this reason, we believe that the relative success of this session was not a consequence of the participants having already undertaken all of the prior activities, but was rather a consequence of them each taking the 'mid-wifely' responsibility for the emerging dialectic. Because of this participant autonomy, we predict that the same success would likely have been achieved if this session had happened first, or if it was presented as a stand-alone session.

CONCLUSIONS AND RECOMMENDATIONS

That there is a demand amongst teacher educators for opportunities for ethical deliberation is quite clear from our research; but then, it perhaps comes as no surprise that the type of person who works in teacher education, more often than not, is naturally (or has become over time) inclined to critical reflection and would always welcome the opportunity and space to do more of it. So, our first conclusion and recommendation, therefore, is that there is a need and demand for ethical deliberation amongst teacher educators and we urge our readers to engage with colleagues in making the space in their busy lives to practise it. Our hope is that as a result of these efforts, more of those involved in training our future teachers feel confident enough to facilitate ethical deliberation with their students. This, in turn, might result at best in those future teachers facilitating similar opportunities for the children that they go on to teach, or at least being better equipped to navigate their way through the moral dilemmas with which they will undoubtedly be faced.

Our second conclusion from this research is that the role and type of dialectic in facilitating ethical deliberation with teacher educators, and probably with trainee teachers too, should be carefully considered. As we have discussed above, the traditional 'gadfly' dialectic, in the form of Socratic dialogue, generally takes the form of a facilitator disabusing their interlocutor (through question, answer, counter-question, and so on) of some mistakenly held belief or presumption. What this generally looks like in practice is that a Socrates-like figure comes along, playing the role of the gadfly, and stings their previously contented interlocutor into a more reflective and critical position. Instead, what we recommend here is the 'mid-wifely' form of dialectic described above by Leigh (2007). Our experience and research suggests that teacher educators are generally in no way contented or living under misapprehensions and false assumptions when it comes to morality, values and ethical dilemmas, and therefore are not in need of, nor would welcome, the 'gadfly' approach. It seems to us that almost all are only too aware of the tensions, the conflicting principles, and the dissonance between public and private morals that drag them this way and that in their professional and personal lives. Thus, our second recommendation is that the facilitator in this situation should avoid the Socrates role, and instead become a co-enquirer who is confident enough to admit that they do not know where the dialogue will lead the group and who sees their role simply as helping to draw out and unpick the processes through which their co-enquirers deliberate.

Our third conclusion from this research is that teacher educators are usually very experienced people who bring with them a veritable treasure trove of incidents, anecdotes and ethical dilemmas. Attempting to initiate role play in this scenario, in our experience, can lead to long meandering discussions that quickly shift focus and shoot off in different directions. This can be particularly difficult to handle for facilitators with groups where multiple people are attempting to contribute their own experiences to the conversation and where, by the time each has had their say, the original scenario has been lost or changed beyond all recognition. Our experience of using role play has frequently resulted in us spending more time establishing, modifying, tweaking, overhauling and revising hypothetical scenarios than we actually spend in executing the role play itself. Our recommendation when facilitating ethical deliberation with teacher educators, therefore, is that the use of role play might only be used in rare situations when the group thinks it appropriate rather than imposed by the facilitator as a conversation starter.

Our final conclusion and recommendation relates to the notion of meta-dialogue: this, we found, was the single most important thing that we discovered in our research. Knezic *et al.* describe Socratic dialogue as having three phases: 'pre-dialogue, main dialogue and post-dialogue. The latter two correspond to 'Socratic-Dialogue Proper' and 'Meta-Dialogue' respectively … The post-dialogue evaluates the proceedings and sometimes further analyses the question' (Knezic *et al.*, 2010, pp. 1105–1106). What we found is that the teacher educators with whom we worked were very strongly motivated to engage in this final post-dialogue discussion and debate about the format of our sessions and workshops and how they should best be facilitated. This motivation probably (though we have no hard evidence to support the hypothesis) stems from them being very accustomed to designing, executing, assessing and reflecting upon educational sessions and lessons.

Consequently, we found that more insightful commentary, questioning, hypothesising and critique arose in a solitary session that we devoted to this post-, or meta-, dialogue than had arisen in several sessions of traditional Socratic dialogue and ethical dilemma role play. Karen Murris identifies the strength of this form of meta-dialogue:

> Through language we address not only our manifold selves in inner dialogue (and others in outer dialogue), but in a community of philosophical enquiry we also use language to reflect on the dialogue itself at meta-dialogical level; its procedures, its values, its thinking strategies and its truth value … It is this thinking about thinking in an enquiry that is necessary for the practice to be philosophical … The role of the educator is that of a 'guide', a 'guardian' and a 'co-enquirer', who in a spirit of open ended enquiry helps to map out the territory of the dialogue, but does not manipulate or steer the course of the enquiry. (Murris, 2008, p. 670)

This meta-dialogical level, Murris argues, requires the facilitator to: 'actively [seek] opportunities to be perplexed, numbed and open to change through reflection and self-reflection. As a pedagogy that responds to the thoughts of its members, genuinely open-ended, critical and self-reflective communities of enquiry are necessary requirements for the practice to continuously renew, transform or diverge' (p. 671). Thus, our final recommendation is that the facilitator of ethical deliberation workshops or seminars (in the context of teacher education) would benefit greatly from abdicating any responsibility as teacher. Instead, we recommend that they be prepared to try (rather paradoxically) beginning with some form of post-dialogue that will harness the huge experience of teacher educators as not only ethical agents but also expert pedagogues. Teacher educators, in our experience, will seemingly quite instinctively call upon their teaching skills to reverse-engineer an ethical dilemma or principle and work out how they themselves would go about teaching a hypothetical session devoted to such a dilemma/ principle. The result, we predict, is likely to be both a much more insightful discussion as well as a much more empowering experience for the participants when they realise that they already possess most of the skills and knowledge required for ethical deliberation.

Part 3
Being a Teacher?

7
The Role of Higher Education in Teacher Education: A Reorientation Towards Ontology

DAVID ALDRIDGE

INTRODUCTION

Recent changes to policy and provision in England and Wales have brought into question the university's place as the home of teacher education (cf. SCETT, 2011; Brighouse, 2013; Kirk, 2013). Advocates of the continuing role of the university, regardless of whether they have seen the increased 'partnership' role of schools as an opportunity or a threat, have tended to speak in terms of a division of labour in which schools take responsibility for practical elements of training and the higher education institution is the site of 'theory' in teacher development. Thus the advance promotional material for the symposium at which an early draft of this chapter was offered asked, 'Does theory, and hence the university, matter in the professional development of teachers?' (reported in Orchard and Foreman Peck, 2011). Contributors to a response to the Coalition government's *White Paper for Schools* advocated 'reconstructing the importance of history and theory in educating teachers' (SCETT, 2011, p. 22); making 'an unequivocal case for educational theory as the foundational knowledge-base of the teacher' (p. 25); 'access to the educational disciplines – history, sociology and comparative studies in particular – for reflecting on the wider

Philosophical Perspectives on Teacher Education, First Edition. Edited by Ruth Heilbronn and Lorraine Foreman-Peck. © 2015 Ruth Heilbronn and Lorraine Foreman-Peck. Editorial Organisation © Philosophy of Education Society of Great Britain. Published 2015 by John Wiley & Sons, Ltd.

responsibilities of members of a profession' (p. 26); an 'intellectual education in the foundation subjects' (p. 27); and an introduction to 'the great inspirational theorists of education, writers such as Paul Hirst, Michael Oakeshott and Brian Simon' (p. 28).

Accepting this division of labour exacerbates the plight of university departments of teacher education. There can be little disagreement that a significant amount of practical experience of some sort is essential for the initial preparation of teachers; on the other hand, in the public discussion of educational policy, theory has often been subjected to a 'discourse of derision' and rejected as so much ideological cant (cf. Ball, 1990, and – for a recent example at the time of writing – Gove, 2013). The most significant attacks on educational theory have come from *within* the academy, motivated variously by more or less rigorous engagements with the 'practice turn', tribal warfare between competing disciplines, or frustration with what currently *passes* for theory in university departments (for an early example of the latter, see Wilson, 1975, and for a later, see Higgins, 2010b, p. 470). Theory has also, from the outset, been commonly rejected as 'irrelevant' by beginner teachers themselves (Stones, 1983; Hogan, 1988). It is hardly surprising, in the face of this, that mounting a rearguard action in defence of theory resonates in some quarters as inauthentic.

I do not intend in this chapter to offer a sustained contribution to the theory/practice dichotomy in education, which has been alternately reconciled, rejected or subverted by a succession of venerable thinkers (for a more or less arbitrary selection, see Hirst, 1983; Pring, 2000; W. Carr, 2006). Neither will I present a critical account of the various different conceptions and interpretations of the term 'theory'. Rather, I intend to present a positive case for a way of conceiving of the 'higher education' of teachers that does not accept this division of labour and that draws on resources that already have a foothold in a broader debate around the nature of higher education and the disputed identity of the university. In the first section, therefore, I present the 'ontological turn' in higher education that has been developed in the work of Ron Barnett and others (Barnett, 2004, 2005; Dall'Alba and Barnacle, 2007; Nixon, 2012). I will argue – following Barnett – for thinking about the university not *epistemologically*, as the site of the delivery of knowledge or skills, but *ontologically*, in terms of what happens to us (both teachers and students) when we learn; in learning, *being* is transformed. I will ultimately argue that what a higher education offers is space for such transformation. This requires, in curriculum terms, a decluttering of programmes of study in favour of a clearing in which dialogue can occur.

I must clarify that arguing for an ontological understanding of education rather than a narrower epistemological conception is not the same as advocating practice over theory. Both practice and theory can be conceived either in terms of an ontological event or as the epistemological achievements of relatively unchanging subjects. Thus Gadamer, to whom the ontological development of this chapter owes a considerable debt, is able to write his *Praise of Theory* (Gadamer, 1998). Gadamer does not assume a standpoint outside of practice, but emphasises that '*theoria* in its original Greek sense of *contemplatio* was conducted in a broader context of life and thus was also a way of comporting oneself' (van Manen, 2007, p. 14). Rather than contemplative detachment, theory can indicate a state when 'the person is not only present but completely present' (Gadamer, 1998, p. 31). Gadamer acknowledges that it is thus hard to differentiate his praise of theory from a praise of practice. Where theory does appear to get short shrift in what follows, it will be when it carries connotations of a neutral standpoint outside of practice, a disciplinary 'method', or a body of skills and competences that can be used or taken into the learner but leave her otherwise more or less unchanged. I introduce the term 'competences' here to indicate that this is also not a matter of distinguishing between *knowing* and *doing*. Doing can also be understood in a restricted epistemological sense. When I do inevitably return to the language of particular pedagogical situations – reading texts, dialogue, and so on – I hope to have shown that their significance is not to be appreciated in terms of individual acts of knowing, or doing (or even *willing*) but in their fullest ontological sense, as transformational events occurring in tradition.

This should also forestall any objections that I might be offering an anti-intellectual approach to teacher education, or aligning myself with the advocates of an 'apprenticeship' model (although I will have some favourable things to say about 'craft'). In the second section of the chapter I will expand on Barnett's work and offer an account of the ontology of teacher education as a complex dialogic event. 'Tradition' has an integral part to play here, and 'classic' educational texts will form essential objects around which dialogue will revolve, but no attempt will be made to incorporate a theoretical canon that might be furnished by the foundational disciplines. In the final section I will consider some implications for teacher educators. I will not ultimately provide a defence of the role of higher education in teacher education. Rather, I will demonstrate that interpreting teacher education in light of the ontological turn poses a significant challenge to university providers, since it entails a transformation of the curriculum or programme of study for teacher education, of notions of students' success and failure on such programmes, and of the educator's identity as an expert.

THE ONTOLOGICAL TURN IN HIGHER EDUCATION

Arguably, the ontological turn does not identify a new development. Much of Barnett's writing resonates with Heidegger's ontological project for a universal higher education (Thomson, 2005). However, Barnett presents the 'turn' as addressing a particular contemporary situation or set of challenges in higher education: he identifies coping with an unknown future as 'a new pedagogical challenge' for the contemporary age (Barnett, 2004, p. 247); furthermore, the changes in this 'new kind of world order' are 'characteristically internal. They are primarily to do with how individuals understand themselves, with their sense of identity (or lack of it)' (p. 248). In addition to change, Barnett introduces the notion of supercomplexity (Barnett, 2000), which consists of challenges that 'could never be resolved' or 'dissolved' because they 'yield a multiplication of answers and further questions' (p. 249). Barnett develops the example of the question 'What is a teacher?', which can be answered from a range of different ideologies and value positions. 'To see universities and teachers as consumers of resources, or even as producers of resources on the one hand, and to see universities as sites of open, critical and even transformatory engagement are, in the end, incompatible positions, no matter what compromises and negotiations are sought' (p. 249).

Change and supercomplexity give rise to a situation of uncertainty. This is not (or not solely) the epistemological condition of asking questions to which the answers are not clear; it is an ontological condition – the condition of *being in question*. Correspondingly, 'the *educational task is, in principle, not an epistemological task*' (Barnett, 2000, p. 252). An education that responds to such uncertainty, or aims to equip students themselves to cope with change, would be concerned with students' '*being* in the world', with their 'ontological dispositions' (p. 248). A 'pedagogy for human being' would need to 'invite the student to take up his or her own stances, and help form the courage to do so' (p. 257). Barnett attests to a growing recognition among colleagues in higher education that what they do cannot be sufficiently understood in terms of knowledge and skills, even 'generic' skills, so that the 'turn' constitutes both a call for new thinking and a recognition of a transformation of higher education already occurring on the ground (2004, pp. 253–254).

The increasing instrumentalisation, marketisation and technologisation of university programmes gives rise to a situation where 'knowledge and skills are seen as attributes that can be decontextualized from the practices to which they relate' (Dall'Alba and Barnacle, 2007, p. 680). In response to this, we are reminded of Heidegger's insight that 'we do not primarily access things conceptually or intellectually, but, instead, through being constantly immersed in activities, projects and practices with things and others' (p. 681). Our previous commitments and projects 'always already' predispose us to experience the world in particular ways. Advocates of a 'practice turn' have stressed that the significance of this insight is as a reversal of the view 'that our fundamental way of engaging with the world is to have a theory' (Donnelly, 1999, p. 936). The term 'practice' perhaps does not adequately capture the unthematised totality of understanding that is implied in the Heideggerian ideas of 'comportment' (Heidegger, 1962, pp. 95–107; Dreyfus, 1991) or 'having-to-do with the world concernfully' (Heidegger, 1962, p. 88). However, Heidegger argues that the activity of 'theorising' is founded on or derived from this originary mode of understanding. The 'theoretical attitude' thus arises from a situation of breakdown or frustration. Absorbed in the activity of making, I reach for the hammer and find it out of its proper place. What previously was not separated from the whole movement of my being directed towards some purposeful end now 'shows up' for me as a problem to be overcome. It is in attempting to solve such problems that we begin to thematise objects as 'occurrent' or 'present' and articulate their specific properties.

Dall'Alba and Barnacle urge that 'being and knowing are inextricable' (Dall'Alba and Barnacle, 2007, p. 682). The world is already 'known' by us, and in this lies the possibility of any new understanding, or any kind of learning. But this knowing is not to be understood as a kind of theory that has not yet been made explicit. Our understanding is rather an orientation of our being (our 'Being-there'), an ontological condition of our openness to the world (Heidegger, 1962, p. 182; Gadamer, 1977, p. 9). To understand the world differently is to be transformed. Learning, then, can be seen as a process of becoming, a reorientation of our being towards new forms of disclosure; the implication is that 'the question for students would be not only what they know, but also who they are becoming' (Dall'Alba and Barnacle 2007, p. 683) and 'what it means to be(come) a teacher, artist, physicist, historian, engineer, architect, and so on, must be a central and ongoing question that continues to be addressed explicitly throughout (and beyond) higher education programmes' (p. 687).

One might imagine that teacher education, dealing as it does with the formation of professional identity rather than simply imparting academic credentials, is well placed to lead the way in an ontological turn. Yet Dall'Alba argues that this is not the case, pointing out that professional programmes 'typically focus on developing specific knowledge and skills to be applied in practice contexts within and beyond the educational program' which are 'insufficient for skilful practice and for transformation of the self that is integral to achieving such practice … A focus on epistemology occurs at the expense of ontological considerations relating to who students are becoming' (Dall'Alba, 2009, p. 41). The competence-based assessment of teacher education in England and Wales has been linked to a climate of performativity (Burnard and White, 2008), and the calls for theory cited earlier are responses to a perceived instrumentalisation of teacher education and a rejection of the claim that all teachers need is the tools to get the job done (SCETT, 2011). But theory – conceived epistemologically – is no less a 'tool', to be applied to the task at hand from a position of detached reflection (W. Carr, 2006).

Student teachers can become sceptical about the claimed benefits of theory for their practice. Pádraig Hogan elaborates that university-based theoretical areas of a course cannot only seem 'remote from one's classroom concerns' but also constitute a set of additional tasks and looming deadlines that detract from many students' more pressing concerns not to make a mess of things in the classroom, or to 'perform' against the teaching standards (Hogan, 1988, p. 191). He writes, concerning the 'bilocation' of students in both schools and universities, that 'the "theory/practice" rift in the experienced world of the student teacher is very often the natural outcome of a conflict of worldviews – particularly institutionalised worldviews – concerning the nature of the educational enterprise itself' and that students can become 'torn apart' by such conflicting priorities (p. 191). This is not to say that existential anxiety is to be avoided in teacher education: students who recognise the moral complexity of educational institutions will rightly be troubled by the lack of easy answers available. Yet rather than embracing theory even as a tool that might be brought to bear on morally ambiguous situations, Hogan notes that students can resort to cynical dismissal and 'an acquiescent, instrumental attitude towards examinations in general, or a severely pragmatic approach to teaching and learning, or a reluctance to handle weaker pupils, or a view of education and schooling coloured mainly by considerations of surviving or beating the system' (p. 191). Theory, when presented as a tool, can be rejected in favour of other tools that get the job done differently.

It would be unfair to claim that this cynicism is the norm, or that students do not for the most part appreciate that their being is in question; many of them experience their initial preparation as a time of acute transformational challenge. But they do not necessarily find in the 'theoretical' content of a programme of study the resources to meet these challenges. Dall'Alba argues that where professional preparation is not viewed from the perspective of ontology, 'the most challenging task of learning professional ways of being ... is left to the students themselves' (Dall'Alba, 2009, p. 50); that is to say, where uncertainty is not endured as a lonely struggle, dialogue concerning ethical ways of being can be pushed out to the refectory in the lunch break, or the student union bar after lectures, or those other spaces on the margins of the higher education experience. The ontological turn does not call for more explicit theorising on educational programmes (even theorising *about* ontology), but a turning of the attention of educators towards how students are transformed in the educational event. To consider how teacher educators' concerns can be brought into the same educational space as the perspectives of their students requires that we expand our ontological overview into the dialogical elements of the event of teacher education.

THE DIALOGIC EVENT OF TEACHER EDUCATION

Hans-Georg Gadamer, who developed the dialogic implications of Heidegger's ontology of understanding, has inspired hermeneutic accounts of teacher education (Hogan, 1982, 1983, 1988; Higgins, 2010b; Nicholson, 2011). It almost goes without saying that most of what teacher educators in higher education do with their students involves dialogue: to recognise dialogue as an *ontological* feature of (all) teacher education is to say something more than this. We should first of all acknowledge that the situation designated by 'dialogue' extends beyond the spoken context: Gadamer claims that in understanding a text, we make it speak, and student teachers will have ways of making their university tutors – and the content of their courses – 'speak' that extend beyond literal face-to-face interactions (cf. Gadamer, 2004, p. 370). Nevertheless, for Gadamer the 'I–Thou' remains paradigmatic in all events of understanding: we do not treat our interlocutor as an object that is to be known about, but as a 'Thou' who can put questions to us, and therefore put us into question.

Additionally, let us recall the claim that we 'always already' understand: coming into dialogue presupposes a shared interest or concern. Putting this another way, it is our *prejudices* that bring us into dialogue. Prejudices have been understood perjoratively and epistemologically, since the Enlightenment, as biases in judgement. Gadamer argues that they are to be understood ontologically as the 'biases of our openness to the world' (Gadamer, 1977, p. 9). As such, they are the inevitable preconditions of any event of understanding. Our prejudices can also be transformed in dialogue, and thus are *we* transformed, since 'It is not so much our judgements as it is our prejudices that constitute our being' (p. 9). Prejudices also determine the questions that we bring with us to the dialogue. Gadamer observes that 'we say that a question too "occurs" to us, that it "arises" or "presents itself" more than we raise it or present it' (Gadamer, 2004, p. 360). Again, note the ontological significance of a question as something that befalls us, if you like, 'over and above our wanting and doing' (p. xxvi). The question is not chosen or applied as a tool to aid the event of understanding, but is constitutive of it. Rather than seeing understanding epistemologically, as something that one or other participant might achieve through dialogue, Gadamer would have us see it as an event in which a shared question emerges. It is this question that captures what Gadamer intends in his much misunderstood claim that understanding entails 'agreement concerning the subject matter' (p. 292). Agreement is both presupposed and provisional in any event of understanding: we come into dialogue because we already agree, yet the dialogue continues because we do not yet agree. Agreement, then, does not require an epistemological act of assent to the other's point of view, but a standing in a related way or orientation towards the subject matter. To understand is to agree over what is at stake, or to 'arrive' at a shared question (which point of arrival will, in that it constitutes a question, be a point of departure). The 'fusion of horizons' thus is a happening that transcends the achievements of individual participants in dialogue and in which their being, their relation to each other and their shared orientation towards the world, is transformed.

Gadamer's dialogic ontology encompasses all events of understanding, including textual interpretation and even our ongoing interpretation of our everyday experiences; note then that teacher education consists of not one dialogue but many, a constellation of overlapping hermeneutic situations in which numerous 'Thous' stand in relation to the student 'I' (Higgins, 2010b; Aldridge, 2013). Nevertheless, some of the wider reaching implications of Gadamer's thought might best be explored in relation to a more literal dialogic context well known to the teacher educator, the 'lesson debrief'. Let us firstly acknowledge that this is a dialogue that gets off the ground because there is sufficient shared concern between the participants. Both student teacher and teacher educator are concerned that the pupils should come to learn something, one would imagine, as well as that the student teacher should eventually make a success of the course. But note also that the 'prejudices' of student and teacher educator will differ significantly. The teacher educator's experience in the classroom may attune her to notice events that the student has missed, or attach a different significance to them. The teacher educator's familiarity with a canon of educational thought may lead her to ask different questions of the student's practice than he does. The student's prior understanding, on the other hand, might be shaped by exposure to a particular model of teaching he has observed in school and is attempting to emulate. Perhaps, on the other hand, he is preoccupied with performative considerations of meeting certain teacher standards and will be inclined therefore to focus on elements of his own practice, rather than the responses of students. But this is to put it crudely. In reality, a complex background of such orientations and implicit questions will be at play, much of which cannot be brought to explicit awareness in any given moment. As Merleau-Ponty elaborates, each participant in this dialogue is 'perched on a pyramid of past life' (Merleau-Ponty, 2002, p. 457): the sum total of each participant's relevant understandings constitutes *what they are* at a particular time, and determines the interpretive possibilities that each will project on to the new situation.

In light of this, we see that the subject matter of the lesson debrief is given in advance in different ways to each participant in the dialogue. Thinking of the issue under discussion as the 'lesson' does not give us very much in common, although we need to start somewhere. We are sometimes encouraged to think of lessons as distinct entities with beginnings, middles and ends, but we do not need to be particularly hermeneutically or educationally sensitive to recognise that the pupils' learning is always already underway, such that whatever is at stake for us in the context of a lesson debrief exceeds the contingent temporal and spatial unities within which we have contrived to do our bit of observing. Shifting fashionable considerations of whether our attention should be focused on 'a lesson', or the 'teaching', or 'learning', or the activities of students themselves, does not do justice to the indeterminacy of the situation (cf. Bennett, 2013). It is better to say that the subject matter of the lesson debrief emerges in dialogue and that participants in the dialogue understand each other to the extent that there is a convergence in the question each participant pursues.

It is in this fusion of horizons that the truth of what each has just observed can be disclosed and an educational experience can occur.

There is always the possibility of misunderstanding. Our prejudices, while enabling understanding, can constrain us. I recall my frustration at students who would repeatedly begin lesson debriefs with the recognition that 'my timings were off' or 'I didn't get as far as I planned'. Thinking further back, I also recall my frustration as a student teacher with a tutor of mine who would repeat the same refrain in lesson debriefs from one school visit to the next. Undoubtedly, there are some remarks about a student's practice that are of such essential significance that they bear constant repetition, but more often in such situations a repeated insight loses its power to show up as an insight at all: what is being revealed here is more like a joke that has got old, or a kind of talking at cross-purposes; a failure of both parties to reach a shared understanding.

Let us now consider those moments of animation, when both observers or participants in the debrief become absorbed in unfolding the mystery of *what went on*. Such moments have the character of a discovery or a disclosure. They are unpredictable and un-formulaic and exceed or transgress any pre-prepared set of criteria (what Gadamer might call a 'method') we might bring for determining the 'success' or 'failure' of the event we have just observed. In these moments (often so difficult to recall or 'write up' after the debrief) we have a sense of having attended together to something that moved, or was 'at work', in the lesson we each experienced. This sense of attending to the movement of the lesson, and the accompanying animation of the dialogue, is equally present in those times when each participant becomes convinced that the other observer has 'got it wrong'. Far from talking at cross-purposes, an exchange like this lays bare something of importance that is at stake between the interlocutors.

The singularity of these events, and the necessity of their breaking through or out of a particular methodological interpretive framework, reminds us that 'a good deal of our theorizing has a narrowing effect on how we think about education' (Fairfield, 2011, p. 2). While for Gadamer a 'method' of some sort is an inevitable starting point, an enabling 'prejudice', no method can exhaust truth. For Heidegger, any event of disclosure is simultaneously a moment of concealment.

As Barnett observes, 'we can never, as it were, freeze-frame the world. Its character must always elude our attempts to understand it; our knowledge of it, no matter how creative, how particular and how imaginative, must always fall short of it' (Barnett, 2004, p. 251). The indeterminacy of the dialogue explored above in the context of teacher education holds equally in the school context. The classroom too is a complex of I–Thou relations (Aldridge, 2013) where learning in any given case will involve a 'fusion of horizons' in a dialogic situation; each child, therefore, inasmuch as they understand something, will understand *differently*. It is not clear, then, that any sort of 'expertise' will be up to the task of interpreting the event denoted by the term 'lesson', at least not where expertise is conceived as having in advance some explicit interpretive framework or method. The analogy that Gadamer employs to convey the to-and-fro motion of the event of understanding is 'play', which suggests that learning will not easily be comprehended through such *repeatable* technical concepts as timing and plans. Both student teacher and their more experienced observer rather stand a chance of understanding the lesson (and each other) to the extent that they are willing or open to be guided by the unfolding of the subject matter that is before them; either stands to be transformed by the disclosure that takes place.

The emergent character of the subject matter is as much the case for the teacher education programme *writ large* as it is for any specific instance of dialogue. There has been any amount of debate over the *subject matter* of the study of education, and whether education constitutes a practice sui generis or a field of endeavour that draws on a range of disciplines – indeed whether it has a subject matter at all (cf. Wilson, 1975; Hogan, 2006). For Gadamer, this is not a problem that must be resolved in advance of the educational situation, but is one that we are always already in the middle of. Different participants bring into dialogue (it might be better to say 'are brought into dialogue by') different prejudices and methods that serve to constitute the subject matter in advance and to shape their contribution to the dialogue and their understanding of the directions it might take. This is as true of the dialogue that is teacher education, with the exception that teacher educators of course 'select' those with whom they will enter into dialogue. They are thus able to exclude from the educational context those whose initial conceptions (at least) of the needs of students, of practices of teaching and learning, and of the professional existence of the teacher, seem simply too distant from their own to reach any fruitful point of convergence. Nevertheless, the possibility of learning something (or for that matter teaching it) requires an openness to the discovery of a deficiency in one's prior conception (including the teacher educator's) and a transformation of what is at stake in the dialogue.

Whatever the difference in presuppositions and background, in dialogue there is always the possibility of mutual understanding, even if this will require some work; Gadamer does not subscribe to the thesis that some horizons are simply incommensurable with others. He refers to the shared language that operates behind the backs of any two participants as the 'tradition', and this can be understood both on a small scale (as the tradition, say, of a particular discipline or local history) or at the broadest level as the shared humanity or linguisticality of the participants. The work of understanding requires finding this common ground or recovering what is shared. Gadamer describes fusions of horizons as 'linguistic circles merging more and more', which suggests individual raindrops coalescing on a windowpane and progressing ever further towards greater convergence (Gadamer, 1977, p. 17). Agreement is thus an event that occurs in the history of a tradition. Participants in dialogue are transformed in their relation to the subject matter before them, but also reflexively in relation to the tradition behind them (Gallagher, 1992, pp. 105–107). In their retrieval of the tradition, new ways of being that were preserved as possibilities in the tradition are disclosed for them. Thus dialogue is educationally transformative for the participants, but the tradition itself is also transformed. It is misleading to think of understanding as the achievement of detached subjects who can be separated from their participation in the tradition that makes understanding possible; ontologically, it is better to speak of the 'conversation that we ourselves are' (Gadamer, 2004, p. 370).

This emphasis on the role of the tradition in understanding mitigates any objection that an ontological approach to teacher education could be construed as dismissive of the disciplines and their distinctive methodologies. The work of understanding requires a retrieval of the resources of tradition, not as a body of knowledge we can draw on, but as an 'effective history' that has made us what we are. Higgins, following Oakeshott, has drawn attention to the rich conversations that have served to constitute the Western educational milieu – including 'figures such as Socrates, Augustine, Vico and Addams' (Higgins, 2010b, p. 442). In working to understand education or to be understood, student teachers will need to have recourse to the tradition that has shaped the perspective that they currently hold, and thus better understand themselves. Teacher educators, in seeking to evoke or entice student teachers into new understandings of education, will need to find the resources that speak to the shared concerns that emerge in the educational event, which may require in some cases an expansion of their own conception of what constitutes the tradition. The ontological relevance of the 'classic works' or 'defining texts' of education thus emerges: they become the objects around which the dialogue of education and the exploration of tradition can circulate (and enable us to see this dialogue as something we are more likely to recognise as an *educational* activity comprising teacher, student and an object of study). Note that this does not entail a conservative approach to these texts: a work becomes a classic because it preserves a question that has the power to disturb us; it preserves the difficulties or tensions within the tradition. The 'disciplines' have relevance here, then, not as particular traditions into which we must be inducted, but as voices within the broader tradition that can come into tension and whose limitations are revealed in dialogue.

The teacher educator might be encouraged at this point to draw up a list of classic works, texts and achievements around which the dialogue of teacher education could be conducted. To do so would be to confuse a 'classic' with a 'canon', and to risk a conservative approach to the work of teacher education (see How, 2011). The canon, by definition, is prescribed; it is given in advance and serves to constrain the possibilities for dialogue. It is through the consolidation of canons that 'disciplines' are able to accumulate around a relatively stable set of questions or core concerns. The 'classic', on the other hand, has an indeterminate or contingent status. A classic might speak to a particular dialogic context, but this is a power that can be gained or lost through the transformation of the participants in dialogue and that is not necessarily transferable across contexts. The classics to which the participants in any educational dialogue will find themselves 'belonging' cannot be given in advance or set in stone. The challenge for the teacher educator, then, is that the 'programme of study' for teacher education, if it is to be ontologically transformative, *resists* design. Granted that we must start somewhere, we can think of the 'content' of any teacher education programme only as a *point of departure* for dialogue. Students' own experiences and influences, on teaching practice and in their prior engagements with young people, will constitute another.

If we have found ourselves reinstating anything like the great theoretical works or the disciplines at this point into our ontological account, it is as participants in a transformative dialogue rather than in the sense of objects that might be claimed in any sort of *knowing*; and it is without the security of being able to know in advance *which* components are likely to serve the development of any particular teacher or group of teachers at any particular time. The selection of texts would not, I would urge, be governed by any a priori distinctions in terms of importance between works of subject pedagogy (or even subject knowledge), the reports of major empirical studies, or more general works of educational philosophy, but would be guided by the demands of the emerging situation and the composition of the group of student teachers. Neither could any assumptions be made about cultural literacy. Either Rousseau or E.D. Hirsch, for example, might often prove valuable, but neither could be considered essential, and it is quite possible that the situation might call, rather, for an engagement with cinematic or literary depictions of the inspirational, exemplary or problematic teacher.

IMPLICATIONS FOR THE BEING OF STUDENTS AND TEACHER EDUCATORS IN HIGHER EDUCATION

It might be objected that this overtly humanistic account of teacher education downplays certain essential technical elements; this is recognised and – to an extent – intended. Recall firstly the chapter's stated aim of exploring the distinctive contribution of 'higher education' to teacher formation. It could hardly be argued that the technical elements of teaching – being able to use appropriate learning technologies (including writing on whiteboards), being able to project's one's voice across the learning space, managing a mark book or spreadsheet effectively – can be addressed as well if not better by observing experts in schools. While I wish in no way to denigrate the importance of clusters of such competences, I want to highlight that no single technical skill or capacity can be demonstrated to be essential to good teaching practice. Among students who complete Post-Graduate Certificate in Education (PGCE) courses, I hazard that there are those who struggle to be audible, whose whiteboard handwriting is all but illegible, or whose natural inclination is to gather together their records of students' achievement on the back of an envelope. That such students do complete PGCE courses can be attributed to the realisation (of student teachers and teacher educators alike) that they can draw on other resources to compensate for these apparent deficiencies. Many of us remember from our own schooldays an eccentric teacher who managed to inspire us more than others when, on paper, almost everything seemed to be against them.

Regarding those students who do not complete the course (teacher educators tend to refer to them being *counselled out* rather than *failing*), perhaps we might attribute this to a cumulative technical deficit, where they are failing to master whole suites of competences rather than particular skills. An example might be 'behaviour management'. A student who does not make progress in mastery of the classroom climate is not likely to last the course. This is not to say that successful student teachers' classes will all run smoothly, of course, but that a teacher will find it hard to compensate in other ways for not developing some combination of tone, demeanour, facial expression, manner of speech and a way of relating to young people that enables her pupils to be comfortable in her presence, discourages them from making continual challenges to her authority, or otherwise motivates them to get on with the task at hand in relative calm. But teacher educators have, of course, observed nearly as many ways of achieving this as there are student teachers. Not succeeding here is not a simple matter of failing to master a suite of skills or competences: the student who is committed to mastery will persevere, experiment with other approaches, and find new ways of relating to her pupil charges.

This brings us to the first significant contribution that the ontological turn can make to our conceptualisation of the education of teachers: the recognition that *lasting the course is not primarily or even signifi-cantly a matter of competence.* Recognition of the dialogic ontology of teacher education undermines a distinction between the 'technical' and the 'theoretical' elements of the experience: what seems to be operative in whether a student 'makes the distance' is better thought of not epistemologically but in ontological terms as a disposition towards the task at hand, what Barnett, following Nietzsche, calls 'the will to go on' (2004, p. 254). Hugh Sockett has identified that 'Counselling out is not then a process of weeding out undesirables but helping those individuals come to realize they have misjudged their attachment to the profession, their temperament, or their sense of themselves, and their need to seek other environments in which they can construct meaningful work and meaningful living' (Sockett, 2012, p. 211). A student without the will to go on is not necessarily deficient in virtue or constancy; recall the close ontological connection between 'coming to understand' and 'taking a stand' in relation to the subject matter. A student's understanding of the endeavour of education is enabled against a background of commitments and stances that are projected as possibilities for future being. Understanding is transfor-mational in that it involves both the discovery and the affirmation of such possibilities: it is an event of self-disclosure. With this in mind, a student's discovery that they 'do not have it in them' to embrace the requirements of a particular vocation can be seen as a potentially pro-found event of authentic becoming rather than a shortcoming or fail-ure. It is a will to go on *elsewhere.*

This is better realised when we acknowledge the context of ethical supercomplexity discussed above (Barnett, 2000, 2004). A career in education, or at least more specifically the situation of *schooling* for which teachers are being prepared, implicates us in an environment of moral complexity that cannot without some fraud on the part of teacher educators be portrayed as an unambiguous 'good'. Many of the arrangements and techniques sanctioned or prescribed by institutions or adopted by experienced teachers in their attempts to make a success of classroom management, for example – whatever the term 'management' might mean in relation to children – could be perceived as corrupting, repressive, and distorting of moral purpose, and it is an 'open' question as to whether the endeavour of schooling might be enacted free of any such effects. I cannot rehearse all of the literature here, but that there is such a wealth of relevant literature attests to the openness of the question, which is all that is significant for my argument (see, however, Moore and Atkinson, 1998, for an exceptional discussion). In this situation of supercomplexity, it is entirely possible that the educated teacher might turn *away* from schooling as well as *towards* it. Some sorts of selection processes might help teacher educators to populate their courses with students who begin the course with a certain kind of orientation towards the task of schooling (and note that this is a very different process from attempting to ascertain whether they have a certain 'skill set'), but the indeterminate nature of the dialogue that is teacher education means that no such process could anticipate the educational transformations that will occur along the way.

This is not to say that the majority of trainees will not be able to find the sort of moral purpose that is essential to sustaining the 'will to go on' in such an environment. But it does draw attention to what might be a specifically 'educational' (particularly in the sense of a higher education) element of teacher development. The desire (on the part of both educators and beginner teachers) for a student to make a 'success' of a professional training course could operate in tension with the kind of transformations outlined above. Within a school context, it is hard to see how students experiencing the kind of existential anxiety implied by discovering a 'turning away' from the task at hand will resist adopting the sort of cynical stance identified by Hogan (1988), or emulating the coping mechanisms that seem to work for colleagues around them. The only alternative would appear to be dropping out – and thus 'failing' where those around them have appeared to 'succeed'. An institution of higher education, on the other hand, ought to be well placed to affirm the kind of self-disclosure implied in such a moment of anxiety. It might also afford the context where teachers at any point their career might find the support and the resources to uncover new possibilities for 'a life to which one can say "yes"' (Gadamer, 1998, p. 31), and the will to risk these possibilities, even where such paths might constitute an ethical challenge to the institution or system in which they are placed.

This hardly means that teacher educators should either celebrate failure or make a mockery of their own selection processes (what *enemies of promise* we would be!), but it might encourage us to call into question what is implied in the idea of the 'successful completion' of a programme of teacher education. It would certainly encourage us to see not only beginning teachers as potential student teachers, since maintaining the will to go on remains a challenge throughout a teacher's career. It might also point to a further conception of the role of the teacher educator in higher education, which could be thought of in terms of the evocation (in the sense of 'calling forth') of possibilities for the teacher. Both Pádraig Hogan (2005) and Paul Smeyers (2002) have pointed to the capacity of the educational event to 'open up worlds' for the learner. This is not a predictable or methodical process; different material excites or interests different students at different times and the opening of a world is not an outcome that could be intended or designed in any particular occasion or moment. The will to go on with teaching is not something that can be furnished, and this is not best understood in terms of the delivery of a certain set of skills but as a poetic process, or something more akin to a courtship (Hogan, 1995, 2010). The range of resources and materials that might serve as the focal point for this evocative dialogue includes, of course, the 'classics' of the educational disciplines, but can also be widened in scope so that we might find ourselves agreeing with David Carr when he writes – as a 'flat-earther', against the grain – that 'students may stand to gain far more from a sympathetic reading of Dickens, Orwell and Lawrence in relation to their understanding of education than they are likely to get from studying Skinner, Bruner or Bloom's taxonomy' (Carr, 1995, p. 329).

The ontological language employed thus far has been shot through with *topological* metaphor – understanding has been conceived as a matter of orientation and relation, of horizons and backgrounds. The primary metaphor operative in Barnett's advocacy of an ontological higher education is 'space' (Barnett, 2004, 2005). Students and teacher educators often recognise that the university offers 'space for reflection' in terms of affording time (to think), or displacement (the university is a certain 'distance' from the school), but there is a further ontological possibility that is potentially far more destabilising for current practice – the *emptiness* of space. The higher education context offers a freedom from curriculum that serves to open up dialogic possibilities. The indeterminacy implied in a dialogic ontology of understanding is in tension with the prescription of programme content (Aldridge, 2013): dialogue continues to the extent that participants allow themselves to be conducted by the subject matter as it emerges, rather than following a predetermined path or script. Higher education might then be valued precisely as a space that is unconstrained and flexible, rather than as a site in which theory or knowledge are delivered. The challenge for educators in such a context is to attend to a student's emerging understanding of the task of teaching and to respond individually and appropriately. They must develop an ear for the varied and changing standpoints and situations from which students interpret educational texts, and draw on resources that can encourage, inspire or disturb students in different situations, all the while remaining open to the possibility of being surprised by the way in which the subject matter is disclosed in the event.

It isn't hard to see how the opening up of such a space could unsettle the teacher educator – it is a space in which anything that might be called 'teaching expertise' counts for little. Rather, the educator becomes the learner: he needs not, as Heidegger advises us, to have 'a larger store of information' than his students, but 'to learn to let them learn'. The strength of the teacher is to be 'more teachable than his apprentices' and to be 'less sure of his material than those who learn are of theirs' (Heidegger, 2011, p. 269). In the same essay, Heidegger calls attention to the 'craft of thinking', which encourages us to attempt a rehabilitation of a metaphor that has become unpopular in university departments that educate teachers. The cabinetmaker 'makes himself answer and respond above all to the different kinds of wood and to the shapes slumbering within wood' (p. 268); the educator's craft is characterised by an orientation of receptivity and openness rather than authority, so that he 'often produces the impression that we really learn nothing from him' (p. 269).

Barnett also draws attention to the *awkwardness* and *strangeness* of the dialogic space of higher education (Barnett, 2004, p. 257; 2005, p. 795); the contribution of this chapter is to argue that this awkwardness applies as much to teacher educators as to student teachers.

Teacher educators must give up the security that comes with holding the keys to a useful theory or set of theories that could bring about certain desired outcomes more efficiently or provide the solutions to some commonly encountered problems. Students are right to be sceptical of any claims made by those who have moved away from the 'chalk face' for privileged access to such goods – certainly when other experienced teachers remain engaged in the task at hand. The power of the dialogue described above is rather that it has the potential to call into question the value of those desired outcomes or challenge the common understanding of the kinds of 'problems' that arise within a particular institution or system. This means that teacher educators can no less than their students avoid orienting themselves ethically in this complex situation; they too are 'in question'. Rather than affirming a particular mode of being into which teachers, institutions and possibly the whole system of schooling has become confidently (or perhaps despairingly) entrenched, the dialogue that is higher education might have the power to disturb, confront and disclose new possibilities. This requires teacher educators to possess resources of creative poetic thought, an attunement to educational and wider conversational traditions and the diversity within them, and above all a willingness to be challenged by and learn from student teachers and developing professionals.

8
Cultivating Human Capabilities in Venturesome Learning Environments

PÁDRAIG HOGAN

INTRODUCTION

I would like to begin by exploring a pedagogical variant of the notion of capabilities, as articulated by Amartya Sen and Martha Nussbaum (1993), and by distinguishing it clearly from that of competencies. The familiar notion of competencies directs attention to the mastery of measurable skills and performances. That of capabilities, especially as developed by Nussbaum, directs attention to the progressive cultivation of human capacities to think critically, to attend with discernment, to anticipate with circumspection, to act with moral insight and energy, and so on. Nussbaum has identified a list of ten key capabilities, ranging from that of being able to live a life of normal length at the basic end, to that of being able to participate in an effective way in the choices that govern one's life at the more developed end (Nussbaum, 2000, pp. 77 ff.). Sen is hesitant about identifying a specific list of capabilities. He stresses instead – as a pioneering kind of economist – the departure of a capabilities approach to human welfare from more traditional utilitarian approaches (e.g. Benthamite) or resource-based approaches (e.g. GDP per head). The more general nature of Sen's stance is reaffirmed in one of his most recent works: 'In contrast with the utility-based or resource-based lines of thinking, individual advantage

Philosophical Perspectives on Teacher Education, First Edition. Edited by Ruth Heilbronn and
Lorraine Foreman-Peck. © 2015 Ruth Heilbronn and Lorraine Foreman-Peck. Editorial Organisation
© Philosophy of Education Society of Great Britain. Published 2015 by John Wiley & Sons, Ltd.

is judged in the capability approach by a person's capability to do the things he or she has reason to value' (Sen, 2009, p. 231). But Sen also credits different developments of the capabilities approach, and specifically Nussbaum's:

> The capability approach is a general approach, focusing on information on individual advantages, judged in terms of opportunity rather than a specific 'design' for how a society should be organized. A number of very distinguished contributions have been made by Martha Nussbaum and others in recent years on matters of social assessment and policy through powerful use of the capability approach. (p. 232)

Sen's endorsement in this passage of investigations by others into the promise of a capabilities approach in different fields of research and human endeavour expands and refines the possibilities for enquiry. In the philosophy of education such investigations have been carried on by Geoffrey Hinchliffe, Lorella Terzi and others (Hinchliffe and Terzi, 2009). Mindful of these developments, I see a particular merit in exploring the potential of a capabilities approach to release educational thought and action from the constricting legacy of a generation or more of preoccupation with competencies. In an educational sense, capabilities can be understood as those human accomplishments, promoted by deliberate learning, that enable informed choices to be made and judicious action to be taken, particularly in unfamiliar or challenging circumstances.

I'm keen to illustrate that pedagogy, in an age of increasing plurality and uncertainty, needs to stress capabilities more so than competencies, and that educational policy needs to support this strongly. In making this case I'll be elucidating the idea of venturesome environments of learning. I'll be challenging the kinds of pedagogical attitudes, practices and professional cultures that an attachment to a competencies policy has promoted in schools internationally in recent decades. I will also be stressing the necessity to take a step beyond critique, however, because education is first and foremost a constructive practice – as distinct from a phenomenon available for critical scrutiny and analysis.

VENTURESOME LEARNING ENVIRONMENTS
AND THEIR DOMAINS OF RELATIONS

The phrase 'venturesome learning environment' refers to something that lies at the heart of education, when viewed as a distinct practice in its own right. First, the phrase refers to a learning environment where it is *safe* for each participant to venture his or her considered thoughts, without fear of belittlement if what is ventured is faulty. Such an environment is particularly hospitable to new questions, new perspectives on the matter under exploration, and new possibilities for learning. There is a shared expectation then that such contributions will be freely and purposefully ventured.

Second, the phrase refers to the quickening of mind and heart that occurs among learners where particular practices of learning have become 'conversational', in Michael Oakeshott's sense of the word: where 'thoughts of different species take wing and play around one another, responding to each other's movements and provoking one another to fresh exertions' (Oakeshott, 1981, p.198). This reference to 'different species' of thought highlights the point that genuine conversation acknowledges from the start the plurality of the human condition, and that plurality must be allowed its due scope in the conduct of educational endeavours.

Third, in the medium to longer term, the phrase refers to a distinct kind of ethical and imaginative landscape that accompanies fruitful experiences of learning: namely those experiences through which particular capabilities and fluencies are brought to progressively higher levels of accomplishment. Dewey uses the phrase 'collateral learning' to highlight the overlooked but lasting influence exerted by the attitudes that accompany any instance of teaching and learning (Dewey, 1995, p. 48). But this collateral dimension – for example, the enduring likes and dislikes quietly picked up during a geometry or French lesson – is itself influenced by the imaginative colour of those regions to which thoughts and efforts are memorably beckoned during the lesson. It may be influenced also by the forgettable quality of thoughts that remain earthbound through lacklustre, predictable teaching practices.

Informal learning environments – in homes, in workplaces, in recreational contexts – could well be venturesome in the sense described. But here I want to emphasise that formal learning environments *need* to be so, at least in some meaningful degree, to be properly described as educational. It is with formal environments of learning that I am centrally concerned here. These can, of course, range from pre-school to further education to graduate school.

Not surprisingly, this emphasis on the quality of learning environments brings pedagogical practices and relations to centre stage. It is important to acknowledge from the beginning that such practices and relations are always socially and historically situated; that is to say, pedagogical practices and relations are always subject to what Gadamer calls an 'effective history' of influences (*Wirkungsgeschichte*) (Gadamer, 1975, pp. 267 ff.). These include influences from policy measures, from administrative procedures, from parental pressures, from gendered assumptions, from preconceived ideas about social class or ethnic background, from the tenor of responses by students and teachers, from examination requirements, and so on.

Many of these influences are constricting ones, as some of the other contributions to this volume emphasise. Teachers as practitioners are often frustrated by such constrictions. But many teachers may have become so habituated in inherited attitudes and practices as to be unaware, or only partially aware, of what possibilities are being constricted, or of how relations of learning have become systematically distorted. Christiane Thompson's perceptive observations on the 'decomposition of pedagogical relations' are pertinent in this connection (see Thompson, 2013).

In looking more closely at the characteristics of venturesome learning environments, I would like to identify, from the standpoint of teaching as a distinct kind of practice, four broad domains of relations. These are not readymade, separate categories. Rather, they are four domains of *human capability* that, when they interweave productively, enable venturesome learning environments to be fostered and sustained. Every pedagogical relationship involves such domains, though where educational practice is inadequately understood, or is carried out in an instrumentalist way, both the inescapability and the significance of this point are likely to be missed. The four domains are: (a) the teacher's relations with the subject or material being taught; (b) the teacher's relations with his/her students; (c) the teacher's relations with colleagues, parents, educational authorities and a wider range of others; (d) the teacher's relation to him/herself, within which the character and significance of the other three domains are decided (Hogan, 2010, pp. 59 ff.).

In all four there is, properly speaking, a particular kind of love. To speak with Hannah Arendt, one might rightly call this a love of engagement with the world (Arendt, 1993, p. 196). This is a kind of love that gives itself in different ways to the betterment of humankind's lot and to enrichments of human experience. It contrasts with, without excluding, more ascetic forms of love that leave the world much as it is and concentrate mainly on worship and veneration of the divine. Where teaching is concerned, love of engagement with the world involves a desire and a will to become fluent, as a practitioner, in *four specific kinds of engagement*, each of which mingles with the others in cultivating venturesome learning environments. I would like to explore, in a preliminary way, each of the four.

Teachers' Relations with Their Teaching Subjects
In the teacher's relations with a subject – economics, physics, history – the heart of the matter is bypassed if these relations are mainly seen as an issue of competence in a body of knowledge or skills, ready and waiting for transmission. If the subject in question is not alive and communicative *within* the teacher's ongoing engagements with it, it is unlikely that students will experience the worlds of possibility, challenge and discovery to be opened up by the subject. That is to say, the teacher needs to build relations to the subject as to a neighbourhood, or range of neighbourhoods, in which she has become at home; but not in the sense of a cosy repose for thought and action. Such neighbourhoods are characterised not by horizons that are everywhere familiar, but by invitations that beckon and demands that lead quite beyond such horizons. Yet, they remain neighbourhoods into which students must be invited ever anew, evoking and sustaining the students' genuine potentials and energies. This is very much a labour of love, and of a perceptive, persevering kind.

But even where a teacher's relations with a particular subject, or range of subjects, are richly alive, the character of these relations might still be restrictive in an educational sense. Becoming progressively more at home in the imaginative worlds opened up by a subject one loves can bring its own difficulties if one is to be *pedagogically capable* as a teacher. These might colloquially be described as difficulties in 'talking to the locals': the increasingly pluralist multitudes of pupils who populate classrooms, but who also wander more familiarly amid the busy offerings of twenty-first-century entertainments industries. Some practical strategies for tackling such difficulties are referred to in the second part of this chapter. The major research project reviewed there represents a large-scale effort to enhance the capabilities of both students and teachers by making the learning environments they share more participatory and venturesome.

But another kind of criticism can be brought against an engrossed love of one's subject. This is the claim that such a love gives the upper hand to conservative influences over more critical and questioning ones in a teacher's beliefs and attitudes. Variants of critical theory, from the work of the earlier Habermas to that of Terry Eagleton, would charge that inheritances of learning, no matter how cherished they might be, are never without embedded presuppositions. Such presuppositions, critical theory points out, often involve institutionalised distortions and invidious distinctions that silence rather than empower marginalised voices.

Criticisms like these highlight a few key points if a teacher's relations with his or her teaching subjects are to be healthy and enriching. In the first place, such relations involve personal commitments, or labours of love. That is to say, they are essentially more than, and different from, the technical notion of 'up-skilling'. Such labours are committed to enabling others to share in the *inherent benefits*, not merely the external rewards, of a particular human pursuit. For instance, if I'm a teacher of history, the external rewards to be gained by my students include high grades in their exams, commendation from teachers and parents, perhaps a coveted place on a college course. But such rewards apply in other subjects as well. The *inherent* benefits are those that enable my students to discover something of the historian in themselves: to open up the intriguing world of motivations, aspirations and value-conflicts lying beneath the data of historical record; to appreciate something of the shifting interplays ever at work between forces of continuity and forces of change; to understand how influences from the past both disclose and constrain the possibilities of the present and the future. In short, the inherent benefits mark, in each case, an unforced calling forth of a student's own capabilities. This recognises that the profile of potentials differs from one person to the next; but also that a plurality of possibilities, as well as being a feature of groups, is a feature of human experience as it unfolds in each individual.

Second, there is a marked contrast here with conventional conceptions of a teacher's fluency in a subject. Conventional conceptions tend to view fluency less as the yield-to-date of a labour of love and more as a competency. The underlying understanding of conventional conceptions of fluency is mainly technical in character; that is to say, fluency in all essential respects can be captured by tests, and indexed by the results of such tests. Such an understanding can present itself as innocent of any ideological baggage, and thus as an important virtue of procedure in workplace cultures pervaded by quantitative analysis and evaluations. But this species of understanding remains largely blind to the insight, common in different ways to Dewey, Heidegger, Wittgenstein and many other philosophers, that no form of human understanding is without decisive presuppositions, implicit interpretations and predisposing 'fore-conceptions' (Heidegger, 1973, pp. 191–192).

Third and more positively, a love of one's subject that is pedagogically productive is in itself an active, sometimes even a turbulent love. It includes a recurrent to-and-fro in one's own experience between a receptive openness to the voices that speak from inheritances of learning and a more critical interrogation of such voices. It contributes in a particular way to a deepening of self-understanding that will be reviewed more closely below, under the fourth domain of relations. The import of this point for policy priorities in the professional development of teachers is also taken up in the second part of the paper.

Teachers' Relations with Their Students

Teachers' relations with students are more accurately understood as a lively *interplay* than as any kind of transmission. One might say that they are an ever-renewed dialogue, enabling the students to experience something genuine of the imaginative neighbourhood opened up by the teacher. But this would be wrong, or at least inadequate.

It would be rather one-sided, overlooking the point that an educational dialogue opens up a *new* imaginative neighbourhood, constituted and coloured by the contributions of the *various* contributors. Granted, the teacher may have frequently travelled these regions before in his/ her own relations with the subject. But if the teacher's relations with the students are genuinely a dialogue, he/she now travels the same path anew and finds that it becomes a somewhat different path through a previously familiar landscape, but now with some unexpected features.

Crucial to such relations, then, is that they seek to enable students to become active and responsible participants in their own learning. For students, this kind of enablement means taking un-coerced steps towards the discovery of their own potentialities and limitations, in response to the voices and challenges that engage them in a buoyant community of learning. In other words, as touched on briefly already, it involves them in discovering something of the geographer in themselves, or of the biologist, or mathematician or linguist; or discovering something of their own aptitude for designing and making – say in wood, in textiles or other materials; or discovering something of a literary, scientific or religious sensibility in themselves. This can, of course, sometimes be a discovery of limitation. Take, for instance, the emergent recognition that one hasn't a strong aptitude for maths, or languages, or some other subject that one may still have to study as a 'core subject' until the minimum school-leaving age. Facing up to this recognition, while continuing to give one's best efforts to the subject in question, is itself a capability of first importance: one that is unlikely to be cultivated where overt or unremarked forms of belittlement feature regularly in learning environments. This is not to make an argument for specialisation at an early age. Nor is it to advocate streaming, or tracking. Rather, it is to say that plurality *within* learning environments needs to be sustained, at least until the students' mid-teens, by greater differentiation in pedagogical practices. Such practices would involve the students themselves, as far as possible, as active and responsible participants in the learning environments that constitute their daily experiences in school. Again, this is an issue to be taken up in the second part of the chapter, at a level where research and practice become joined.

Where learning environments are predominantly compliant or authoritarian, passive or aggressive, it is unlikely that relations between teachers and students will be marked by dialogue. Pedagogical dialogue is a form of persevering action. It is marked by an enduring ethical commitment to building and sustaining the kinds of relations that make learning environments places where it is safe to venture and rewarding to listen. This kind of commitment is very necessary where the best efforts of students continually come up with wrong answers, or a series of dead-end paths, or where the teacher makes an error of judgement. It is even more necessary where frustrations in a learning environment lead to outbursts of acrimony, or where a more deep-seated resentment on the part of some students continually threatens to subvert the learning ethos. In such circumstances insights and actions that may run quite counter to the intuitions lodged in traditional pedagogies are called for. For instance, as Burbules puts it, 'maintaining the relational conditions for further discussion is frequently more important, in the long run, than settling the specific question at hand' (Burbules, 1993, p. 144).

It is important to stress, then, that it is the *realisation*, or bringing about, of such relations – among students themselves as well as with their teachers – that allows environments of learning to become properly fertile. This realisation remains inescapably incomplete, however. It is the ever-partial attainment of an aim-in-view. It identifies a crucially important human capability, but not one that can be accomplished with an assured finality. It remains ever vulnerable, moreover, to setbacks, distortions, and even collapse. As Griffiths (2013) has illustrated, pedagogical relations in group settings are particularly susceptible to contingencies, favourable or adverse. Recognition of this contingent dimension, however, sits well with a conception of teaching and learning that regards it as conversational. The teacher, of course, carries a central responsibility for how such conversation is experienced in a classroom, or school laboratory, or other formal learning environment. But the points made above are an important reminder that the most fruitful conversations are not something that can be *conducted* to a pre-designed pattern. Rather, they are something we 'fall into' when the circumstances are hospitable, or, in the case of learning environments, where they are as far as possible *made* hospitable through insightful efforts. It is thus that thoughts can 'take wing', as Oakeshott says, and that learning environments can take on their own unforced momentum and tenor.

Teachers' Relations with Colleagues, Authorities, Parents and Wider Community

Where relations with colleagues, parents, educational authorities and others in wider society are concerned, this, like the former two domains, could readily be subdivided. Critical analysis of this domain, moreover, illustrates how ubiquitous issues of power are in it. The history of education in Western civilisation is replete with examples of unequal power relations as an inherited and renewed norm: between older and younger teachers, between teaching colleagues in pursuit of professional advancement, between teachers and school managements, between teachers and parents, between teachers and policy authorities, and so on.

But critical analyses of this kind fall short of their own best purposes if they neglect to analyse the interplay of power with *other* human motives. The shortfall is more serious if analysis fails to make explicit the question implied in all critique of human practices: Critique for the sake of what? Recall here that education is a *practice*, as distinct from a natural phenomenon, or biological process. It is when the practical question 'Critique for the sake of what?' is engaged with that the real possibilities of this third domain of relations come properly into view. To put this coming-into-view succinctly: one's teaching colleagues are rightly regarded as sources of constructive criticism and ideas; parents and guardians are properly seen as supportive partners; educational authorities as potential sources of coherent and accountable policy; and the public mainly as a body whose trust is necessary but has to be earned. This, I should stress, is less a theory of professional relations than an uncovering of the kind of work that actually needs to be done in the everyday conduct of professional practice.

None of this is to ignore the very real kinds of acrimony referred to in the second last paragraph. Nor is it to overlook the fact that even the best instances of a practice will probably fall short of the ideals mentioned in the last one. Jockeying for advantage, the venting of personal powers and perks, and the furthering of one's own way are features of most workplaces. But to make these the controlling forces in elucidating the conduct of relations in any socially beneficial practice is to disfigure the practice itself. Or it is to describe a practice that has already been disfigured. Being critically alert to how such disfigurements can become institutionalised provides an invaluable vantage point to teachers. In the first place, it helps to clarify the coherence of teaching as a practice and to challenge, as Carr does, the discouraging idea that education is an 'essentially contested concept' (D. Carr, 2010, pp. 89 ff.). Second, such alertness discloses navigational markers to teachers who are keen to work collegially in building and sustaining learning environments that are hospitable to venturing. A central insight here is that teaching is seen less as instruction carried on by individuals in isolation from each other, and more as a cooperative promotion of learning by a diversity of colleagues. Such diversity will mean wide differences of outlook in matters political, economic, religious, and so on. Notwithstanding these, the cooperative efforts of teachers *as educational practitioners* are properly dedicated to something coherent amid this diversity. In a sentence, that coherence lies in promoting a profusion of human flourishing through promising and defensible practices of learning. Recognising the importance of this, the cultivation of collegial relations that contribute to venturesome learning environments played a central part in the research project that will be reviewed in the second part of this chapter.

Teachers' Relations to Self

This fourth domain of relations can also be described as the teacher's self-understanding. Here the other three relations come together – profitably or otherwise – to orient in one way or another the teacher's thinking and actions. For instance, my relation as a teacher to the subjects I teach might be a cherished one that continually attracts me to new encounters. But I might be disposed in a different way towards my students, frequently resenting their lack of appreciation of my efforts. In this case the very richness of the first domain of relations could possibly become a refuge for the teacher from the second domain. That refuge may even become a prison if the world into which the teacher is drawn offers ever fewer ideas or possibilities for sharing its treasures with those who are still largely strangers to it. On the face of it, this kind of distortion of the teacher's self-understanding is occasioned by an exclusive kind of academic love. From a pedagogical perspective, however, it is more accurate to say that the distortion occurs where an exclusive form of love becomes more than that: where it becomes *exclusionary*. In other words, the teacher's relations with the students are such, or have become such, that the teacher sees most if not all of them as unworthy of entry to the riches of the world in question; or as incapable of meeting even the rudimentary demands for entry. Or the teacher sees little possibility of recasting his or her own presentations of the subject so that its demands might in some way become negotiable by the students. Thus the teacher fails to see that his or her authority has to be earned – as illustrated by Kodelja (2013).

This kind of intractability in the teacher's self-understanding straddles the first and second domains of relations (relation to subject, relation to students). A common way of viewing the kind of difficulty faced by the teacher here is to describe it as lack of 'pedagogical content knowledge', to use a well-known phrase associated with Lee Shulman. Pedagogical content knowledge, in Shulman's own words, refers to 'the blending of content and pedagogy into an understanding of how particular topics, problems or issues are organised, represented, and adapted to the diverse interests and abilities of learners, and presented for instruction' (Shulman, 2004, p. 228). As a particular form of know-how, pedagogical content knowledge furnishes many ideas and strategies for planning, illustrating, monitoring, giving and receiving feedback, and other aspects of a teacher's practice. It marks a decisive advance in the world of educational research. Yet, for all that, it seems more a possession than a disposition: a *form of having* as distinct from a *way of being and acting*. By contrast, the case I am arguing here involves an ontological shift of emphasis: from the possession and deployment of understanding and skill to more original and challenging *ways of being human*, and of relating to ideas and people.

The investigation of a research and development project, below, will take up in a practical context the philosophical arguments I have been advancing above about venturesome learning environments.

More particularly, it will review some findings on the kinds of relations that cultivate human capabilities in such environments. From its early days this project was informed by specific philosophical ideas. But it was also keen to revise and refine such ideas, thus providing them with a stronger practical warrant and making them more robust candidates for the professional commitments of teachers and the attentions of educational policy makers.

THE POSSIBLE AND THE PRACTICAL: RESEARCH ON LEARNING ENVIRONMENTS IN A POLICY CONTEXT

'Teaching and Learning for the 21st Century' (TL21 for short) is the name of a €1.3 million research project that was launched in December 2003 by the National University of Ireland Maynooth and 15 post-primary schools in three clusters of five – urban, suburban and rural. An interim report, titled *Voices from School*, was published in 2005 and the final report on the active phase of the project, titled *Learning Anew*, was published in 2008 (Hogan *et al.*, 2005, 2008). The project then entered a dissemination phase, called the 'TL21 Transfer Initiative' (2008–09 to 2011–12). This later phase involved a wider number of schools, organised in clusters around five government-funded Education Centres for continuing professional development (CPD). These Education Centres have become partners in the TL21 Transfer Initiative. It also involved periodic discussions on our part with policy-making and managerial bodies in Irish education. This latter dimension has been crucial, not least because it has been an experience of reciprocal learning relations, increasingly embodying many of the features explored above. In fact, without work on such relations, which can of course sometimes hit a discordant note, it is difficult to see how trust and influence can grow between research and policy making.

The two main aims of the TL21 project, and equally of the TL21 Transfer Initiative, have been (1) to strengthen post-primary teachers' capabilities as the authors of their own work, and (2) to enable post-primary students to take a more active and responsible hand in their own learning. The main interventions of both the TL21 project and the Transfer Initiative have been CPD workshops for teachers, participatory in nature and organised in a linked sequence over two-year time spans. For those participating in the workshops there is an optional accreditation track. Those who choose this can proceed to a Postgraduate Diploma/MEd by carrying out a series of action research assignments on their own practice.

In the first series of workshops, some notable patterns quickly manifested themselves in the professional attitudes and practices of the participating teachers. These patterns were evident in each of the domains of learning relations reviewed above. Taking each domain in turn, the patterns were as follows.

First, as regards teachers' relations to the subjects they were teaching, many of the initial participants maintained a lively personal interest in developments in their subjects. Yet too often that interest remained in a different compartment from their own work with their students in these subjects. Commercially prepared textbooks and other resources in the different subjects were a prevailing influence on both what was taught and how it was taught. At the outset of the project, teachers' attitudes and practices frequently revealed a relation to their subjects that seemed unduly influenced by what they perceived the examinations system to reward. Teachers thus tended to concentrate on a narrow range of achievements in the subject in question (e.g. in Mathematics, Science, English, Irish), springing mainly from rote learning and drill-and-practice teaching (Hogan *et al.*, 2008, pp. 5–6). Such capabilities as were being cultivated were all too often conformist in character and tended to neglect the inherent benefits of the subject.

Second, where relations with students were concerned, for the most part the participating teachers enjoyed good relations with their students. But they hardly ever discussed their pedagogical ideas and practices with students. Rarely, moreover, did they involve students in other than routine practices of learning. Such practices were carried through in efficient but predictable ways, and were seldom evaluated afterwards by the teachers (pp. 5–6).

Third, the lack of discussion with students about how teaching and learning were to be planned and experienced was also evident as a prevailing pattern in teachers' relations with colleagues. Such relations were generally good and topics like sport, family and current affairs featured daily in conversations between teaching colleagues, as did incidents of misbehaviour among students. But only occasionally were there professional discussions about the ideas that shaped their own thoughts and actions as practitioners.

Finally, at the beginning of the research project features such as these described in the last three paragraphs disclosed a prevalent self-understanding among teachers that was more acquiescent than questioning, more individualist than professionally collegial, more domesticated than venturesome.

Against this background I want to turn now to some central findings from the TL21 project, including its dissemination phase, the TL21 Transfer Initiative. I will highlight the kinds of changes in professional attitudes and practices, and in environments of learning, that it succeeded in promoting. The findings are drawn chiefly from the final report on the research-intensive stage of the project, *Learning Anew* (Hogan *et al.*, 2008).

First of all, to begin with the students, the use of new teaching and learning strategies – mainly from the assessment for learning family – brought about significant improvements in students' attitudes to their work and also promoted their active involvement in that work. When properly availed of, assessment for learning approaches necessarily involve a discerning provision of constructive feedback to students. In fact, the adept use of such approaches can hardly fail to influence for the better the reciprocal relations of teachers and students. We discovered that their regular use, however, can make the enhancement of capability, both for students and teachers, an enduring feature of classroom environments. The kinds of changes that were most evident among students in the project's schools were a decrease in student-initiated conflicts with teachers; greater cooperation between students in group work and pair work; more positive attitudes to learning among students; better practices of learning, including improved completion of homework; and better attendance rates in some instances where attendance rates were poor (Hogan *et al.*, 2008, pp. 41 ff.).

Second, where the participating teachers were concerned, some found that their initial attempts in using new approaches were resisted by students. Here, the project's workshops and informal networking provided valuable opportunities for teachers to share with each other the challenges they were experiencing, and to identify possible solutions.

It became clear that the best improvements in students' learning were recorded where teachers began with just one or two changes in approach and subsequently introduced others in a gradual way. These incremental changes in the teachers' practices also led to significant shifts in their professional attitudes. Although no explicit efforts were made to change teachers' relations to their teaching subjects, these relations began to change in unforced ways. The changes came about as teachers found themselves relying progressively less on textbooks and ready-made curriculum materials and began to devise, to use and to share their own pedagogical resources. The use of interactive ICT resources, already familiar to most students, featured prominently in this connection (pp. 28–34, 55–57).

Where teachers pursued new approaches with students over an extended period, changes in learning environments were sometimes striking, including regular features like a readiness on students' part to ask questions, to venture an answer that might be wrong, to accept ideas and correction from other students, and to propose suggestions for project work and homework (pp. 45–46, 48–49). School leaders reported that where small-scale changes were succeeding and gathering some momentum, opportunities were created to expand the scope of developments so as to influence the learning environment of their schools more widely (pp. 17–19). Profiting from such opportunities was the chief concern of the leadership dimension of the project, and this is even more the case now in the work of the TL21 Transfer Initiative with a wider number of schools.

Third, in order to engage with and strengthen teachers' capabilities, regular CPD workshops for teachers were a central feature of this research project. But these workshops themselves had a number of distinguishing features. They included expectations for active participation, clearly defined learning tasks, purposeful collaboration on these tasks, continuity between workshops in a developmental sequence, feedback and evaluation during and between workshops (p. 100). The kinds of learning communities that such features promoted modelled in practice the venturesome learning environments aimed for by the project as a whole. They also nurtured on a wide scale teachers' confidence and capacity to pursue similar aims in their own classrooms. This enabling momentum in teachers' self-understanding – from being reliable but largely acquiescent followers towards becoming perceptive and cooperative critics of their own practice – is probably the most seminal of the project's achievements to date. The reasons for this are important and call now for some closer, but necessarily concise analysis.

Even when supported by convincing evidence from schools, findings like these can bypass the eyes and ears of policy makers unless accompanied by some strategies that bring policy makers themselves into the practical research arena. With this in mind, a representative range of video recordings was gathered from classrooms and school laboratories, and from interviews with students, teachers and school principals. These were first presented at a colloquium and exhibition in the university in June 2007, to illustrate and review the kinds of developments that were taking place in the schools. Two further such events took place in May 2008 and June 2012, with periodic bilateral meetings with interested parties in the intervals. Such parties included policy makers, managerial bodies, teacher union leaders, key figures from the National Council for Curriculum and Assessment, the schools' inspectorate, as well as principals and teachers from participating schools, and they attended these colloquia in large numbers. They watched evidence in the form of DVD clips from school classrooms and laboratories; they viewed exhibitions of students' work; they spoke informally to teachers; and they participated more formally in plenary presentation-and-discussion sessions.

And here the research team discovered an unexpected finding. Because such colloquia in themselves help to build learning relations, notably between researchers and policy makers, they are a productive way to advance – and to enlighten – the idea of *evidence-informed* policy. This idea contrasts with the controversial and sometimes coercive idea of 'evidence-based' policy, criticised by Biesta (2010b) and others. The former's emphasis on colloquia and exhibitions, on giving voice to students, teachers, school leaders and others, invites policy makers into a world they all too rarely experience: namely, the fuller dimensions of a research-friendly practitioners' world. An evidence-informed approach such as we have embraced does not eschew quantitative analysis, however; rather it finds the proper use of such analysis crucial for accurate evaluation and assessment. But from the outset its understanding of capabilities – of both teachers and students – remains inseparable from viewing educational purposes as things to be reviewed, revised and enhanced in the light of practitioners' own capable monitoring of practical research initiatives.

The substantial success achieved by our colloquia, and by the idea of research-informed policy that the colloquia helped to advance, is of course encouraging. It gives reason to hope that, by pursuing educational research along the lines described above, progress might be made in promoting the notion of venturesome learning environments as *a policy priority* in a country's national educational policy. Hand in hand with this go brighter hopes for promoting CPD networks that enable teachers and students to become proficient in the kinds of relations of learning we have been exploring. But such hopes can never be taken for granted. At their heart lies the conviction – to many politicians an audacious one – that education is a practice in its own right with its own inherent purposes. The dominant tenor of educational reform in most Western countries in recent decades indicates a contrary view (Hargreaves and Shirley, 2009). For the most part, reform measures have been curiously blind to the importance of relations in learning. They have routinely ignored the experienced quality of learning and have effectively made teaching-to-the-test the mainstay of educational practice. Far from cultivating creative approaches among teachers, they have tended to homogenise and standardise teaching itself. Far from making learning environments places where it is safe to venture an idea that might be wrong, or where different imaginative neighbourhoods might be frequently opened up, such environments are made conducive to conformity and prone to individualism.

Despite the recurring infertility of such remedies, they manifest a populist plausibility that makes them attractive to governments. In the United States, for instance, the staying power of the controversial 'No Child Left Behind' initiative of 2001 and the propagation of the 'Race to the Top' initiative of 2009 reveal this plausibility. Although the latter carries a more positive thrust than the former, both treat educational practitioners, including school leaders, as servile operatives to be controlled by carrot and stick in delivering targets imposed from above. Insightful educational debate becomes largely redundant in such circumstances.

However, more promising alternatives, with a more convincing warrant and a more learner-centred focus, have now begun to make news internationally. Notable here is the 'Fourth Way' thinking reported and analysed in the last few years by Andy Hargreaves and Dennis Shirley (2009); also Pasi Sahlberg's *Finnish Lessons* (2011) on the underlying reasons for Finland's prominence among the current educational success stories of Western democracies. Central to such alternatives is the placing of trust in teachers and the promotion of participatory and purposeful learning among students. Classical ancestors of such alternatives can of course be found in the kinds of learning environments cultivated by Socrates in ancient Athens and memorably captured in the early dialogues of Plato, such as the *Gorgias, Protagoras, Apology, Crito* and *The Republic* Book 1 (Plato, 1937). But the enormous promise of such pedagogical thinking and action was decisively and continually eclipsed by the forces of empire, church and state over two millennia of Western civilisation. The eclipse was not total, however. There were many distinguished if diverse figures who explored some variants of such promise – in their actions, in their writings, or in both – in the educational history of the West. Here one could broadly speak of an educational tradition that includes Heloise and her teacher Abelard in the twelfth century, Erasmus and Montaigne in the sixteenth, Vico, Rousseau and Kant in the eighteenth, Pestalozzi, Froebel and Peabody in the nineteenth, Dewey and Freire in the twentieth.

CONCLUSION

A rearticulation of the promise of this variegated but coherent educational tradition for the pluralist circumstances of the twenty-first century begins with a manifold recognition. Such a recognition underlies the arguments on relations of learning and environments of learning that have been made throughout this chapter. More specifically, the recognition in question is a threefold one, making explicit at a policy level what a commitment to venturesome learning environments involves at a practitioner level. First, there is the recognition that education is a primary and public good in a democratic society, as distinct from an ancillary service to the economy or to the current government in power. Second, there is the recognition that teaching is a practice – or family of practices – in its own right, as distinct from a subordinate range of activities to be controlled in all essentials by a body of superiors. That this practice must be accountable to democratic society is intrinsic to such recognition, but accountable for fruits that are genuinely of the practice itself, quite a distinct matter from acquiescence in externally imposed demands. Third, there is the recognition that the first and enduring priority of educational practice is to enhance the quality of human experiences of learning. This is an undertaking that seeks to evoke and nourish the ownmost potentials of each – but in communal, pluralist learning environments – in response to what is addressed to such potentials from inheritances of learning, old and new.

9
Towards a Theory of Well-Being for Teachers

LORRAINE FOREMAN-PECK

INTRODUCTION

It is an uncontroversial presumption that good education requires good teachers. As the UK White Paper *The Importance of Teaching* asserts, 'no education system can be better than the quality of its teachers' (DfE, 2010, p. 3). The government's idea of a good teacher is encapsulated in a set of revised standards published in May 2012 (DfE, 2012b). These set out what teachers must know and be able to do, thus interpreting 'good' to mean 'competent'. In addition, the standards require teachers to demonstrate certain behaviour and attitudes within and outside school, such as tolerance and respect for the rights of others.

The view that good teachers should also be good people and embody certain virtues and qualities of character appropriate to the work of a teacher is also recognised in an earlier policy discussion document (DfE, 2011b). In this document it is suggested that the current requirements for entrants into the teaching profession should include qualities of character such as humility, respect, empathy and resilience. Furthermore, it is suggested that certain personal virtues and qualities are necessary for 'effectiveness', especially sustained commitment, resilience, perseverance, motivation, strong interpersonal skills and willingness to learn (DfE, 2011b, pp. 4–5). These do indeed seem to be prerequisites for learning how to be a competent teacher. But if one

Philosophical Perspectives on Teacher Education, First Edition. Edited by Ruth Heilbronn and Lorraine Foreman-Peck. © 2015 Ruth Heilbronn and Lorraine Foreman-Peck. Editorial Organisation © Philosophy of Education Society of Great Britain. Published 2015 by John Wiley & Sons, Ltd.

takes a more expansive view of the nature of teaching, which emphasises a moral and relational view of teaching, then other virtues come into play. From this standpoint, virtues such as justice, tolerance, courage, patience, optimism, integrity, trustworthiness, open-mindedness, and being able to learn from experience are as important as being competent (Noddings, 2005; Heilbronn, 2010, p. 9; Higgins, 2011). We could argue that the latter virtues are necessary for the kind of interaction that teaching calls for, and are just as important as those qualities of character associated with being effective.

Despite the focus on the personal qualities of teachers, there is a conspicuous lack of discussion about the more overarching concept of a teacher's well-being, even though there is a substantial literature attesting to the emotionally challenging nature of teaching, which may lead individuals to feel exhausted, enervated and burnt out (Reid, 1962; van Manen, 1995; Nias, 1996; Hargreaves, 2000; Day and Leith, 2001; Kelchtermans, 2005). From this omission we can infer that it is assumed that the right qualities and virtues will enable those so endowed to withstand the rigours of a teacher's life. This is an inadequate idea because the 'competence plus virtues and personal qualities model' of teaching does not go far enough in acknowledging the essentially contextual or contingent nature of teaching (Squires, 1999), the kind of understanding and skills needed to meet contingent challenges and the essential role of support from experienced mentors or tutors. As such, it is an unbalanced view. One consequence of the competence plus virtues/personal qualities account of a teacher as a person is that if a teacher is having difficulties, this may be thought of reductively, as a technical deficiency (incompetence) or a personal matter (incorrect virtues or qualities), rather than one located in the preparation for teaching or the conditions of work.

There have been, over the past decade, a proliferation of UK and international policy initiatives promoting pupils' well-being in schools (Coleman, 2009; Soutter, O'Steen and Gilmore, 2012). The English White Paper *The Importance of Teaching* (DfE, 2010) and the Standards for the Award of Qualified Teacher Status (DfE, 2012b), whilst recognising the importance of good teachers to the well-being of pupils and to the competitive global economy, does not recognise that teacher well-being is an issue, except obliquely in its mention of the unacceptably high attrition rates of teachers in training and in the early years (DfE, 2011b , p. 10). Yet one could argue that lack of well-being is a cause of attrition, rather than lack of 'good' personal characteristics such as perseverance, motivation or resilience. At its most basic, a lack of happiness and personal fulfilment may lead to the judgement that perseverance is not worthwhile.

Furthermore, it should be noted that even though the government has recognised the stultifying effect of its micro management of the education system, the relaxation of control of schools that it is currently recommending does not drill down to teacher level. Teachers and mentors may feel an uncomfortable clash between personal and responsible autonomy and conformity to institutional priorities. Teacher mentoring and performance review is still 'procedural and systems-led', rather than providing for the development of an individual's sense of professional autonomy (Dymoke and Harrison, 2006). School-based teacher coaching for the Master's in Teaching and Learning[1] for instance, focuses on performativity (Anderson and Gristy, 2013). While competence in teaching is important, the person of the teacher as an individual with a singular personality and interests, working in conditions of near isolation and close regulation, is neglected. Even before the introduction of the present tough accountability systems for schools and teachers, Nias argued that the solitary nature of teachers' conditions of work made the idea of the teacher's investment in her personal resources important, and this stressed the importance of the teacher as a 'person' (Nias, 1987, 1996).

The aim of the chapter is to give an account of what 'teacher well-being' could mean, and to suggest ways in which the personal well-being of teachers can be fostered. In order to develop an account, I first sketch out some ways in which 'well-being' has been conceptualised, look at the way well-being is challenged by the conditions and nature of a teacher's work, and then offer a positive account of possible ways in which to help teachers develop a sense of well-being.

WHAT IS MEANT BY 'WELL-BEING'?

Even though there has been a proliferation of national and international policy initiatives addressing schools' and other social services' role in promoting well-being, there is no consensus about its meaning

(Ereaut and Whiting, 2008; Coleman, 2009; Soutter *et al.*, 2012). It is an elastic concept that is shaped in different directions according to the discipline or concern it is related to. Economists, for example, define it as being satisfied with life, and that depends on being able to satisfy one's preferences for goods and services. Some psychologists, concerned to carry out empirical studies, have analysed the concept into operational component parts. For example, Seligman *et al.* (2009) suggest the following tri-part division of well-being into: the hedonistic or the 'Pleasant Life', the 'Engaged Life' and the 'Meaningful Life'. The Pleasant Life involves pleasurable experiences and their associated emotions such as joy. The Engaged Life involves a loss of self-consciousness or the experience of flow, and occurs when one is using one's 'highest talents' to meet the challenges that come one's way, facilitating learning. The Meaningful Life is about serving a 'higher purpose'; some cause or belief that is larger than oneself.

The nature of well-being or flourishing has been the subject of philosophical writings since Aristotle. An important argument for the case being presented here is given by White (2007). He addresses the issue of whether 'well-being' can be a purely subjective phenomenon, and if it is not, in what sense it can be 'objective' such that one is entitled to claim that a person is not flourishing even if she thinks she is. White argues that we can reach agreed judgements about whether a person is flourishing or not in a similar way that art critics can reach broad agreement about the merits of particular works of art. That literary critics and art experts do reach agreements is attested to by various awards for outstanding work, such as the Royal Society of Arts annual exhibition, the Booker Prize and the Tate Modern Art award. This is not to say that there are people who do not share the same judgements, but the warrant for awarding prizes lies in the extensive experience and expertise of other artists who are panel members. This is an important point, since it means that well-being is a concept that has, broadly speaking, publicly shared criteria, even if these are hard to articulate. It is true that there is no identifiable single body of experts for judging whether someone is leading a flourishing life as there is in the case of the art critics and art practitioners. However, White argues that we can easily conceive of expertise as being distributed among society's members. For example, doctors and parents can agree that the teenage heroin addict is not leading a flourishing life even if she says she is. In the context of teaching we can also point to objective judgements. For instance, Higgins points to the moral phenomenological character of teaching. This can be described as the idea of having to perform ('the show must go on'); the necessity for 'free-floating attention'; and, as we noted earlier, the ability to respond to the unexpected event, to improvise successfully (Higgins, 2011, pp. 373–374). An inability in these areas is likely to lead to a lack of success and therefore to a judgement by other experienced teachers that the teacher is not flourishing, at least as a teacher.

In the context of counselling young people, well-being has been stipulated as meaning 'maximising one's potential, leading a happy and successful life and making a contribution to society' (Phoenix, 2013). Other definitions are more precise, with implications for action. For instance, the National Institute for Health and Clinical Excellence (NICE, 2009), in the context of a review of social and emotional well-being in secondary education pupils, define it as a tripartite concept consisting of emotional well-being (happiness and confidence, not feeling depressed); psychological well-being (a feeling of autonomy, control over one's life, problem-solving skills, resilience, attentiveness and a sense of involvement with others); and social well-being (the ability to have good relationships with others, to avoid disruptive behaviours, delinquency, violence or bullying).

It should be apparent that these various accounts of well-being have an emotional content in common, to do with personal control, success or fulfilment, good relationships, approval of society, and engaging in worthwhile work. Many emotions are based on cognitive factors and cannot therefore be separated from a person's perceptions, attitudes, values and beliefs, and as a result emotions can be judged to be reasonable or unreasonable (Hanfling, 1976). On Hanfling's account of the emotions, how we feel can be affected by how we conceptualise situations, and there are various means of doing this – for instance, through reading, or reflecting, or engaging in meaningful conversations with others. This conceptual point is supported by empirical findings (Tickle, 1991; Nias, 1996). Tickle's 1991 study of the emotions of a group of teachers in their first year led him to conclude that the management of their emotions depended on how they perceived their success and failures in the interaction with individual pupils and in the mastery or otherwise of classroom techniques. The newly qualified teachers he studied experienced a range of emotions such as joy, elation, excitement, depression and despair. The challenge for novice teachers, he concluded, was to research the emotional aspects of their 'selves' that were inextricably linked to their practices (Tickle, 1991, p. 327). On the account of the emotions presented here, this inevitably means reflecting on the situations that engender positive and negative emotions, and being self-reflexive.

CHALLENGES TO TEACHERS' WELL-BEING

The personally challenging dimension to being a teacher has been well attested to (van Manen, 1995; Nias, 1996; Hargreaves, 2000; Day and Leith, 2001; Kelchtermans, 2005). It was early noted by the philosopher of education, Louis Arnaud Reid: 'Teaching is an encounter in which the teacher's own personal life is involved and this can be deeply disturbing' (Reid, 1962, p. 91). The 'encounter' referred to is often with pupils who may not share the teacher's values – may indeed have values they disapprove of and may come from backgrounds that they do not fully understand. These encounters often take place in 'crowded conditions with large numbers of pupils' (Nias, 1996). Such encounters are likely to engender strong emotions the object of which may not be completely in the teacher's awareness. The teacher, in order to be effective and concerned, has to develop good relationships with individual pupils, groups of pupils and colleagues. Such a complex demand is often seen reductively, as a matter of discipline and maintaining order. As Higgins and others have remarked, in the classroom setting successful management often involves some theatrical ability – that is, the ability to simulate an emotion such as displeasure while not actually feeling it. The emotional and physical wear and tear involved in developing an 'acting persona' is brilliantly depicted by Smith, a career teacher of English, who wrote: 'Teachers are actors. Teachers need a performing personality. Control, I could already see, was part of the act and the act was part and parcel of the personality' (Smith, 2001, p. 29). Smith writes of his schoolteacher father that his ability to captivate a class depended on his 'Welsh wit and repartee', his 'buzz and bursts of energy' and his 'nervous impulses'. His father's determination to win a class was evident in the 'tension in his face' (p. 67). Other writers have remarked that teaching can be very stressful because it involves a huge number of interpersonal interactions with others, usually the less mature, on a daily basis, many of which are unpredictable (Higgins, 2010a, p. 373; Luntley, 2000). The sheer number of interactions may lead to anxiety, anger and fear of failure. Decisions have to be made instantly on the basis of incomplete evidence (Tickle, 1991). Exhaustion, or 'burn out', is an occupational hazard (Higgins, 2010a).

Added to these challenges to a teacher's character is the context in which teaching takes place. The UK has seen the imposition of measures to control teachers and schools, through feedback on performance, benchmarking and teachers' performance review. Here the emphasis is on the managerialist imperatives of compliance and accountability. Teachers are subject to competitive pressure in that their performance is measured and assessed according to their previous performance and the projected performance of pupils and this is compared with other benchmarked schools. 'Naming and shaming' is still prevalent. Teachers are therefore in competition with their previous best performance and with their colleagues in other schools (Hodgson, 2012, p. 537).

A more subtle challenge to well-being, which is relevant to those involved in the induction or continuing professional development of teachers, is that managerialism promotes dialogue unsuited to exploring challenges to well-being, such as values conflict. Managerialist dialogue is concerned with audit and compliance. Open dialogue, on the other hand, is about asking enquiry questions and setting one's own agenda, in the context of finding out how to understand and improve practice. Wadsworth describes open dialogues or 'multilogues' in the context of evaluating a social service as participants engaging on an equal footing in cycles of reflecting, observing, discussing, theorising, concluding, planning, acting, reflecting, observing and so on (Wadsworth, 2001, p. 52). It is addressed to the question 'What is good in what we have done and was there a better way of doing it?', rather than 'Have we met our objectives'? It makes room for the expression and exploration of situations that engender feelings of success and feelings of doubt. It involves comparative evaluative thinking in which evaluative criteria for wise judgement can be developed.

Given the possibilities for challenge to a teacher's well-being, such as unpredictable or contingent events and interactions, possible values conflict, discipline and maintenance of order, a heavy-handed managerialist system and an unsympathetic audit language, we can see that if teachers cannot come to terms with these, cognitively and emotionally, they are unlikely to experience well-being in their roles and sustain a long-term commitment to teaching.

WHAT ARE THE ELEMENTS OF WELL-BEING FOR TEACHERS?

From a consideration of the nature of teaching and the conditions of a teacher's work, and the concepts of well-being found in the literature, we can begin to outline an account of the necessary elements of a teacher's well-being, in an analogous way to the NICE account for secondary school pupils. The following is a tentative account along these lines:

Emotional well-being – knowing what one feels; knowing oneself; knowing how to adopt a teaching persona when necessary; knowing what one is good at; being confident; being optimistic; being open-minded; knowing what one values; valuing and enjoying teaching successes.

Psychological well-being – feeling a sense of autonomy and control over one's life; being equipped to tackle teaching problems; being resilient; being attentive to others and to the teaching environment; working with a sense of a 'higher purpose'; achieving 'flow' tempered by free-floating awareness in classroom interaction.

Social well-being – developing and valuing good and caring relationships with pupils; engaging in worthwhile work with colleagues; supporting colleagues emotionally and practically; being able to ask for help and advice; using a non-audit vocabulary to talk about teaching.

In the typical school setting many of these 'well-being' elements, such as self-knowledge, are weakly realised or totally absent. For novice and experienced teachers, the opportunity to reflect on these elements will only occur in training, mentoring and performance review, unless they are lucky enough to find good colleagues. However, without the recognition of the importance of these elements to a teacher's flourishing, they are unlikely to be addressed. Furthermore, as already mentioned, the nature of 'official' dialogue undertaken is unlikely to address anything except competence. The White Paper (2010), for example, whilst envisaging an increased emphasis in the training of teachers for observing, being observed, working and planning with other teachers and, crucially, for reflection, clearly has in mind only a concern with competence. The one example of mentoring given is the case of underperforming teachers, and the White Paper's authors recommend 'giving' direct and detailed feedback on performance and strategies to improve. The other 'well-being' aspects of teaching are left out of account.

Coleman has drawn attention to the fact that there is often some trepidation in talking about well-being, especially emotional well-being in the context of pupils' well-being. However, he points out that it hardly makes sense to talk about the emotional well-being of pupils without attending to the emotional well-being of staff: 'A moment's thought will make it obvious that the emotional health of one half of a community will be influenced by the emotional health of the other half' (Coleman, 2009, p. 290). In the sketch of the suggested elements of a teacher's well-being above, it is claimed that emotional well-being is connected to self-knowledge. Given that this is probably the most contentious and difficult element of well-being suggested in the framework, the following section attempts to deal with this aspect, while not in any way denying the importance of the other aspects. We have already claimed that dialogue with a mentor or tutor is important for teacher development and that an 'audit' language is unsuited to talk about feelings, or other matters that are not narrowly classroom- and performance-based. In order to see how dialogue or reflective conversations can help teachers develop self knowledge and other elements of 'well-being', an account of the 'self' drawing on the work of Kekes (1995) is outlined, and then a more expansive concept of reflective conversations about practice is discussed.

DEVELOPING SELF-KNOWLEDGE

Kekes argues that self-knowledge consists of knowing one's character, and that character is formed partly by genetic inheritance and partly by postnatal conditioning and upbringing. The resulting capacities, desires, values and qualities we have are given or 'fortuitous'. In contrast are patterns of values, desires, preferences and attitudes that we have shaped ourselves by reflecting on our fortuitous inheritance. We have done this through reflection and judgement and have made efforts to promote some aspects of our character and suppress others. Kekes argues that the more deliberate and less fortuitous our character, the greater is our control over our desires, capacities, values and actions. Increasing control is important to the extent that we wish to increase patterns of our character that 'aid rather than hinder living according to our conception of a good life' (Kekes, 1995, p. 117). Self-knowledge is a conscious and a self-conscious process. We can know facts about ourselves in the way that we know facts about other people. Knowing ourselves differs, however, in that such knowledge is evaluative and conative, or action guiding. If we know that we hate crowds, for example, we will, unless there are countervailing reasons, try to avoid them. Self-knowledge consists of looking backwards and forwards. We gain knowledge by looking back and attempt to learn how to remove impediments in our character to desired futures.

In looking back we are attempting to find significance. Kekes argues that there are several aspects involved: metaphysical or fundamental beliefs, such as beliefs about human beings; social facts, such as the customs and conventions of the society in which we live; beliefs about our individual pasts and autobiographical facts; and our personal characteristics, capacities, values and desires. Most of the time, most of this knowledge is in the background, known tacitly. The boundary between what is in the background and what becomes significant to us and is then in the foreground of our attention shifts or is permeable depending on our interpretations of experiences and our responses to them. Kekes suggests that the most volatile elements in the background are our personal characteristics, namely our capacities, values, beliefs and desires.

One way in which we come to learn about ourselves and our emotional responses is through reflecting on the incidents, situations or people who have engendered them. Life in general provides much raw material for reflection, and how we have responded in the past to events or situations that have engendered an emotional response foreshadows the way in which we may respond to challenges in teaching or the school environment. There is a close connection between our everyday self and our professional self. We have, so far, stressed those common aspects of a teacher's work that may present challenges to well-being. However, common challenges may be experienced differently by different people and what is problematic for one person may not be for another. Furthermore, Tripp (2012) argues that events that engender emotional disturbance do not necessarily have a dramatic quality, but if they are critical for us they do involve a desire to take action. They represent significant turning points, but first they have to be understood. This involves reflection on the event and reflection on one's emotional response to the event. It is through reflective dialogue or a reflective conversation with more experienced and sympathetic mentors or teachers that such understanding may come about. It follows that the nature of the reflective conversation is important.

REFLECTION

McIntosh (2010) claims that it is quite usual for education, nursing and social work students to be set general written exercises, such as a diary, asking them to reflect on their experiences, without being given any idea of how to go about it or what the purpose of the exercise is. Underlying the request is a vague idea that somehow students will make connections for themselves between their experiences, their feelings and the theories being propounded in their taught course. The act of reflecting through writing is therefore carrying a heavy load in the difficult area of resolving issues to do with values conflict and, for teacher trainees, the emotional challenges of dealing with discipline, coming to terms with the education system's demands and rationalising one's practice. It is also an activity that many students find very difficult to do in a meaningful way. McIntosh's description of a reflective written exercise contrasts markedly with reflection conceived as a conversation between a trainee teacher and a mentor or school-based tutor. In such a conversation the mentor or tutor leads and can decide what the agenda is to be. The focus of the conversation is usually the observed lesson taken by the teacher trainee, but may be based on written accounts such as a diary (Tripp 2012). The conversational form allows for either a compliance- and competence-focused dialogue or an open dialogue or a mix of both. We have already argued that aspects of well-being can best be addressed in open dialogues.

Reflective conversations can also be carried out with a group in the context of initial teacher education and training or continuing professional development. This possibility is not developed here except to point out that context partly determines what is a prudent topic for discussion. In group discussions it may not be in the trainees' or students' best interest, nor that of the group, for individual students to publicly disclose or discuss their feelings about incidents or experiences of teaching that have engendered them. In group contexts, individuals maybe enabled to reflect privately on their own situation and feelings through the discussion of a resource such as a text or film or case study, which may, for example, highlight aspects of teaching.

In mentoring dialogues, however, there is a weaker boundary between the personal and the professional, especially where the personal impinges on the professional. As we noted earlier, learning to teach can be, in Reid's words, 'deeply disturbing'. Even so, mentoring should not be confused with therapy or counselling. Mentoring can be thought of as a fairly straightforward transmission of skills, as in the apprenticeship model, or as a judgement of the achievement of standards or competencies, narrowly conceived. The model proposed here is a reflective practitioner model, augmented by the idea of a dialogical relationship between mentor and mentee, in which the mentor supports the development of the practical judgement of the mentee by engaging in grounded reflection on practice. The mentor's role is, as Heilbronn says, not to hand out judgements, but, borrowing from Dewey, to help trainees develop a sense of 'relative values or perspective' (Heilbronn, 2008, p. 113).

The subject matter of the mentoring dialogue, although led by the mentor, starts with the mentee's experience. This may involve a fairly predictable focus on lesson management and presentation issues such as ' timing' (see Chapter 7), or the evaluation of the success of the methods used. In Squires' (1999) model of teaching, these issues are addressing the function or role of the teacher and the suitability or value of the procedures or methods and materials. Many times, however, the subject matter of the dialogue will be the trainee's response to the contingent or unpredictable event that, as we have argued, importantly characterises teaching and is a major source of its challenge. Such incidents or events may be ignored but if, as we have been arguing, the idea of well-being is important, then part of the mentoring purpose is to develop a view about the reasonableness or otherwise of what one is experiencing, and what action is appropriate. In terms of emotional well-being, this means acknowledging what one feels is important. Where there are challenges or 'emotional disturbances', we could argue that they may be caused by underlying incongruencies with our basic beliefs about the nature of human beings, customs and conventions, and beliefs about our own values and desires (Kekes, 1995), and bringing these to the surface may lead to self-knowledge, which has the potential for either changing our self-perception and attitudes, changing our world, or both.

An example may serve to illustrate these points. A trainee on teaching practice had to spend at least ten minutes before the start of each lesson begging and borrowing chairs from neighbouring classrooms before she could begin her lesson. The trainee experienced frustration and helplessness. The mentor experienced anger. Polite requests to the head of department for more chairs were fruitless. We could argue that the emotions felt were reasonable in that our basic beliefs about how trainees and mentors should be treated were violated. Furthermore, the situation engendered despair in the mentor when it became obvious that the school could not or would not solve this situation, responding that 'it's always been like this'. The implication was that colleagues were uncaring and ineffectual. In this situation it is difficult to see how a trainee could experience a sense of well-being.

WELL-BEING AND PROFESSIONAL DEVELOPMENT

We have argued that the idea of teacher well-being should be considered as an important aspect of professional development. It is, however, largely absent in theorising about teacher training and education. As a concept it is easily confused with therapy or counselling, and as a practical approach it is difficult to see how it could be operationalised without becoming therapy. While the mentoring relationship should be concerned with a teacher's professional self, students do offer personal comments and sometimes ask for personal advice. To mention two examples out of a multitude of possible instances, one student asked the author if in her opinion he was an alcoholic. Another mentioned the difficulties of living with her mother-in-law. While these aspects of trainees' experiences were affecting their general well-being, they were not, in the author's judgement, centrally affecting their well-being as developing teachers, and were therefore not judged to be within the remit of a mentor. This position begs two questions: first, supposing the 'alcoholic student' or the 'harassed daughter-in-law' were not flourishing on their courses, what then would the role of the mentor have been? And second, what *is* legitimately within the remit of the mentor?

In the cases where students' personal problems are seriously affecting their ability to develop as teachers, referral to a support service or a recommendation to discontinue is a usual course of action, supported by the university, at least on university courses of initial teacher education. The second question of what is in a mentor's remit is more difficult, in that the area of the contingent is more difficult to specify; difficult since, as we have argued, what crops up as significant for an individual is personal and occurs in varied contexts, and so is largely unpredictable. This presents a problem from the point of view of how there can be any continuity or accumulation of teachers' knowledge and expertise: if all contingent problems are unpredictable, how do we come to learn for ourselves, and from one another, how to understand them and how to tackle them?

In order to attempt to theorise in this area we may invoke the idea of a type and a token. Contingent events may be particular in their concrete manifestation, but they may also belong to a type. Thus the 'problem of the chairs' is a concrete manifestation of a type of problem to do with the management of a school. The content of a reflective conversation is informed by the mentor's knowledge of how schools are managed and organised, by what is known about how they can best be organised, and what it is reasonable to expect in a well-managed school. The 'problem of the chairs' is a management problem affecting the developing professional self of the trainee teacher, and is therefore within the remit of the mentor. It is also a problem that can and ought to be solved, although it is another question about who is best placed to do this, and how to go about it.

Other types of contingent problem types within a mentor's remit include teacher–pupil, or pedagogical, relationships, collegial relationships, and the reception of curriculum content by pupils. Experienced mentors will have accumulated a fund of knowledge derived from their experiences, reading and research that they can bring to bear on these areas. Where their knowledge and understanding is lacking, they can at least suggest lines of enquiry that may illuminate the problem.

CONCLUSION

The assumption that a set of competences, plus a set of personal virtues and personal qualities, together with a performance-based mentoring support would be enough to carry trainee teachers through the emotional demands of teaching, is critiqued. It is argued that the essentially contingent and unpredictable challenges of teaching that threaten teachers' sense of well-being require mentoring support, which is of a fundamentally different kind from that which is solely performance based.

NOTE

1 The Masters in Teaching and Learning is a government-funded initiative for qualified teachers in England, currently in its final phase. It aims to support teachers' development in the first five years of teaching and is practice- and classroom-based. Similar programmes have been running in other parts of the UK.

References

Aldridge, D. (2013) The Logical Priority of the Question: R. G. Collingwood, Philosophical Hermeneutics and Enquiry-Based Learning. *Journal of Philosophy of Education*, 47.1: 71–85.

Aloni, M. (2008) The Fundamental Commitments of Educators. *Ethics and Education*, 3.2: 149–159.

Anderson, J. and Gristy, C. (2013) Coaching Staff in Schools: What Can We Learn from the New Role in the Masters in Teaching and Learning In-School Coach and the Higher Education Tutor Working Alongside Them? *Journal of Education for teaching: International Research and Pedagogy*, 39.1: 107–122.

Anderson, R. (2009) The Idea of a University. In K. Withers (ed.), *First Class? Challenges and Opportunities for the UK's University Sector* (London: IPPR), pp. 37–45.

Anscombe, G.E.M. (1958) Modern Moral Philosophy. *Philosophy*, 33.124: 1–19.

Apple, M.W. (2004) Schooling, Markets, and an Audit Culture. *Educational Policy*, 18.4: 614–621.

Apple, M.W. (2005) Education, Markets, and an Audit Culture. *Critical Quarterly*, 47.1: 1–29.

Arcilla, R.V. (2010) *Mediumism: A Philosophical Reconstruction of Modernism for Existential Learning* (Albany, NY: SUNY Press).

Arendt, H. (1958) *The Human Condition* (Chicago: University of Chicago Press).

Arendt, H. (1993) The Crisis in Education. In *Between Past and Future* (Harmondsworth: Penguin).

Aristotle (1980) *The Nicomachean Ethics* (Oxford: Oxford University Press).

Aristotle (1981) *The Politics* (London: Penguin).

Arrowsmith, W. (1971) Teaching and the Liberal Arts: Notes Toward an Old Frontier. In D. Bigelow (ed.), *The Liberal Arts and Teacher Education: A Confrontation* (Lincoln: University of Nebraska Press).

Ball, S.J. (1990) *Politics and Policy Making in Education* (London: Routledge).

Philosophical Perspectives on Teacher Education, First Edition. Edited by Ruth Heilbronn and Lorraine Foreman-Peck. © 2015 Ruth Heilbronn and Lorraine Foreman-Peck. Editorial Organisation © Philosophy of Education Society of Great Britain. Published 2015 by John Wiley & Sons, Ltd.

Ball, S.J. (2000) Performativities and Fabrications in the Education Economy: Towards the Performative Society? *Australian Educational Researcher*, 27.2: 1–23.

Ball, S. (2001) Performativities and Fabrications in the Education Economy: Towards the Performative Society. In D. Gleeson and C. Husbands (eds), *The Performing School: Managing Teaching and Learning in a Performance Culture* (London: RoutledgeFalmer).

Barnett, R. (2000) *Realizing the University in an Age of Super Complexity* (Buckingham: Open University).

Barnett, R. (2004) Learning for an Unknown Future. *Higher Education Research and Development*, 23.3: 247–260.

Barnett, R (2005) Recapturing the Universal in the University. *Educational Philosophy and Theory*, 37.6: 785–797.

Barone, T. (2001) *Touching Eternity: The Enduring Outcomes of Teaching* (New York: Teachers College Press).

Bateson, G. (1972) *Steps to an Ecology of Mind: Collected Essays in Anthropology, Psychiatry, Evolution, and Epistemology* (Chicago: University of Chicago Press).

Bauer, W. (ed.) (2003) *Educational Philosophy and Theory*, 35.2 (A special issue on *Bildung*).

Bennett, T. (2013) *The Beaufort Wind Scale – Why We Need an Observation Revolution*. TESConnect Blog. Online at http://community.tes.co.uk/tom_bennett/b/weblog/archive/2013/05/24/the-beaufort-wind-scale-why-we-need-an-observation-revolution.aspx?s_cid=MON_News_COM (accessed 20 October 2014).

BERA/RSA (2014) *National Inquiry into Teacher Education – Interim Report*, January (London, BERA/RSA).

Biesta, G.J.J. (2004) Against Learning: Reclaiming a Language for Education in an Age of Learning. *Nordisk Pedagogik*, 23.1: 70–82.

Biesta, G.J.J. (2006) *Beyond Learning: Democratic Education for a Human Future* (Boulder, CO: Paradigm Publishers).

Biesta, G.J.J. (2007) Why 'What Works' Won't Work: Evidence-Based Practice and the Democratic Deficit of Educational Research. *Educational Theory*, 57.1: 1–22.

Biesta, G.J.J. (2009a) Good Education in an Age of Measurement: On the Need to Reconnect with the Question of Purpose in Education. *Educational Assessment, Evaluation and Accountability*, 21.1: 33–46.

Biesta, G.J.J. (2009b) Witnessing Deconstruction in Education: Why Quasi-Transcendentalism Matters. *Journal of the Philosophy of Education*, 43.3: 391– 404.

Biesta, G.J.J. (2010a) Why 'What Works' Still Won't Work: From Evidence-Based Education to Value-Based Education. *Studies in Philosophy and Education*, 29.5: 491–503.

Biesta, G.J.J. (2010b) *Good Education in an Age of Measurement: Ethics, Politics, Democracy* (Boulder, CO: Paradigm Publishers).

Biesta, G.J.J. (2011) Disciplines and Theory in the Academic Study of Education: A Comparative Analysis of the Anglo-American and Continental Construction of the Field. *Pedagogy, Culture & Society*, 19.2: 175–192.

Biesta, G.J.J. (2012) Giving Teaching Back to Education. *Phenomenology and Practice*, 6.2: 35–49.

Biesta, G.J.J. (2013) Becoming Educationally Wise: Towards a Virtue-Based Approach to Teaching and Teacher Education. In A.-L. Østern, K. Smith, T. Ryghaug, T. Krüger and

M.B. Postholm (eds), *Teacher Education Research between National and Global Trends* (Trondheim: Akademika), pp. 29–51.

Biesta, G.J.J. (2014) *The Beautiful Risk of Education* (Boulder, CO: Paradigm Publishers).

Biesta, G.J.J., and Priestley, M. (2013) Capacities and the Curriculum. In M. Priestley and G.J.J. Biesta (eds), *Reinventing the Curriculum: New Trends in Curriculum Policy and Practice* (London: Bloomsbury), pp. 39–50.

Blacker, D. (1997) *Dying to Teach: The Educator's Search for Immortality* (New York: Teachers College Press).

Bloom, H. (1973) *The Anxiety of Influence: A Theory of Poetry* (Oxford: Oxford University Press).

Boghossian, P. (2012) Socratic Pedagogy: Perplexity, Humiliation, Shame and a Broken Egg. *Educational Philosophy and Theory*, 44.7: 710–720.

Borden, S. L. (2007) *Journalism as Practice: MacIntyre, Virtue Ethics, and the Press* (Farnham: Ashgate).

Bousquet, M. (2008) *How the University Works: Higher Education and the Low-Wage Nation* (New York and London: New York University Press).

Brighouse, T. (2013) Government Induced Crisis in Initial Teacher Education: New Visions For Education Group. Online at http://www.newvisionsforeducation.org.uk/2013/04/15/government-induced-crisis-in-initial-teacher-education/ (accessed 20 October 2014).

Bruford, W.H. (1975) *The German Tradition of Self-Cultivation: Bildung from Humboldt to Thomas Mann* (Cambridge: Cambridge University Press).

Bryman, A. (2012) *Social Research Methods*, 4th edition (Oxford, Oxford University Press).

Buchmann, M. (1988) Argument and Contemplation in Teaching. *Oxford Review of Education*, 14.2: 201–214.

Burbules, N.C. (1993) *Dialogue in Teaching: Theory and Practice* (New York: Teachers College Press).

Burnard, P. and White, J. (2008) Creativity and Performativity: Counterpoints in British and Australian Education. *British Educational Research Journal*, 34.5: 667–682.

Buus, J. (2005) Teaching: Profession or Vocation? *Catholic Education*, 8.3: 326–345.

Campbell, E. (1997) Connecting the Ethics of Teaching and Moral Education. *Journal of Teacher Education*, 48.4: 255–263.

Campbell, E. (2003) *The Ethical Teacher* (Maidenhead: Open University Press).

Camus, A. (1962) *Exile and the Kingdom* (London: Penguin Books).

Carr, D. (1992) Practical Enquiry, Values and the Problem of Educational Theory. *Oxford Review of Education*, 18.3: 241–251.

Carr, D. (1993) Questions of Competence. *British Journal of Educational Studies*, 41.3: 253–271.

Carr, D. (1995) Is Understanding the Professional Knowledge of Teachers a Theory–Practice Problem? *Journal of Philosophy of Education*, 29.3: 311–329.

Carr, D. (2000) *Professionalism and Ethics in Teaching* (London and New York: Routledge).

Carr, D. (2005) Personal and Interpersonal Relationships in Education and Teaching: A Virtue Ethical Perspective. *British Journal of Educational Studies*, 53.3: 255–271.

Carr, D. (2006) Professional and Personal Values and Virtues in Education and Teaching. *Oxford Review of Education*, 32.2: 171–183.

Carr, D. (2009) Revisiting the Liberal and Vocational Dimensions of University Education. *British Journal of Educational Studies*, 57.1: 1–17.

Carr, D. (2010) Education, Contestation and Confusions of Sense and Concept. *British Journal of Educational Studies* 58.1: 89–104.

Carr, D. and Steutel, J. (1999) *Virtue Ethics and Moral Education* (London: Routledge).

Carr, W. (1987) What Is an Educational Practice? *Journal of Philosophy of Education*, 21.2: 163–175.

Carr, W. (2006) Education Without Theory? *British Journal of Educational Studies*, 54.2: 136–159.

Casanave, C.P. and Sosa, M. (2007) *Respite for Teachers: Reflection and Renewal in the Teaching Life* (Ann Arbor: University of Michigan Press).

Chan, A.S. and Fisher, D. (eds) (2009) *The Exchange University: Corporatization of Academic Culture* (Vancouver: University of British Columbia Press).

Clarke, A.E. (2007) Grounded Theory: Critiques, Debates, and Situational Analysis. In W. Outhwaite and S.P. Turner (eds), *Social Science Methodology* (London: Sage), pp. 423–442.

Coleman J. (2009) Well-Being in Schools: Empirical Measure, or Politician's Dream? *Oxford Review of Education*, 35.3: 281–292.

Collini, S. (2012) *What Are Universities for?* (London: Penguin).

Crawford, M.B. (2009) *Shopclass as Soulcraft: An Inquiry into the Value of Work* (New York: Penguin).

Crocco, M. and Costigan, A. (2007) The Narrowing of Curriculum and Pedagogy in the Age of Accountability: Urban Educators Speak Out. *Urban Education* (November) 42.6: 512–535.

Dall'Alba, G. (2009) Learning Professional Ways of Being: Ambiguities of becoming. In G. Dall'Alba (ed.), *Exploring Education Through Phenomenology: Diverse Approaches* (Oxford: Wiley-Blackwell), pp. 41–52.

Dall'Alba, G. and Barnacle, R. (2007) An Ontological Turn for Higher Education. *Studies in Higher Education*, 32.6: 679–691.

David, M. and Sutton, C.D. (2011) *Social Research: An Introduction*, 2nd edition (London: Sage).

Davis, A. (1999) *Educational Assessment: A Critique of Current Policy. Impact No. 1.* (London: Philosophy of Education Society of Great Britain).

Davis, A. (2008) *Educational Assessment: A Critique of Current Policy. Impact No. 16.* (London: Philosophy of Education Society of Great Britain).

Day, C. and Leith, R. (2001) Teacher and Teacher Educators Lives: the Role of Emotion. *Teaching and Teacher Education*, 17.4: 403–415.

DCSF. (2008) *Personalised Learning a Practical Guide* (Nottingham: Department of Children, Schools and Families).

de Certeau, M. (1984) *The Practice of Everyday Life*, Vol. 1 (Berkeley and Los Angeles: University of California Press).

Deakin Crick, R. (2008) Key Competencies for Education in a European Context. *European Educational Research Journal*, 7.3: 311–318.

Dearden, R. F. (1972) Education as a Process of Growth. In R.F. Dearden, P.H. Hirst and R.S. Peters, *Education and the Development of Reason* (London: Routledge and Kegan Paul).

Delpit, L. (1995) The Silenced Dialogue: Power and Pedagogy in Educating Other People's Children. In *Other People's Children: Cultural Conflict in the Classroom* (New York: Free Press), pp. 21–47.

Dewey, J. (1916) *Democracy and Education: An Introduction to the Philosophy of Education* (New York: Macmillan).

Dewey, J. (1960) *The Quest for Certainty* (USA: Capricorn Editions).

Dewey, J. (1995) *Experience and Education* (New York: Macmillan).

Dewey, J. (2008) *Democracy and Education* (UK: Filiquarian Publishing).

DfE (1988) Education Reform Act (London: HMSO).

DfE (2010) The Importance of Teaching: The Schools White Paper. Online at https://www.gov. uk/government/publications/the-importance-of-teaching-the-schools-white-paper-2010 (accessed 20 October 2014).

DfE (2011a) Including All Learners: The Three Principles in the Inclusion Statement: General Article. Department for Education. Online at http://www.education.gov.uk/schools/teaching andlearning/curriculum/b00199686/inclusion/challenges (accessed 20 October 2014).

DfE (2011b) Training our Next Generation of Outstanding Teachers. An Improvement Strategy for Discussion. Online at https://www.gov.uk/government/publications/training-our-next-gene ration-of-outstanding-teachers-an-improvement-strategy-for-discussion (accessed 20 October 2014).

DfE (2012a) Initial Teacher Training Allocations for Academic Year 2013 to 2014. Online at https://www.gov.uk/government/publications/initial-teacher-training-allocations-for-academic-year-2013-to-2014-final (accessed 20 October 2014).

DfE (2012b) Teachers' Standards in England. Online at http://www.education.gov.uk/schools/ teachingandlearning/reviewofstandards/a00205581/teachers-standards1-sep-2012 (accessed 20 October 2014).

DfE (2012c) Systematic Synthetic Phonics and the Year 1 Phonics Screening Check. Department for Education. Online at. http://www.education.gov.uk/schools/toolsandinitiatives/emails toschools/a00205297/phonics-07-11-11 (accessed 20 October 2014).

Dinnerstein, D. (1991) [1976] *The Mermaid and the Minotaur: Sexual Arrangements and Human Malaise* (New York: Harper Perennial).

Donne, J. (1975) *Devotions upon Emergent Occasions*, ed. Anthony Raspa (Montreal: McGill-Queen's University Press). Online at http://litmed.med.nyu.edu/Annotation?action=view&an nid=1128 (accessed 20 October 2014).

Donnelly, J.F. (1999) Schooling Heidegger: On Being in Teaching. *Teaching and Teacher Education*, 15.8: 933–949.

Donoghue, F. (2008) *The Last Professors: The Corporate University and the Fate of the Humanities* (New York: Fordham University Press).

Dreyfus, H.L. (1991) *Being-in-the-World: A Commentary on Heidegger's Being and Time Division I* (Cambridge, MA: MIT Press).

Dunne, J. (1993) *Back to the Rough Ground* (Notre Dame, IN: University of Notre Dame).

Dunne, J. (2003) Arguing for Teaching as a Practice: A Reply to Alasdair MacIntyre. *Journal of Philosophy of Education*, 37.2: 353–371.

Dunne, J. (2006) Newman Now: Re-examining the Concepts of 'Philosophical' and 'Liberal' in the Idea of a University. *British Journal of Educational Studies*, 54.4: 412–428.

Durkheim, E. (1961) *Moral Education; A Study in the Theory and Application of the Sociology of Education* (New York: Macmillan).

Dylan, B. (1965) It's Alright Ma (I'm Only Bleeding) (Special Rider Music).

Dymoke, S. and Harrison, J.K. (2006) Professional Development and the Beginning Teacher: Issues of Autonomy and Institutional Conformity in the Performance Review Process. *Journal of Education for Teaching: International Research and Pedagogy*, 32.1: 71–92.

Edmundson, M. (2003) *Teacher: The One Who Made All the Difference* (New York: Vintage).

Egan, K. (2008) *The Future of Education: Reimagining our Schools from the Ground Up* (New Haven, CT: Yale University Press).

Ellis, V. (2012) Living with Ghosts: 'Disciplines', Envy and the Future of Teacher Education. *Changing English: Studies in Culture and Education*, 19.2: 155–166.

Ellis, V. and Orchard, J.L. (2014) Learning to Teach 'from Experience': Towards a Genealogy of the Idea. In V. Ellis and J. Orchard (eds), *Learning Teaching from Experience: Multiple Perspectives and International Contexts*. London: Bloomsbury Academic.

Ellsworth, E. (1989) Why Doesn't This Feel Empowering? Working Through the Repressive Myths of Critical Pedagogy. *Harvard Educational Review*, 59.3: 297–324.

Emerson, R.W. (1985) [1841] Self-Reliance. In L. Ziff (ed.), *Ralph Waldo Emerson: Selected Essays* (New York, Penguin), pp. 175–204.

Ereaut, G. and Whiting, R. (2008) *What Do We Mean by 'Wellbeing' and Why Might It Matter?* Report for the Department for Children, Schools and Families, No. DCSF-RW073 (London: DCSF).

ESRC (1997) [1994] *What Pupils Tell Us about Teachers and Lessons* (London: Economic and Social Research Council).

Estola, E., Erikkilä, R. and Syrjälä, L. (2003) A Moral Voice of Vocation in Teachers' Narratives. *Teachers and Teaching: Theory and Practice*, 9.3: 239–256.

Fairfield, P. (2011) *Introduction.* In P. Fairfield (ed.), *Education, Dialogue and Hermeneutics* (London and New York: Continuum), pp. 1–4.

Fielding, M. (2008) Personalisation, Education and the Market. *Soundings*, 38.1: 56–69.

Folbre, N. (2010) *Saving State U: Fixing Public Higher Education* (New York: The New Press).

Foot, P. (1978) *Virtues and Vices and Other Essays in Moral Philosophy* (Oxford: Basil Blackwell).

Foreman-Peck, L. and Winch, C. (2010) *Using Educational Research to Inform Practice* (Oxford: Routledge).

Freedman, S.G. (1990) *Small Victories: The Real World of a Teacher, Her Students, and Their School* (New York: HarperCollins).

Freire, P. (1970) *Pedagogy of the Oppressed* (New York: Continuum).

Freire, P. (2000) *Pedagogy of the Oppressed*, 30th Anniversary edition, trans. M.B. Ramos (New York: Continuum).

Fromberg, D.P. (1998) Play Issues in Early Childhood Education. In C. Seefeldt (ed.), *The Early Childhood Curriculum: A Review of Current Research*, 2nd edition (Columbus, OH: Merrill), pp. 190–212.

Fromberg, D.P. (2002) *Play and Meaning in Early Childhood Education* (Boston: Allyn & Bacon).

Furlong, J., Campbell, A., Howson, C., Lewis, S. and McNamara, O. (2006) Partnership in English Initial Teacher Education: Changing Times, Changing Definitions – Evidence from the Teacher Training Agency National Partnership Project. *Scottish Educational Review*, 37 (Special): 32–45.

Furlong, V.J. (1985) *The Deviant Pupil: Sociological Perspectives* (Milton Keynes: Open University Press).

Gadamer, H.-G. (1975) *Truth and Method*, trans. G. Barden and J. Cumming (London: Sheed and Ward).

Gadamer, H.-G. (1977) The Universality of the Hermeneutic Problem. In *Hans-Georg Gadamer: Philosophical Hermeneutics*, ed. D.E. Linge (Berkeley, CA: University of California Press).

Gadamer, H.-G. (1998) *Praise of Theory* (New Haven, CT: Yale University Press).

Gadamer, H.-G. (2004) *Truth and Method* (London and New York: Continuum).

Gallagher, S. (1992) *Hermeneutics and Education* (Albany: State University of New York Press).

Garrison, J. (1995) Dewey's Philosophy and the Experience of Working: Labor, Tools and Language. *Synthèse*, 105.1: 87–114.

Garrison, J. and Good, J.A. (2010) Traces of Hegelian *Bildung* in Dewey's Philosophy. In P. Fairfield (ed.), *John Dewey and Continental Philosophy* (Carbondale, IL: Southern Illinois University Press), pp. 44–68.

Ghaye, A. and Ghaye, G. (1998) *Teaching and Learning through Critical Reflective Practice*. (London: David Fulton).

Giroux, H. (2007) *The University in Chains: Confronting the Military-Industrial-Academic Complex* (The Radical Imagination) (Boulder, CO: Paradigm Publishers).

Giroux, H. and Purple, D. (1983) *The Hidden Curriculum. Education Illusion or Insight* (Berkeley, CA: McCutchan).

Good, J.A. (2006) *A Search for Unity in Diversity: The 'Permanent Hegelian Deposit' in the Philosophy of John Dewey* (Lanham, MD: Lexington Books).

Gove, M (2013) I refuse to surrender to the Marxist teachers. *Mail Debate*, 23 March 2013. Online at http://www.dailymail.co.uk/debate/article-2298146/I-refuse-surrender-Marxist-teachers-hell-bent-destroying-schools-Education-Secretary-berates-new-enemies-promise-opposing-plans.html (accessed 20 October 2014).

Gray, D.E. (2009) *Doing Research in the Real World*, 2nd edition (London: Sage).

Greene, M. (1973) *Teacher as Stranger: Educational Philosophy for the Modern Age* (Belmont, CA: Wadsworth).

Greene, M. (1978) Teaching: The Question of Personal Reality. *Teachers College Record*, 80.1: 23–35.

Greene, M. (1987) Teaching as Project: Choice, Perspective, and the Public Space. In F. Bolin and J.M. Falk (eds), *Teacher Renewal: Professional Issues, Personal Choices* (New York: Teachers College Press).

Greene, M. (1988) *The Dialectic of Freedom* (New York: Teachers College Press).

Griffiths, M. (2013) Critically Adaptive Pedagogical Relations: The Relevance for Educational Policy and Practice. *Educational Theory*, 63.3: 221–236.

Gunnarsson, B. (2009) *Professional Discourse* (London: Continuum).

Gur-Ze'ev, I. (2010) *Diasporic Philosophy and Counter-Education* (Rotterdam: Sense Publishers).

Hammershøj, L.G. (2009) Creativity as a Question of *Bildung*. *Journal of Philosophy of Education*, 43.4: 545–558.

Hanfling, O. (1976) *The Grammar of Feelings* (Milton Keynes: Open University Press).

Hansen, D.T. (1994) Teaching and the Sense of Vocation. *Educational Theory*, 44:3: 259–275.

Hansen, D.T. (1995) *The Call to Teach* (New York: Teachers College Press).

Hare, W. (1993) *What Makes a Good Teacher: Reflections on Some Characteristics Central to the Educational Enterprise* (London, ON: The Althouse Press).

Hargreaves, A. (2000) Mixed Emotions: Teachers' Perceptions of Their Interactions with Students. *Teaching and Teacher Education*, 16.8: 811–826.

Hargreaves, A. and Shirley, D. (2009) *The Fourth Way: The Inspiring Future for Educational Change* (Thousand Oaks, CA: Corwin Press).

Hartley, D. (1994) Mixed Messages in Education Policy – Sign of the Times. *British Journal of Educational Studies*, 42.3: 230–244.

Heidegger, M. (1927) *Sein und Zeit*, trans. J. Macquarrie and E. Robinson as *Being and Time* (Oxford: Blackwell).

Heidegger, M. (1962) *Being and Time* (Oxford: Blackwell).

Heidegger, M. (1973) *Being and Time*, trans. J. Macquarrie and. E. Robinson (Oxford: Basil Blackwell).

Heidegger, M. (2011) What Calls for Thinking? In D.F. Krell (ed.), *Heidegger: Basic Writings* (London and New York: Routledge) pp. 257–277.

Heilbronn, R. (2008) *Teacher Education and the Development of Practical Judgement* (London: Continuum).

Heilbronn, R. (2010) The Nature of Practice-based Knowledge and Understanding. In R. Heilbronn and J. Yandell (eds), *Critical Practice in Teacher Education: A Study of Professional Learning* (London: Institute of Education, IoE Press).

Heilbronn, R. (2011) *Evaluation of Student Teachers' Written Texts on the Good Teacher – 2008–2011* (London: Institute of Education, University of London). Unpublished coursework evaluation.

Heilbronn, R. (2013) Wigs, Disguises and Child's Play: Solidarity in Teacher Education. *Ethics and Education*, 8:1 31–41.

Higgins, C. (2003) Teaching and the Good Life: A Critique of the Ascetic Ideal in Education. *Educational Theory*, 53: 131–154.

Higgins, C. (2010a) The Good Life of Teaching: An Ethics of Professional Practice. Special Issue, *Journal of the Philosophy of Education*, 44.2/3: 189–208.

Higgins, C. (2010b) Teaching as Experience: Toward a Hermeneutics of Teaching and Teacher Education. *Journal of Philosophy of Education*, 44.2–3: 435–478.

Higgins, C. (2011) *The Good Life of Teaching: An Ethics of Professional Practice* (Oxford: Wiley Blackwell).

Hillier, Y. (2012) *Reflective Teaching in Further and Adult Education*, 3rd edition (London: Continuum).

Hinchliffe, G. and Terzi, L. (eds) (2009) Capabilities and Education. Special Issue, *Studies in Philosophy and Education*, 28.5.

Hirst, P.H. (1965) Liberal Education and the Nature of Knowledge. In R.D. Archambault, *Philosophical Analysis and Education* (London: Routledge and Kegan Paul).

Hirst, P. (1983) Educational Theory. In P. Hirst (ed.), *Educational Theory and Its Foundation Disciplines* (London: Routledge and Kegan Paul), pp. 3–24.

Hobson, A. (2003) Student Teachers' Conceptions and Evaluations of Theory in Initial Teacher Training (ITT). *Mentoring & Tutoring: Partnership in Learning*, 11.3: 245–261.

Hodgson, N. (2012) The Only Answer Is Innovation: Europe, Policy, and the Big Society. *Journal of Philosophy of Education*, 6.4: 532–545.

Hogan, P. (1982) Teacher Education and Higher Learning. *Studies – An Irish Quarterly Review*, 71.282: 109–120.

Hogan, P. (1983) The Central Place of Prejudice in the Appraisal of Student Teachers. *Journal of Education for Teaching*, 9.1: 30–45.

Hogan, P. (1988) Communicative Competence and Cultural Emancipation: Reviewing the Rationale for Educational Studies in Teacher Education. *Oxford Review of Education*, 14.2: 187–199.

Hogan, P. (1995) *The Custody and Courtship of Experience – Western Education in Philosophical Perspective*. Dublin.

Hogan, P. (2005) The Politics of Identity and the Epiphanies of Learning. In W. Carr (ed.), *The RoutledgeFalmer Reader in Philosophy of Education* (Abingdon and New York: Routledge), pp. 83–96.

Hogan, P. (2006) Education as a Discipline of Thought and Action: A Memorial to John Wilson. *Oxford Review of Education*, 32.2: 253–264.

Hogan, P. (2010) *The New Significance of Learning: Imagination's Heartwork* (Abingdon and New York: Routledge).

Hogan, P. (2013) Cultivating Human Capabilities in Venturesome Learning Environments. *Educational Theory* 63.3: 237–252.

Hogan, P., with Brosnan, A., de Róiste, B., MacAlister, A., Malone, A., Quirke-Bolt, N., Smith, G. (2005) *Voices from School*, Interim Report on the Project, *Teaching and Learning for the 21st Century,* 2003–2007 (Maynooth Education Department, National University of Ireland Maynooth).

Hogan, P., Brosnan, A., de Róiste, B., MacAlister, A., Malone, A., Quirke-Bolt, N. and Smith, G. (2008) *Learning Anew: Final Report of the Research and Development Project 'Teaching and Learning for the 21st Century* (Maynooth, Education Department, National University of Ireland Maynooth). Online at www.nuim.ie/TL21 (accessed 20 October 2014).

Holligan, C. (1997) Theory in Initial Teacher Education: Students' Perspectives on Its Utility, a Case Study. *British Journal of Educational Research*, 23.4: 533–551.

Holmes, E. (2005) *Teacher Well-Being: Looking After Yourself and Your Career in the Classroom* (London: RoutledgeFalmer).

Hostetler, K. (ed.) (1997) *Ethical Judgment in Teaching* (Boston, MA: Allyn & Bacon).

How, A. (2011) Hermeneutics and the 'Classic' Problem in the Human Sciences. *History of the Human Sciences*, 24.3: 47–63.

Howe, K. and Miramontes, O. (1991) A Framework for Ethical Deliberation in Special Education. *Journal of Special Education*, 25.1: 7–25.

Huebner, D. (1987) The Vocation of Teaching. In F.S. Bolin and J.M. Falk (eds), *Teacher Renewal: Professional Issues, Personal Choices* (New York: Teachers College Press), pp. 17–29.

Inchausti, R. (1993) *Spitwad Sutras: Classroom Teaching as a Sublime Vocation* (Westport, CT: Bergin and Garvey).

Isenberg, J. and Quisenberry, N. (1988) Play: Essential for All Children. The Association for Childhood Education International. Online at http://www.freepatentsonline.com/article/Childhood-Education/93348877.html (accessed 20 October 2014)

Jackson, P.W. (1966) The Way Teaching Is. In *The Way Teaching Is (Report of the Seminar on Teaching)* (Washington, DC: National Educational Association), pp. 7–27.

Jackson, P.W. (1986) The Mimetic and the Transformative: Alternative Outlooks on Teaching. In *The Practice of Teaching* (New York: Teachers College Press), pp. 115–145.

James, W. (1899) *Talks to Teachers on Psychology and to Students on Some of Life's Ideals* (New York: Henry Holt and Company).

Jenkinson, S. (2001) *The Genius of Play: Celebrating the Spirit of Childhood* (Glasgow: Hawthorne Press).

Jersild, A.T. (1955) *When Teachers Face Themselves* (New York: Teachers College, Columbia University).

Johns, C. and McCormack, B. (2002) Unfolding the Conditions where the Transformative Potential of Guided Reflection (Clinincal Supervision) Might Flourish or Founder. In C. Johns and D. Freshwater, *Transforming Nursing Through Reflective Practice* (Oxford: Blackwell Science).

Johnson, S.M. (1990) *Teachers at Work: Achieving Success in Our Schools* (New York: Basic Books).

Jones, A. (2004) *Talking Cure: The Desire for Dialogue* (New York: Peter Lang).

Kakkori, L. and Huttunen, R. (2012) The Sartre–Heidegger Controversy on Humanism and the Concept of Man in Education. *Educational Philosophy and Theory*, 44.4: 351–365.

Kant, I. (2003) *On Education* (New York: Dover Publications).

Kegley, J. (2011) The Ethical Subject/Agent as Rational Individual but Also as So Much More. *Journal of Speculative Philosophy*, 25.1: 166–129.

Kekes, J. (1995) *Moral Wisdom and the Good Life* (New York: Cornell University Press).

Kelchtermans, G. (2005) Teachers' Emotions in Educational Reforms: Self-Understanding, Vulnerable Commitment and Micropolitical Literacy. *Teacher and Teacher Education*, 21.8: 995–1006.

Kirk, G. (2013) *The Value of University–School Partnership in Teacher Education – a UCET Position Paper*. Universities' Council for the Education of Teachers. Online at http://www.ucet.ac.uk/4658 (accessed 2 January 2014).

Kirp, D.L. (2003) *Shakespeare, Einstein, and the Bottom Line: The Marketing of Higher Education* (Cambridge, MA: Harvard University Press).

Kitchner, K.S. (1992) Psychologist as Teacher And Mentor: Affirming Ethical Values throughout the Curriculum. *Professional Psychology: Research and Practice*, 23.3: 190–195.

Knezic, D., Wubbels, T., Elbers, E. and Maaike, H. (2010) The Socratic Dialogue and Teacher Education. *Teaching and Teacher Education*, 97.2: 1104–1111.

Kodelja, Z. (2013) Authority, the Autonomy of the University, and Neoliberal Politics. *Educational Theory*, 63.3: 317–330.

Kohl, H. (1984) *Growing Minds: On Becoming a Teacher* (New York: Harper & Row).

Korthagen, F. (1999) Linking Reflection and Technical Competence: The Logbook as an Instrument in Teacher Education. *European Journal of Teacher Education*, 22.2–3: 191–207.

Kozol, J. (2007) *Letters to a Young Teacher* (New York: Crown).

Lamm, Z. (1976) *Conflicting Theories of Instruction: Conceptual Dimensions* (Berkeley, CA: McCutchan).

Lawn, M. and Furlong, J. (2009) The Disciplines of Education in the UK: Between the Ghost and the Shadow. *Oxford Review of Education*, 35.5: 541–552.

Leigh, F. (2007) Platonic Dialogue, Maieutic Method and Critical Thinking. *Journal of Philosophy of Education*, 41.3: 309–323.

Levinas, E. (1987) *Time and the Other*, trans. R. Cohen (Pittsburgh: Duquesne University Press).

Løvlie, L., Mortensen, K.P. and Nordenbo, S.E. (eds) (2003) *Educating Humanity:* Bildung *in Postmodernity* (Oxford: Blackwell).

Luby, A. (2006) We must beware of Geeks bearing gifts. *Times Educational Supplement*, 9 June 2006.

Lum, G. (1999) Where's the Competence in Competence-Based Education and Training? *Journal of Philosophy of Education*, 33.3: 403–418.

Lum, G. (2003) Towards a Richer Conception of Vocational Preparation. *Journal of Philosophy of Education*, 37.1: 1–12.

Luntley, M. (2000) *Performance, Pay and Professionals, IMPACT No. 2*. Philosophy of Education Society of Great Britain.

MacAllister, J. (2012a) Virtue Epistemology and the Philosophy of Education. *Journal of the Philosophy of Education*, 46.2: 251–270.

MacAllister, J. (2012b) School Discipline, Educational Interest and Pupil Wisdom. *Educational Philosophy and Theory*, 45.1: 20–35.

MacIntyre, A. (1984) *After Virtue: A Study in Moral Theory*, 2nd edition (South Bend, IN: University of Notre Dame Press).

Macintyre, A. (2007) [1981] *After Virtue: A Study in Moral Theory*, 3rd edition, with a new prologue (South Bend, IN: University of Notre Dame Press).

MacIntyre, A. (2009) The Very Idea of a University: Aristotle, Newman and Us. *British Journal of Educational Studies*, 57.4: 247–362.

Mannoni, O. (2003) [1969] I Know Well, but All the Same … . In M.A. Rothenberg, D.A. Foster and S. Zizek (eds), *Perversion and the Social Relation*, trans. G.M. Goshgarian (Durham, NC: Duke University Press), pp. 68–92.

Margonis, F. (2007) A Relational Ethic of Solidarity? *Philosophy of Education* 62.70. Online at http://ojs.ed.uiuc.edu/index.php/pes/article/view/1437/184 (accessed 20 October 2014).

Martin, M.W. (2000) *Meaningful Work: Rethinking Professional Ethics* (New York: Oxford University Press).

Martinez, D., Desiderio, M. and Papakonstantinou, A. (2010) Teaching: A Job or a Profession? The Perceptions of Educators. *The Educational Forum*, 74.4: 289–296.

Matchett, N. (2008) Ethics across the Curriculum. *New Directions for Higher Education*, 142 (Summer): 25–38.

McCulloch, G., Helsby, G. and Knight, P. (2000) *The Politics of Professionalism: Teachers and the Curriculum* (London: Continuum).

McCune, L. and Zanes, M. (2001) Learning, Attention and Play. In S. Golbeck (ed.), *Psychological Perspectives on Early Childhood Education* (Mahwah, NJ: Lawrence Erlbaum), pp. 92–106.

McIntosh, P. (2010) *Action Research and Reflective Practice* (London and New York: Routledge).

McIntyre D. (1991) The Oxford University Model of Teacher Education. *South Pacific Journal of Teacher Education*, 19.2: 117–129.

McIntyre, D. and Hagger, H. (1992) Professional Development through the Oxford Internship Model. *British Journal of Educational Studies*, 40.3: 264–283.

Merleau-Ponty, M. (2002) *Phenomenology of Perception* (London: Routledge).

Misak, C. (2008) Experience, Narrative, and Ethical Deliberation. *Ethics*, 118 (July): 614–632.

Mitchell, S. (2006) Socratic Dialogue, the Humanities, and the Art of the Question. *JOURNAL*, 5.2: 181–197.

Moore, A. and Atkinson, D. (1998) Charisma, Competence and Teacher Education. *Discourse*, 19.2: 171–182.

Morphew, C.C. and Eckel, P.D. (2009) *Privatizing the Public University: Perspectives from across the Academy* (Baltimore, MD: Johns Hopkins University Press).

Mulder, M., Weigel, T. and Collins, K. (2007) The Concept of Competence in the Development of Vocational Education and Training in Selected EU Member States: A Critical Analysis. *Journal of Vocational Education and Training*, 59.1: 65–85.

Murdoch, I. (1985) [1970] *The Sovereignty of Good* (London: Routledge).

Murris, K.S. (2008) Philosophy with Children, the Stingray and the Educative Value of Disequilibrium. *Journal of Philosophy of Education*, 42.3–4: 667–685.

NCL (2011) National Teaching Schools Prospectus. National College for School Leadership and Children's Services. Online at http://www.essexclerks.org.uk/sites/default/files/Teaching%20Schools%20Prospectus.pdf (accessed 20 October 2014).

NCL (2012) How Teaching Schools Are Already Starting to Make a Difference. National College for Leadership and Children's Services. Online at http://webarchive.national archives.gov.uk/20130123124929/http://www.education.gov.uk/nationalcollege/docinfo?id=177293&filename=green-shoots.pdf (accessed 20 October 2014).

NCL (2013) How Teaching Schools Are Making a Difference: Part 2. National College for Leadership and Children's Services. Online at http://webarchive.nationalarchives.gov.uk/20130123124929/http://www.education.gov.uk/nationalcollege/docinfo?id=178116&filename=green-shoots-part-two.pdf (accessed 20 October 2014).

Newfield, C. (2008) *Unmaking the Public University: The Forty-Year Assault on the Middle Class* (Cambridge, MA: Harvard University Press).

Newman, J. (1996) [1852/58] *The Idea of a University* (New Haven, CT: Yale University Press).

Nias, J. (1987) Teaching and the Self. *Cambridge Journal of Education*, 17.3: 178–185.

Nias, J. (1996) Thinking about Feeling: the Emotions of Teaching. *Cambridge Journal of Education*, 26.3: 293–306.

NICE (2009) Promoting Young People's Social and Emotional Well-being in Secondary Education: Consultation on the Evidence (London: National Institute for Health and Clinical Excellence). Online at http://www.nice.org.uk (accessed 2 September 2013).

Nicholson, G. (2011) The Education of the Teacher. In P. Fairfield (ed.), *Education, Dialogue and Hermeneutics* (London and New York: Continuum), pp. 61–76.

Nietzsche, F. (1990) [1874] Schopenhauer as Educator. In W. Arrowsmith (trans. and ed.), *Unmodern Observations* (New Haven, CT: Yale University Press), pp. 147–226.

Nixon, J. (2012) *Interpretive Pedagogies for Higher Education: Arendt, Berger, Said, Nussbaum and Their Legacies* (London: Bloomsbury Academic).

Noddings, N. (2003) Is Teaching a Practice? *Journal of Philosophy of Education*, 37.2: 241–252.

Noddings, N. (2005) Caring in Education. In *The Encyclopedia of Informal Education*. Online at www.infed.org/biblio/noddings_caring_in_education.htm (accessed 20 October 2014).

Nussbaum, M.C. (2000) *Women and Human Development: The Capabilities Approach* (Cambridge: Cambridge University Press).

Oakeshott, M. (1981) The Voice of Poetry in the Conversation of Mankind. In *Rationalism in Politics and Other Essays* (London: Methuen).

Oakley, J. and Cocking, D. (eds) (2001) *Virtue Ethics and Professional Roles* (Cambridge: Cambridge University Press).

Oancea, A. and Bridges, D. (2009) Philosophy of Education in the UK: the Historical and Contemporary Tradition. *Oxford Review of Education*, 35.5: 553–568.

Oancea, A. and Orchard, J. (2012) The Future of Teacher Education. *Journal of Philosophy of Education*, 46.X: 574–588.

OED (1983) *The Shorter Oxford English Dictionary*, vol. 2 (Oxford: Oxford University Press).

Orchard, J. and Foreman-Peck, L. (2011) Philosophical Perspectives on the Future of Teacher Education. *Research Intelligence*, 116: 26–27.

Painter-Morland, M. (2008) *Business Ethics as Practice: Ethics as the Everyday Business of Business* (Cambridge: Cambridge University Press).

Palmer, P. (1998) *The Courage to Teach: Exploring the Inner Landscape of a Teacher's Life* (San Francisco, CA: Jossey-Bass).

Papastephanou, M. (2006) Education, Risk and Ethics. *Ethics and Education*, 1.1: 47–63.

Parry, R. (2008) Episteme and Techne. In E.N. Zalta (ed.), *The Stanford Encyclopedia of Philosophy* (Fall 2008 edition). Online at http://plato.stanford.edu/archives/fall2008/entries/episteme-techne (accessed 20 October 2014).

Parsons, F. (1909) *Choosing a Vocation* (Boston: Houghton Mifflin).

Peters, M. (2010) Re-imagining the University in the Global Era. *Policy Futures in Education*, 8.2: 151–165.

Peters, R.S. (1965) Education as initiation. In R. D. Archambault (ed.), *Philosophical Analysis and Education* (London: Routledge & Kegan Paul), pp. 87–111.

Peters, R.S. (1973) *The Philosophy of Education* (Oxford: Oxford University Press).

Peters, R.S. (1974) *Psychology and Ethical Development. A Collection of Articles on Psychological Theories, Ethical Development and Human Understanding*. London: George Allen & Unwin.

Phoenix, A. (2013) Research on Childhood and Well-being: Gender and Racialised Identities. Unpublished Lecture given at OUDES, 4 March 2013.

Plato (1937) *The Dialogues of Plato* (in two volumes), trans. B. Jowett (New York: Random House).

Plato (1987) *The Republic*, revised 2nd edition (London: Penguin Books).

Plowden, B. (1967) *The Plowden Report: Children and Their Primary Schools* (London: Central Advisory Council for Education).

Popkewitz, T.S. (ed.) (2013) *Rethinking the History of Education: Transnational Perspectives on Its Methods, Questions and Knowledge* (New York: Palgrave Macmillan).

Preskill, S. (1998) Narratives of Teaching and Quest for the Second Self. *Journal of Teacher Education*, 49.5: 344–357.

Pressman, E. S. (dir.) (1994) *My So-Called Life: The Substitute* [episode of television series]. Shout! Factory, DVD, 2007.

Priestley, M., Robinson, S. and Biesta, G.J.J. (2012) Teacher Agency, Performativity and Curriculum Change: Reinventing the Teacher in the Scottish Curriculum for Excellence? In B. Jeffrey and G. Troman (eds), *Performativity in UK Education: Ethnographic Cases of its Effects, Agency and Reconstructions* (Painswick: E&E Publishing), pp. 87–108.

Pring, R. (2000) *Philosophy of Educational Research* (London: Continuum).

Pring, R. (2007) Reclaiming Philosophy for Educational Research. *Educational Review*, 59.3: 315–330.

Readings, B. (1996) *The University in Ruins* (Cambridge, MA: Harvard University Press).

Reid, L.A. (1962) *Philosophy and Education: An Introduction* (London: Heinemann).

Reynolds, D. (1991) Changing Ineffective Schools. In M. Ainscow (ed.), *Effective Schools for All* (London: David Fulton).

Robson, C. (2011) *Real World Research*, 3rd edition (Chichester: John Wiley & Sons).

Rogers, D. and Webb, J. (1991) The Ethic of Caring in Teacher Education. *Journal of Teacher Education*, 42.3: 173–181.

Ronnie, D. (2013) *The Professional Identity of Teacher Educators: A Career on the Cusp?* (Abingdon: Routledge).

Rorty, R. (1999) Education as Socialization and as Individualization. In *Philosophy and Social Hope* (New York: Penguin), pp. 114–126.

Rose, M. (2005) [1990] *Lives on the Boundary: A Moving Account of the Struggles and Achievements of America's Educationally Underprepared*, with a new Afterword (New York: Penguin).

Ruch, R. (2003) *Higher Ed, Inc.: The Rise of the for-Profit University* (Baltimore, MD: Johns Hopkins University Press).

Sahlberg, P. (2011) *Finnish Lessons: What Can the World Learn from Educational Change in Finland?* (New York: Teachers College Press).

Sen, A. (2009) *The Idea of Justice* (Cambridge, MA: The Belknap Press of Harvard University Press).

Sen, A. and Nussbaum, M.C. (1993) *The Quality of Life* (Oxford: Clarendon Press).

SCETT (2011) In Defence of Teacher Education. Standing Committee for the Education and Training of Teachers. Online at http://www.scett.org.uk/ (accessed 20 October 2014).

Schön, D. (1983) *The Reflective Practitioner: How Professionals Think in Action* (New York: Basic Books).

Schön, D. (1987) *Educating the Reflective Practitioner* (London: Jossey-Bass).

Schwarz, G.E. (1998) Teaching as Vocation: Enabling Ethical Practice. *Educational Forum*, 63.1: 23–29.

Seligman, M.E.P, Ernst, R.M., Gillham, J., Reivich, K. and Linkins, M. (2009) Positive Education: Positive Psychology and Classroom Interventions. *Oxford Review of Education*, 35.3: 293–311.

Semel, S. (ed.) (2010) *The Foundations of Education: The Essential Texts* (Routledge: London).

SG (2011) *Teaching Scotland's Future: A Report of a Review of Teacher Education in Scotland.* Scotland Government Report, G. Donaldson (Chair). Onlinehttp://www.scotland.gov.uk/Resource/Doc/337626/0110852.pdf (accessed 20 October 2014).

Shaffer, T.L. (1987) *Faith and the Professions* (Provo, UT: Brigham Young University Press).

Shulman, L.S. (2004) *The Wisdom of Practice Essays on Teaching, Learning, and Learning to Teach* (San Francisco: Jossey-Bass).

Slaughter, S. and Rhoades, G. (2004) *Academic Capitalism and the New Economy: Markets, State, and Higher Education* (Baltimore, MD: Johns Hopkins University Press).

Slee, R., Weiner, G. and Tomlinson, S. (1998) *School Effectiveness for Whom: Challenges to the School Effectiveness and Improvement Movement* (Falmer: Falmer Press).

Smeyers, P. (2002) The Origin: Education, Philosophy and a Work of Art. In M.A. Peters (ed.), *Heidegger, Education and Modernity* (Oxford: Rowman and Littlefield).

Smith, J. (2001) *The Learning Game* (London: Abacus).

Smith, R. (2011) The Play of Socratic Dialogue. *Journal of Philosophy of Education*, 45.2: 221–233.

Sockett, H.T. (1993) *The Moral Base for Teacher Professionalism* (New York: Teachers College Press).

Sockett, H. (2012) *Knowledge and Virtue in Teaching and Learning: The Primacy of Dispositions* (New York and Abingdon: Routledge).

Soutter, A.K., O'Steen, B. and Gilmore, A. (2012) Wellbeing in the New Zealand Curriculum. *Journal of Curriculum Studies*, 44.1: 111–142.

Squires, G. (1992) *Teaching as a Professional Discipline: A Multi-dimensional Model* (Oxford: Taylor and Francis).

Squires, G. (1999) *Teaching as a Professional Discipline: A Multi-dimensional Model* (London: Routledge).

Standish, P. (1995) Why We Should Not Speak of an Educational Science. *Studies in Philosophy and Education*, 14: 267–281.

Standish, P. (2007) Rival Conceptions of the Philosophy of Education. *Ethics and Education*, 2.2: 159–171.

Steiner, G. (2005) *Lessons of the Masters* (Cambridge, MA: Harvard University Press).

Steinkamp, N. and Gordjin, B. (2003) Ethical Case Deliberation on the Ward: a Comparison of Four Methods. *Medicine, Health Care and Philosophy*, 6.3: 235–246.

Stern, S. (2009) Pedagogy of the Oppressor. *City Journal*, Spring 2009, 19.2. Online at http://city-journal.org/2009/19_2_freirian-pedagogy.html (accessed 20 October 2014).

Stobart, G. (2007) *Testing Times: The Uses and Abuses of Assessment* (London: Routledge).

Stones, E. (1983) Perspectives in Pedagogy. *Journal of Education for Teaching*, 9.1: 68–76.

Swiffen, A. (2009) What Would Hegel Do? Desire and Recognition in the Pedagogical Relation. *Journal of Curriculum Theorizing*, 25.2: 48–61.

Taylor, C. (1989) *The Sources of the Self: The Making of the Modern Identity* (Cambridge, MA: Harvard University Press).

Thompson, C. (2005) The Non-transparency of the Self and the Ethical Value of *Bildung*. *Journal of Philosophy of Education*, 39.3: 519–533.

Thompson, C. (2006) Adorno and the Borders of Experience: The Significance of the Nonidentical for a 'Different' Theory of *Bildung*. *Educational Theory*, 56.1: 69–87.

Thompson, C. (2013) Evaluations and the Forgetfulness of Pedagogical Relations: Remarks on Educational Authority. *Educational Theory*, 63.3: 283–298.

Thompson, M. (1992) Do 27 Competences Make a Teacher? *Education Review*, 6.2: 4–8.

Thomson, I. (2005) *Heidegger on Ontotheology: Technology and the Politics of Education* (Cambridge: Cambridge University Press).

Thornberg, R. (2006) Hushing as a Moral Dilemma in the Classroom. *Journal of Moral Education*, 35.1: 89–104.

Tickle, L. (1991) New Teachers and the Emotions of Learning Teaching. *Cambridge Journal of Education*, 21.3: 319–329.

Tierney, W.G. (2007) *New Players, Different Game: Understanding the Rise of for-profit Colleges and Universities* (Baltimore, MD: Johns Hopkins University Press).

Tomlinson, J. and Little, V. (2000) A Code of the Ethical Principles Underlying Teaching as a Professional Activity. In R. Gardner, J. Cairns and D. Lawton (eds), *Education for Values: Morals, Ethics and Citizenship in Contemporary Teaching* (London: Kogan Page), pp. 147–157.

Totterdell, M. (2000) The Moralization of Teaching: a Relational Approach as an Ethical Framework in the Professional Preparation and Formation of Teachers. In R. Gardner, J. Cairns and D. Lawton (eds), *Education for Values: Morals, Ethics and Citizenship in Contemporary Teaching* (London: Kogan Page), pp. 127–146.

Tripp, D. (2012) *Critical Incidents in Teaching: Developing Professional Judgements*, 2nd edition (London and New York: Routledge).

Tuchman, G. (2009) *Wannabe U: Inside the Corporate University* (Chicago, IL: University of Chicago Press).

van Manen, M. (1995) On the Epistemology of Reflective Practice. *Teachers and Teaching: Theory and Practice*, 1.1: 33–50.

van Manen, M. (1991) *The Tact of Teaching: The Meaning of Pedagogical Thoughtfulness*. (Albany: State University of New York Press).

Van Manen, M. (2007) Phenomenology of Practice. *Phenomenology & Practice*, 1.1: 11–30.

Verger, A., Altinyelken, H. and de Koning, M. (2013) *Global Managerial Education* (Amsterdam: Education International).

Vinterbo-Hohr, A. and Hohr, H. (2006) The Neo-Humanistic Concept of *Bildung* Going Astray: Comments to Friedrich Schiller's Thoughts on Education. *Educational Philosophy and Theory*, 38.2: 215–230.

Wadsworth, Y. (2001) Becoming Responsive – Some Consequences for Evaluation as Dialogue across Distance. *New Directions for Evaluation*, 92: 45–58.

Walker, R.L. and Ivanhoe, P.J. (eds) (2007) *Working Virtue: Virtue Ethics and Contemporary Moral Problems* (Oxford: Oxford University Press).

Waller, W. (1932) *The Sociology of Teaching*. (London: John Wiley & Sons).

Wang, M.T. and Holcombe, R. (2010) Adolescents' Perceptions of School Environment, Engagement, and Academic Achievement in Middle School. *American Educational Research Journal*, 47.3: 633–662.

Warnick, B. (2008) *Imitation and Education* (Albany: State University of New York Press).

Washburn, J. (2006) *University, Inc.: The Corporate Corruption of Higher Education* (New York: Basic Books).

Waters, L. (2004) *Enemies of Promise: Publishing, Perishing, and the Eclipse of Scholarship* (Chicago: University of Chicago Press).

White, J. (1990) *Education and the Good Life; Beyond the National Curriculum* (London: Kogan Page).

White, J. (2007) Wellbeing and Education: Issues of Culture and Authority. *Journal of the Philosophy of Education*, 41.1: 17–28.

Whitehead, A. (1967) [1929] Universities and Their Function. In *The Aims of Education and Other Essays* (New York: The Free Press), pp. 91–102.

Wiedmaier, D., Moore, C., Onwuegbuzie, A., Witcher, A., Collins, J. and Filer, C. (2007) Students' Perceptions of Characteristics of Effective College Teachers. *American Educational Research Journal*, 44.1: 113–160.

Williams, B. (1985) *Ethics and the Limits of Philosophy* (Cambridge, MA: Harvard University Press).

Wilson, J. (1975) *Educational Theory and the Preparation of Teachers* (Windsor: NFER).

Wilson, P.S. (1971) *Interest and Discipline in Education* (London: Routledge).

Wilson, R. (2010) Tenure, RIP: What the vanishing status means for the future of education. Online at http://chronicle.com/article/Tenure-RIP/66114/?key=QTglLlM9bCROYyNteiBLe idVO3B6KRgrbyBCZn0aYlhR (accessed 20 October 2014).

Winch, C. (2000) *Education, Work and Social Capital* (London: Routledge).

Winch, C. (2010) For Philosophy of Education in Teacher Education. Unpublished paper delivered to the Oxford Branch of the Philosophy of Education Society of Great Britain, Oxford, May 2010.

Winch, C. (2012) For Philosophy of Education in Teacher Education. *Oxford Review of Education*, 38.3: 305–322.

Winstanley, C. (2012) Alluring Ideas: Cherry Picking Policy from Around the World. *Journal of Philosophy of Education*, 46.4: 516–531.

Witz, A. (1992) *Professions and Patriarchy* (London: Routledge).

Zeichner, K. (2003) Teacher Research as Professional Development for P-12 Educations in the US. *Educational Action Research*, 11.2: 301–325.

Index

Philosophical Perspectives on Teacher Education, First Edition. Edited by Ruth Heilbronn and
Lorraine Foreman-Peck. © 2015 Ruth Heilbronn and Lorraine Foreman-Peck. Editorial Organisation
© Philosophy of Education Society of Great Britain. Published 2015 by John Wiley & Sons, Ltd.